Scholastic Almanac 2011: Facts & Stats is produced by becker&mayer! LLC, 11120 NE 33rd Place, Suite 101, Bellevue, WA 98004.
www.beckermayer.com

Manager and Senior Designer, Juvenile Design Group: Rosanna Brockley
Editor: Delia Greve
Project Director: Jacqueline A. Ball, J. A. Ball Associates, Inc.
Writers: Jackie Ball, Lynn Brunelle, Jim Brunelle, Delia Greve, Monique Peterson, Sandra Will
Head Designer: Mathew McInelly
Designer: Matthew Fisher

ISBN 978-0-545-23761-1

10 9 8 7 6 5 4 3 2 1   10 11 12 13 14

Printed in the U.S.A.   40
First printing, September 2010
Cover design by Kay Petronio

08155   8/1/10

Due to the publication date, statistics are current as of June 2010.

SCHOLASTIC

ALMANAC 2011

FACTS & STATS

SCHOLASTIC INC.
NEW YORK · TORONTO · LONDON · AUCKLAND
SYDNEY · MEXICO CITY · NEW DELHI · HONG KONG

SCHOLASTIC

ALMANAC 2011 FACTS & STATS

- AUCKLAND
- HONG KONG

SCHOLASTIC
TO
NEW YORK · MEXICO
SYDNEY

Scholastic Almanac 2011: Facts & Stats is produced by becker&mayer! LLC, 11120 NE 33rd Place, Suite 101, Bellevue, WA 98004.
www.beckermayer.com

Manager and Senior Designer, Juvenile Design Group: Rosanna Brockley
Editor: Delia Greve
Project Director: Jacqueline A. Ball, J. A. Ball Associates, Inc.
Writers: Jackie Ball, Lynn Brunelle, Jim Brunelle, Delia Greve, Monique Peterson, Sandra Will
Head Designer: Mathew McInelly
Designer: Matthew Fisher

ISBN 978-0-545-23761-1

10 9 8 7 6 5 4 3 2 1

Printed in the U.S.A.   40
First printing, September 2010
Cover design b

08155

Due to the

rrent as of June 2010

10 11 12 13 14

CONTENTS

Animals

You Animal

From aphids to zebras, animals come in a great assortment of shapes and sizes. The amazing variety of animal life on Earth is called biodiversity. Scientists have counted and named 1.5 million species, and most estimate there are from 5 to 20 million more. In fact, at the present rate of describing new species, it could take hundreds of years to finish identifying them.

Bug Bites

More than half of these species are insects. The world is so full of bugs that scientists are suggesting they be eaten in places where food is scarce. Why not? They're plentiful and full of protein. Researchers say that grubs, ants, wasps, and other insects are already eaten in 113 countries.

Polar Bears in Danger

Animals that eat only bugs are called insectivores. Herbivores eat plants. Carnivores eat other animals, and omnivores eat pretty much everything. All animals have to eat, and they all need something else: a healthy habitat. Sometimes human activity or development destroys animal habitats. On May 14, 2008, polar bears were added to the endangered species list because their habitat is being threatened by global climate change. At present, there are 8,811 animals classified as threatened or endangered in the world.

Pet Projects

Until about 12,000 years ago, all dogs were wolves. After years of breeding for specific characteristics, there are now more than 400 breeds, from chihuahuas to German shepherds. Domestic cats go back about 5,000 years. Experts say they've changed very little since ancient times. See page 31 for the top dogs—and cats—in the United States. Did your pet make the list?

TAKE a LOOK

Do you know your hogs from your hounds? What's a group of each of them called? And if you've got a "murder" or a "charm" of animals on your front lawn, should you run or stick around? Find the answers on page 29.

CHECK IT OUT!

The next time you're around a cat, notice the way it walks. How is the movement different from the way a dog walks? Hint: Only camels and giraffes move like cats. (The answer is on page 350.)

THE ANIMAL KINGDOM
Detailed Classification

Porifera SPONGES

Cnidaria COELENTERATES

Platyhelminthes FLATWORMS

Nematoda ROUNDWORMS

Mollusca MOLLUSKS

Annelida TRUE WORMS

Hydrozoa HYDRAS, HYDROIDS

Scyphozoa JELLYFISH

Anthozoa SEA ANEMONES, CORAL

Turbellaria FREE-LIVING FLATWORMS

Monogenea PARASITIC FLUKES

Trematoda PARASITIC FLUKES

Cestoda TAPEWORMS

Polyplacophora CHITONS

Gastropoda SNAILS, SLUGS

Bivalvia CLAMS, SCALLOPS, MUSSELS

Cephalopoda OCTOPUSES, SQUID

Polychaeta MARINE WORMS

Oligochaeta EARTHWORMS, FRESHWATER WORMS

Hirudinea LEECHES

Insecta INSECTS

Chilopoda CENTIPEDES

Diplopoda MILLIPEDES

Symphyla SYMPHYLANS, PAUROPODS

Collembola, SPRINGTAILS
Thysanura, SILVERFISH, BRISTLETAILS
Ephemeroptera, MAYFLIES
Odonata, DRAGONFLIES
Isoptera, TERMITES
Orthoptera, LOCUSTS, CRICKETS, GRASSHOPPERS
Dictyptera, COCKROACHES, MANTIDS
Dermaptera, EARWIGS
Phasmida, STOCK INSECTS, LEAF INSECTS
Psocoptera, BOOK LICE, BARK LICE
Diplura, SIMPLE INSECTS

Protura, TELSONTAILS
Plecoptera, STONE FLIES
Grylloblattodea, TINY MOUNTAIN INSECTS
Strepsiptera, TWISTED-WINGED STYLOPIDS
Trichoptera, CADDIS FLIES
Embioptera, WEBSPINNERS
Thysanoptera, THRIPS
Mecoptera, SCORPION FLIES
Zoraptera, RARE TROPICAL INSECTS
Hemiptera, TRUE BUGS
Anoplura, SUCKING LICE

Mallophaga, BITING LICE, BIRD LICE
Homoptera, WHITEFLIES, APHIDS, SCALE INSECTS, CICADAS
Coleoptera, BEETLES, WEEVILS
Neuroptera, ALDERFLIES, LACEWINGS, ANT LIONS, SNAKEFLIES, DOBSONFLIES
Hymenoptera, ANTS, BEES, WASPS
Siphonaptera, FLEAS
Diptera, TRUE FLIES, MOSQUITOES, GNATS
Lepidoptera, BUTTERFLIES, MOTHS

Insectivora, INSECTIVORES (e.g., shrews, moles, hedgehogs)
Chiroptera, BATS
Dermoptera, FLYING LEMURS
Edentata, ANTEATERS, SLOTHS, ARMADILLOS
Pholidota, PANGOLINS
Primates, PROSIMIANS (e.g., lemurs, tarsiers, monkeys, apes, humans)

Rodentia, RODENTS (e.g., squirrels, rats, beavers, mice, porcupines)
Lagomorpha, RABBITS, HARES, PIKAS
Cetacea, WHALES, DOLPHINS, PORPOISES
Carnivora, CARNIVORES (e.g., cats, dogs, weasels, bears, hyenas)
Pinnipedia, SEALS, SEA LIONS, WALRUSES
Tubulidentata, AARDVARKS

Hyracoidea, HYDRAXES
Proboscidea, ELEPHANTS
Sirenia, SEA COWS (e.g., manatees, dugongs)
Perissodactyla, ODD-TOED HOOFED ANIMALS (e.g., horses, rhinoceroses, tapirs)
Artiodactyla, EVEN-TOED HOOFED ANIMALS (e.g., hogs, cattle, camels, hippopotamuses)

Animals

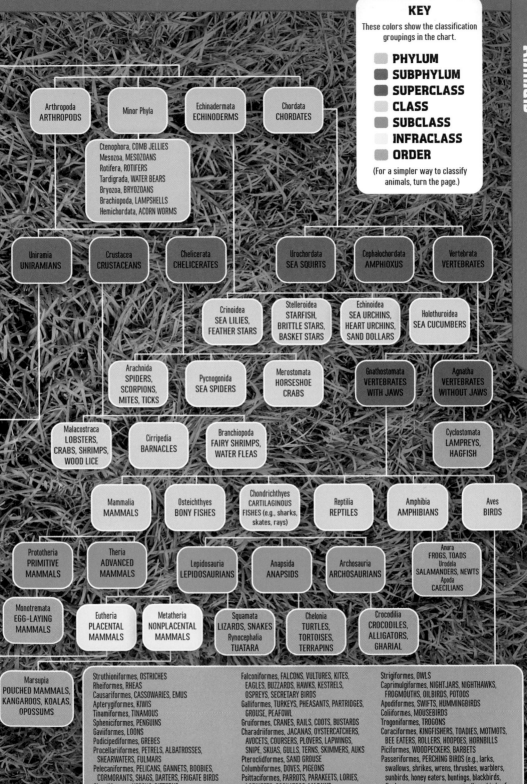

KEY

These colors show the classification groupings in the chart.

- PHYLUM
- SUBPHYLUM
- SUPERCLASS
- CLASS
- SUBCLASS
- INFRACLASS
- ORDER

(For a simpler way to classify animals, turn the page.)

Arthropoda ARTHROPODS

Minor Phyla

Echinadermata ECHINODERMS

Chordata CHORDATES

Ctenophora, COMB JELLIES
Mesozoa, MESOZOANS
Rotifera, ROTIFERS
Tardigrada, WATER BEARS
Bryozoa, BRYOZOANS
Brachiopoda, LAMPSHELLS
Hemichordata, ACORN WORMS

Uniramia UNIRAMIANS

Crustacea CRUSTACEANS

Chelicerata CHELICERATES

Urochordata SEA SQUIRTS

Cephalochordata AMPHIOXUS

Vertebrata VERTEBRATES

Crinoidea SEA LILIES, FEATHER STARS

Stelleroidea STARFISH, BRITTLE STARS, BASKET STARS

Echinoidea SEA URCHINS, HEART URCHINS, SAND DOLLARS

Holothuroidea SEA CUCUMBERS

Arachnida SPIDERS, SCORPIONS, MITES, TICKS

Pycnogonida SEA SPIDERS

Merostomata HORSESHOE CRABS

Gnathostomata VERTEBRATES WITH JAWS

Agnatha VERTEBRATES WITHOUT JAWS

Malacostraca LOBSTERS, CRABS, SHRIMPS, WOOD LICE

Cirripedia BARNACLES

Branchiopoda FAIRY SHRIMPS, WATER FLEAS

Cyclostomata LAMPREYS, HAGFISH

Mammalia MAMMALS

Osteichthyes BONY FISHES

Chondrichthyes CARTILAGINOUS FISHES (e.g., sharks, skates, rays)

Reptilia REPTILES

Amphibia AMPHIBIANS

Aves BIRDS

Prototheria PRIMITIVE MAMMALS

Theria ADVANCED MAMMALS

Lepidosauria LEPIDOSAURIANS

Anapsida ANAPSIDS

Archosauria ARCHOSAURIANS

Anura FROGS, TOADS
Urodela SALAMANDERS, NEWTS
Apoda CAECILIANS

Monotremata EGG-LAYING MAMMALS

Eutheria PLACENTAL MAMMALS

Metatheria NONPLACENTAL MAMMALS

Squamata LIZARDS, SNAKES
Rynocephalia TUATARA

Chelonia TURTLES, TORTOISES, TERRAPINS

Crocodilia CROCODILES, ALLIGATORS, GHARIAL

Marsupia POUCHED MAMMALS, KANGAROOS, KOALAS, OPOSSUMS

Struthioniformes, OSTRICHES
Rheiformes, RHEAS
Causariiformes, CASSOWARIES, EMUS
Apterygiformes, KIWIS
Tinamiformes, TINAMOUS
Sphenisciformes, PENGUINS
Gaviiformes, LOONS
Podicipediformes, GREBES
Procellariiformes, PETRELS, ALBATROSSES, SHEARWATERS, FULMARS
Pelecaniformes, PELICANS, GANNETS, BOOBIES, CORMORANTS, SHAGS, DARTERS, FRIGATE BIRDS
Ciconiiformes, HERONS, BITTERNS
Anseriformes, DUCKS, GEESE, SWANS, SCREAMERS

Falconiformes, FALCONS, VULTURES, KITES, EAGLES, BUZZARDS, HAWKS, KESTRELS, OSPREYS, SECRETARY BIRDS
Galliformes, TURKEYS, PHEASANTS, PARTRIDGES, GROUSE, PEAFOWL
Gruiformes, CRANES, RAILS, COOTS, BUSTARDS
Charadriiformes, JACANAS, OYSTERCATCHERS, AVOCETS, COURSERS, PLOVERS, LAPWINGS, SNIPE, SKUAS, GULLS, TERNS, SKIMMERS, AUKS
Pteroclidformes, SAND GROUSE
Columbiformes, DOVES, PIGEONS
Psittaciformes, PARROTS, PARAKEETS, LORIES, LORIKEETS, COCKATOOS, MACAWS
Cuculiformes, CUCKOOS, TURACOS, HOATZIN

Strigiformes, OWLS
Caprimulgiformes, NIGHTJARS, NIGHTHAWKS, FROGMOUTHS, OILBIRDS, POTOOS
Apodiformes, SWIFTS, HUMMINGBIRDS
Coliiformes, MOUSEBIRDS
Trogoniformes, TROGONS
Coraciiformes, KINGFISHERS, TOADIES, MOTMOTS, BEE EATERS, ROLLERS, HOOPOES, HORNBILLS
Piciformes, WOODPECKERS, BARBETS
Passeriformes, PERCHING BIRDS (e.g., larks, swallows, shrikes, wrens, thrushes, warblers, sunbirds, honey eaters, buntings, blackbirds, finches, weavers, sparrows, starlings, birds of paradise, crows)

9

Show Some Spine

The simplest way to classify animals is to divide them into two groups: those with spinal columns, or backbones, and those without backbones. The bones in the spinal column are called vertebrae, so animals with backbones are called vertebrates. There are at least 40,000 species of vertebrates. There are many millions of species of invertebrates, or animals without backbones.

All mammals, fish, birds, reptiles, and amphibians are vertebrates. Invertebrates include everything else: sponges, jellyfish, insects, spiders, clams, snails, worms, and many, many others.

Vertebrates

Invertebrates

Animals with Most Known Species

Mollusks
100,000

Fish
24,000

Worms
20,000

Birds
9,600

Reptiles
8,700

Mammals
5,000

Insects and
Other Arthropods
1,000,000+

10 Longest Animal Life Spans

Animal	Maximum age (years)
Quahog (marine clam)	400
Giant tortoise	150
Human	122
Sturgeon	100
Killer whale	90
Blue whale	80
Golden eagle	80
Elephant	75
Sea anemone	70
Crocodile	60

For the better part of 200 million years, dinosaurs ruled the world. Yet until the 19th century, they didn't even have a name. In 1842, English scientist Sir Richard Owen concluded that recently discovered fossils of huge jaws and teeth must belong to reptiles unlike any living animals. He named them *Dinosauria* ("terribly great lizards"). Some dinosaurs *were* great. *Supersaurus* could grow to a length of 130 feet (40 m)—as long as a 13-story building is tall—and weigh as much as 10 elephants. But other dinosaurs were the size of chickens. Most dinosaurs were herbivores, and most lived on land. They coexisted peacefully with mammals, most of which were small rodents.

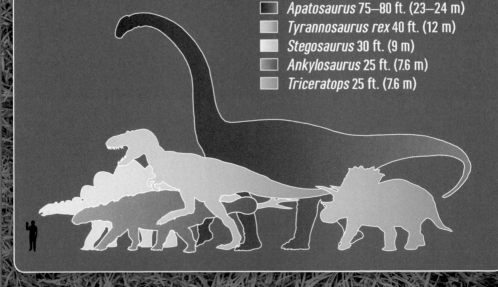

☐ *Apatosaurus* 75–80 ft. (23–24 m)
☐ *Tyrannosaurus rex* 40 ft. (12 m)
☐ *Stegosaurus* 30 ft. (9 m)
☐ *Ankylosaurus* 25 ft. (7.6 m)
☐ *Triceratops* 25 ft. (7.6 m)

Animals

12

Which Dinosaurs Lived When?

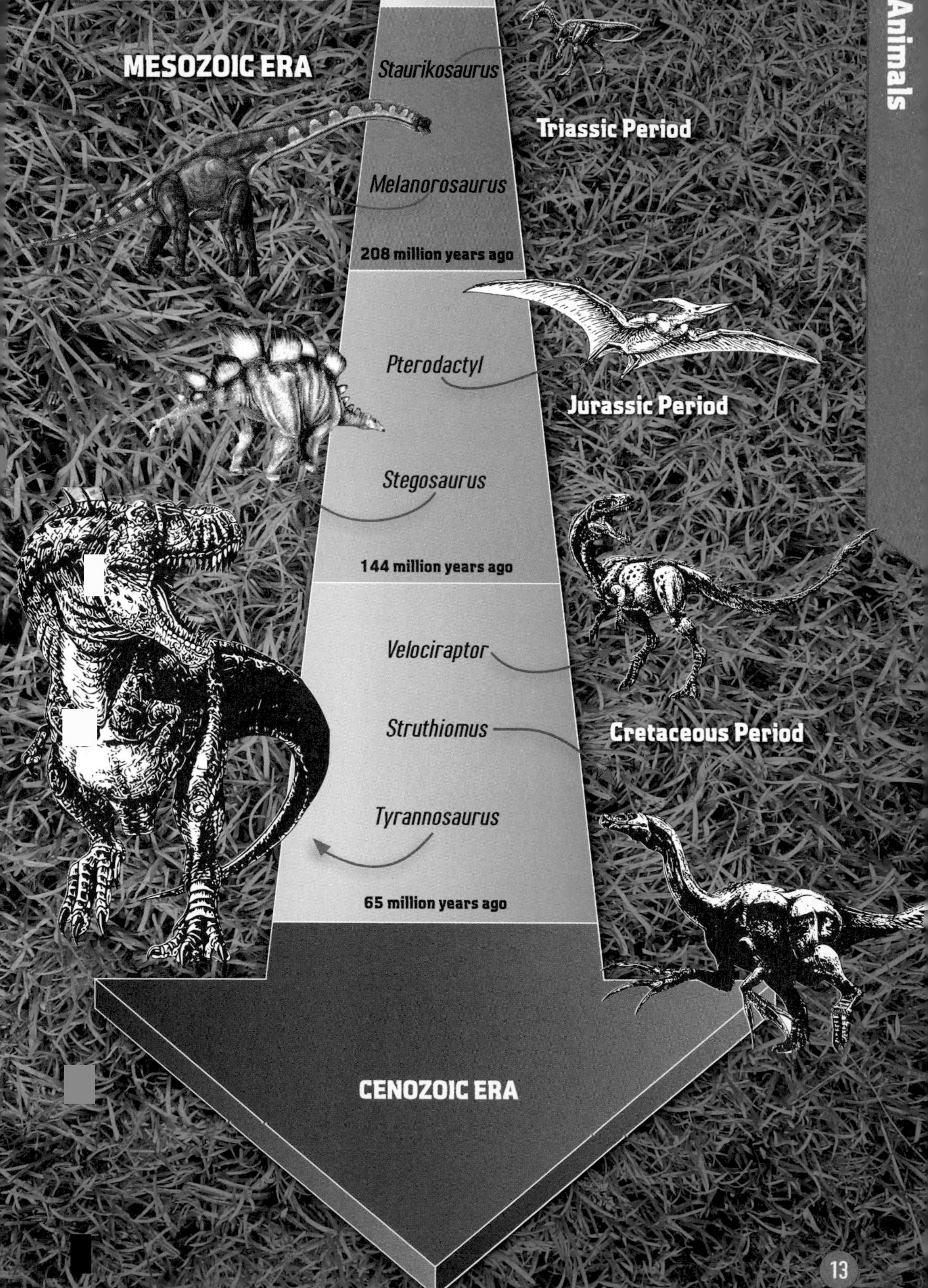

248 million years ago

PALEOZOIC ERA

MESOZOIC ERA

Staurikosaurus

Triassic Period

Melanorosaurus

208 million years ago

Pterodactyl

Jurassic Period

Stegosaurus

144 million years ago

Velociraptor

Struthiomus

Cretaceous Period

Tyrannosaurus

65 million years ago

CENOZOIC ERA

Animals

Sauropods were the giants of the prehistoric world. The *apatosaurus*, *diplodocus*, and *seismosaurus* were all sauropods. These dinosaurs had long necks, long tails, and huge stomachs and chests. Big as they were, the sauropods were peaceful plant eaters.

Theropods were the only meat-eating dinosaurs. One of the fiercest was *Tyrannosaurus rex*, but the *velociraptor* was equally ferocious. It slashed and sliced prey to pieces with the razor-sharp curved claws on its feet.

Stegosaurs' plates and spikes may have done more than keep away enemies. Scientists think blood flowing through the spikes could have been warmed or cooled by the air moving over the stegosaur's back, controlling body temperature.

Ankylosaurs were built for survival. Heavy, bony plates protected their bodies like armor on a tank. Some types had a mass of bone on their tails that they could use as a club.

Ceratopsians looked like rhinoceroses. They had horns on their faces and a curved collar of bone around their neck. Horns over a *triceratops*'s eyes could reach 3 feet (90 cm) long.

Animals

And Then There Were None

For millions and millions of years, dinosaurs dominated. Then they were gone—forever. What happened? The scientific community has been split on different theories for years, but now there seems to be agreement: An asteroid did it. In March 2010, an international panel of scientists announced that an enormous asteroid striking Earth about 65 million years ago caused catastrophic damage to life on our planet.

Scientists estimate that the asteroid was 9 miles (15 km) wide and struck with an impact more powerful than a billion atomic bombs, causing worldwide earthquakes, tsunamis, landslides, and fires. The impact sent millions of tons of sulphur, dust, and soot into the atmosphere, encasing the earth in dark clouds for months. Plants died, and plant-eating dinosaurs starved to death. The meat-eating dinosaurs that fed on the plant eaters starved, too.

CHECK IT OUT !

Tyrannosaurus rex may have had a bad rap. At one time, scientists thought *T. rex* was a lazy scavenger, feeding on dead dinosaurs and snoozing in the sun between meals. Now they say the fierce meat eater was an active predator too, stalking prey and breaking its neck with strong jaws. As to how *T. rex* used its extremely small arms, they're not so sure.

15

Insects

Insects come in an amazing number of shapes and colors, but all you have to do is count to three to tell them apart from other creatures. All insects have three pairs of legs and three body parts: the head, the thorax, and the abdomen. Scorpions, ticks, centipedes, and many other creatures that look like insects are not the real thing.

Insects come in an amazing number of species, too. There are about four times as many insects as every other kind of animal, combined. Why so many? Insects have adapted to survive.

They can live in the hottest, coldest, wettest, and driest places. Their small size lets them survive in tiny spaces with practically no food. Many insects give birth to millions of young at once, so there's always a new generation to keep the species alive. Most have wings to fly away from danger.

Bugs may bug us, but only about 1 percent of insects are harmful. On the other hand, bees, wasps, and butterflies help keep us supplied with fruits and vegetables and help keep our world beautiful by pollinating plants and flowers.

Top 10 Most Common Insects

Animal	Approximate number of known species
Beetles	350,000
Butterflies and moths	150,000
True flies	120,000
Ants, bees, and wasps	50,000
True bugs	40,000
Grasshoppers, crickets, and locusts	20,000
Caddis flies	7,000
Lacewings	4,000
Lice	2,900
Dragonflies and damselflies	2,500

To hide from predators, walking sticks can blend into the twigs and branches on which they live. The largest kinds of walking sticks live in Asia and can grow to be more than 22 inches (56 cm) with their legs fully extended.

Insect eyes can have up to 30,000 lenses. Each lens lets in a separate piece of the scene, and then the parts combine to form a whole picture.

Grasshoppers have about 900 muscles—over 200 more muscles than humans. Many insects can lift or pull objects 20 times their weight.

Scientists say the dragonfly is the fastest-flying insect, capable of reaching 38 miles per hour (61 kph).

Fruit farmers love ladybugs because they eat the aphids that destroy crops. Predators hate their foul taste, which comes from a liquid the spotted insects produce from joints in their legs when threatened.

Mammals

There are more than 4,500 kinds of mammals, including the species you see when you look in the mirror: human. Mammals are different from all other animals in two important ways:

- Babies feed on their mother's milk.

- They have hair or fur.

Most mammals eat only plants, but big cats like the leopard and lion are exclusively meat eaters. Humans and some other species are omnivores. They have flat teeth to grind plants, sharp teeth to pierce animal flesh, and the digestive systems to handle both kinds of food.

All mammals are warm-blooded. Their body temperature stays the same no matter how cold or warm it gets around them. They also have large brains compared to their body size. Scientists say this lets certain mammals, like humans, chimps, apes, and dolphins, learn more than other animals. In February 2010, a panel of scientists declared that dolphins are second only to humans in intelligence and are so bright they should be considered "nonhuman persons."

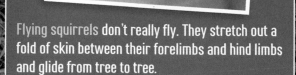

Unlike kangaroos, koalas, and other marsupials, the opossum does not have a pouch.

Flying squirrels don't really fly. They stretch out a fold of skin between their forelimbs and hind limbs and glide from tree to tree.

What do an armadillo's bony shell and a rhinoceros's thick hide have in common? They both protect against sharp-clawed predators.

The echidna and the platypus are the only mammals that don't give birth to live young. They're *monotremes* that lay eggs with leathery shells.

Many scientists say that a bear's winter sleep isn't true *hibernation* because the animal's body temperature falls only slightly. Other mammals, such as chipmunks and woodchucks, undergo a sharp temperature drop when they take their seasonal snooze.

19

Heaviest Land Mammals

Mammal	Weight
African elephant	15,000 lb. (6,804 kg)
Hippopotamus	9,920 lb. (4,500 kg)
White rhinoceros	5,000 lb. (2,268 kg)
Giraffe	3,000 lb. (1,361 kg)
Asian water buffalo	2,600 lb. (1,179 kg)
Arabian camel (dromedary)	1,520 lb. (689 kg)
Grizzly bear	1,500 lb. (680 kg)
Gorilla	500 lb. (227 kg)
Siberian tiger	400 lb. (181 kg)

Heaviest Marine Mammals

Mammal	Weight
Blue whale	150 tons
Fin whale	80 tons
Right whale	70 tons
Sperm whale	60 tons
Humpback whale	40 tons
Sei whale	40 tons
Gray whale	15 tons
Baird's beaked whale	14 tons
Killer whale	10 tons

Animals

Smallest Mammals

Mammal	Weight
Kitti's hog-nosed bat	1.2 in. (3.2 cm)
Pipistrelle bat	1.4 in. (3.6 cm)
Masked shrew	1.8 in. (4.6 cm)
Common (Eurasian) shrew	2.0 in. (5.1 cm)
Harvest mouse	2.0 in. (5.1 cm)
Southern blossom bat	2.0 in. (5.1 cm)
House mouse	2.5 in. (6.4 cm)

Fastest Mammals

Mammal	Maximum speed
Cheetah	70 mph (113 kph)
Pronghorn antelope	61 mph (98 kph)
Springbok	55 mph (89 kph)
Blue wildebeest	50 mph (80 kph)
Lion	50 mph (80 kph)
Brown hare	48 mph (77 kph)
Red fox	30 mph (48 kph)

Birds

If you see an animal with feathers, you can be sure it's a bird. Only birds have them, and they have lots! Scientists say birds have between about 1,000 and 25,000 feathers, which they shed once a year as new ones grow in. Feathers keep birds warm, help them fly, and give them their remarkable variety of colors and markings.

Like mammals, birds are warm-blooded vertebrates. A bird's skeleton is strong because many of the bones are fused together. In humans and other animals, they're separate. At the same time, bird skeletons are lightweight because many of the bones are hollow.

Scientists believe that birds evolved from ancient reptiles—specifically, meat-eating dinosaurs such as *Tyrannosaurus rex* and the *velociraptor.* They say at one time these ferocious dinosaurs may have had feathers!

The feathers of this mallard and of all birds are made of keratin, the same substance that covers a rhinoceros's bony horn and makes up human hair and nails.

Hummingbirds are the only birds that can fly backward. A hummingbird's heart beats 1,000 times a minute.

Parrots have a large cerebrum, the part of the brain that controls learning. Scientists say that may be why they can learn to talk.

Do you have eyes like a hawk? Not a chance! Hawks can see about eight times as well as humans.

Arctic terns migrate the farthest of any bird. Every year they travel about 22,000 miles (35,400 km) from the Arctic to their Antarctic winter home and back again.

All birds have wings, but not all birds can fly. Ostriches, the largest living birds, walk or run. Penguins swim, using their wings as flippers.

When a woodpecker digs for insects in the bark of a tree, it makes a loud hammering sound. It makes the same sound when trying to attract a mate or to claim territory from other birds. Some woodpeckers can make holes large enough to damage trees or even break them in half.

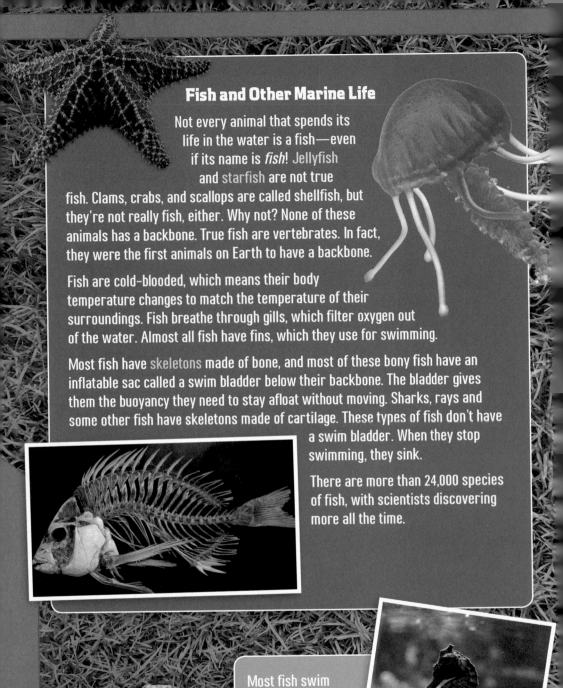

Fish and Other Marine Life

Not every animal that spends its life in the water is a fish—even if its name is *fish*! Jellyfish and starfish are not true fish. Clams, crabs, and scallops are called shellfish, but they're not really fish, either. Why not? None of these animals has a backbone. True fish are vertebrates. In fact, they were the first animals on Earth to have a backbone.

Fish are cold-blooded, which means their body temperature changes to match the temperature of their surroundings. Fish breathe through gills, which filter oxygen out of the water. Almost all fish have fins, which they use for swimming.

Most fish have skeletons made of bone, and most of these bony fish have an inflatable sac called a swim bladder below their backbone. The bladder gives them the buoyancy they need to stay afloat without moving. Sharks, rays and some other fish have skeletons made of cartilage. These types of fish don't have a swim bladder. When they stop swimming, they sink.

There are more than 24,000 species of fish, with scientists discovering more all the time.

Most fish swim horizontally, but the sea horse swims vertically.

Animals

Barracudas and piranhas have razor-sharp teeth that can strip the flesh from a large mammal in minutes.

The whale shark is the largest fish. It grows to more than 50 feet (15.2 m) in length and may weigh several tons. The smallest fish—as well as the smallest vertebrate—is the paedocypris, which is less than one-third of an inch (7.9 mm) long.

Sharks have excellent eyesight, especially in the darkness. Bright colors such as yellow and orange seem to attract them. Based on documented attacks, the five most dangerous species of shark are the great white, bull shark, tiger shark, grey nurse shark, and lemon shark.

Clown fish stay safe from predators by hiding inside the poisonous stinging tentacles of certain sea anemones. Why aren't the clown fish stung? Scientists say they may be protected by a layer of slime on their skin.

Reptiles & Amphibians

Reptiles and amphibians have a lot in common. They're both vertebrates. They're both cold-blooded, and they've both been around for millions of years. However, there are important differences. Most amphibians hatch from eggs laid in water and then spend their adult lives on land. Reptiles are primarily land animals, although some, like sea turtles and sea snakes, spend their whole life in the water.

Another difference is their skin. A reptile's skin is dry and scaly. Most amphibians have moist skin, which is often kept that way by a slimy coating of mucus.

Lizards and snakes are the most common reptiles—there are thousands of different kinds. Alligators, crocodiles, and turtles are also reptiles. Frogs, toads, and salamanders are the most common amphibians.

Since about the 1980s, the population of some frog species has been declining. Scientists don't fully understand why. However, because frogs and all amphibians absorb gases and other chemicals directly through their skin, there is some worry that disappearing frogs could be an indication of serious environmental problems.

Animals

The Gila monster has a poisonous bite, but most reptiles are harmless to humans.

The gray tree frog can freeze solid without harming itself. A substance in its blood works like antifreeze to protect its organs and tissues.

One way to tell a frog from a toad is to look at its skin. A frog's skin is smooth and moist. A toad's is bumpy and dry.

For many years, scientists thought a chameleon changed colors to blend into its surroundings for protection from predators. Now some scientists think that chameleons change colors to stand out to other chameleons. Brighter colors are used to show dominance and attract mates, while drab colors signal surrender.

Animals in Trouble

According to the World Wildlife Federation (WWF), tigers are among the most endangered animals in the world. There are only about 3,200 tigers left in the wild, and almost half of the main subspecies of tiger are now believed to be extinct.

These are the other animals on the WWF's list of ten of the most endangered animals:

Polar bear
Pacific walrus
Magellanic penguin
Leatherback turtle
Bluefin tuna

Mountain gorilla
Monarch butterfly
Javan rhinoceros
Giant panda

Habitat loss, environmental changes, poaching, hunting, and overfishing are the critical threats to these animals' survival.

Names of Male, Female, and Young Animals

Animal	Male	Female	Young
Bear	Boar	Sow	Cub
Cat	Tom	Queen	Kitten
Cow	Bull	Cow	Calf
Chicken	Rooster	Hen	Chick
Deer	Buck	Doe	Fawn
Dog	Dog	Bitch	Pup
Donkey	Jack	Jenny	Foal
Duck	Drake	Duck	Duckling
Elephant	Bull	Cow	Calf
Fox	Dog	Vixen	Kit
Goose	Gander	Goose	Gosling
Horse	Stallion	Mare	Foal
Lion	Lion	Lioness	Cub
Rabbit	Buck	Doe	Bunny
Sheep	Ram	Ewe	Lamb
Swan	Cob	Pen	Cygnet
Swine	Boar	Sow	Piglet
Tiger	Tiger	Tigress	Cub
Whale	Bull	Cow	Calf
Wolf	Dog	Bitch	Pup

Animal Multiples

ants: colony

bears: sleuth, sloth

bees: grist, hive, swarm

birds: flight, volery

cats: clutter, clowder

cows: drove

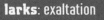

chicks: brood, clutch

clams: bed

cranes: sedge, seige

crows: murder

doves: dule

ducks: brace, team

elephants: herd

elks: gang

finches: charm

fish: school, shoal, drought

foxes: leash, skulk

geese: flock, gaggle, skein

gnats: cloud, horde

goats: trip

gorillas: band

hares: down, husk

hawks: cast

hens: brood

hogs: drift

horses: pair, team

hounds: cry, mute, pack

kangaroos: troop

kittens: kindle, litter

larks: exaltation

lions: pride

locusts: plague

magpies: tidings

mules: span

nightingales: watch

oxen: yoke

oysters: bed

parrots: company

partridges: covey

peacocks: muster, ostentation

pheasants: nest, bouquet

pigs: litter

ponies: string

quail: bevy, covey

rabbits: nest

seals: pod

sheep: drove, flock

sparrows: host

storks: mustering

swans: bevy, wedge

swine: sounder

toads: knot

turkeys: rafter

turtles: bale

vipers: nest

whales: gam, pod

wolves: pack, route

woodcocks: fall

Types of Pets in the United States

Animal	Number of households owning
Dog	44.8 million
Cat	38.4 million
Freshwater fish	14.2 million
Bird	6.4 million
Small animal (rabbits, ferrets, hamsters, guinea pigs, and gerbils)	6.0 million
Reptile	4.8 million
Equine (horses, ponies)	4.3 million
Saltwater fish	800,000

Top 10 Registered U.S. Dog Breeds

Labrador retriever

German shepherd

Yorkshire terrier

Golden retriever

Beagle

Boxer

Bulldog

Dachshund

Poodle

Shih Tzu

Top 10 Registered U.S. Cat Breeds

Persian

Maine coon

Exotic shorthair

Siamese

Abyssinian

Ragdoll

Birman

American shorthair

Oriental shorthair

Sphynx

Birthdays

You Take the Cake

What's more fun than a birthday—especially if it's yours? Birthdays and kids seem to go together like candles and cake. In fact, historians say the tradition of placing one candle for each year of age, with a few more for the future, goes back to an 18th-century birthday celebration for children called *Kinderfest* (*kinder* is the German word for "children"). Birthday cakes, without candles, may date all the way back to honey and nut cakes made by the ancient Romans.

Birthday Pie and Head Bumps

Not every culture celebrates with cake. In Russia, kids might be served a fruit birthday pie with birthday messages carved into the crust. In China, they might be treated to *sou bao*, individual sweet buns shaped and colored to look like peaches. Birthday children in Ghana eat *oto*, a fried patty made from mashed sweet potato and eggs.

Other traditions differ, too. Among some Hindu families in India, it's common to shave a child's head on his or her first birthday. Irish kids might get turned upside down and bumped (*very gently!*) on the head, once for each year.

Top Times to Be Born

Were you born in the United States on a Tuesday or in July? Tuesday used to be the most popular day of the week for births, and July was once the most popular month of the year. However, as of 2006, the U.S. Census Bureau says more births happen on Wednesday than any other day of the week and in August than any other month of the year.

BIRTHSTONES BY MONTH

Each month has its own jewel or semiprecious stone. There are stories and legends about every birthstone. April's birthstone, the diamond, is a symbol of love that was also thought to bring courage. Sailors once believed that the aquamarine, March's birthstone, could protect them from danger at sea. Research the story behind your month's stone.

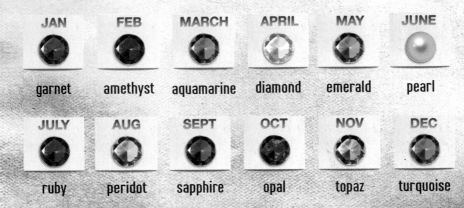

JAN	FEB	MARCH	APRIL	MAY	JUNE
garnet	amethyst	aquamarine	diamond	emerald	pearl

JULY	AUG	SEPT	OCT	NOV	DEC
ruby	peridot	sapphire	opal	topaz	turquoise

(TAKE a LOOK)

You are unique—there's no doubt about that. Still, lots of people share your birthday. In fact, mathematicians calculate that out of a group of 23 people, at least 2 will have the same birthday. Turn the page to learn someone famous who was born on the same day—but not necessarily in the same year—as you.

Are you a twin? In the United States, about 32 out of every 1,000 births are twins. Are you a triplet, quadruplet, or part of an even larger birth group? That rate is about 153 per 100,000.

CHECK IT OUT !

33

January

1 Paul Revere, American patriot, 1735
2 Taye Diggs, actor, 1971
3 J. R. R. Tolkien, author, 1892
4 Doris Kearns Goodwin, historian, 1943
5 Diane Keaton, actor, 1946
6 Joan of Arc, military leader and saint, around 1412
7 Nicolas Cage, actor, 1964
8 Stephen Hawking, physicist, 1942
9 John Knowles Paine, composer, 1839
10 George Foreman, boxer, 1949
11 John MacDonald, first Canadian prime minister, 1815
12 Jack London, author, 1876
13 Orlando Bloom, actor, 1977
14 Albert Schweitzer, scientist and humanitarian, 1875
15 Drew Brees, pro football player, 1979
16 Kate Moss, model, 1974
17 Michelle Obama, U.S. First Lady, 1964
18 Kevin Costner, actor, 1955
19 Edgar Allan Poe, author, 1809
20 Edwin "Buzz" Aldrin, astronaut, 1930
21 Plácido Domingo, operatic tenor, 1941
22 Sir Francis Bacon, explorer, 1561
23 Edouard Manet, painter, 1832
24 Mary Lou Retton, gymnast, 1968
25 Alicia Keys, musician, 1981
26 Ellen Degeneres, TV personality, 1958
27 Hannah Teter, snowboarder, 1987
28 Sarah McLachlan, musician, 1968
29 Oprah Winfrey, media personality, 1954
30 Christian Bale, actor, 1974
31 Justin Timberlake, musician, 1981

February

1 Langston Hughes, writer, 1902
2 Christie Brinkley, model, 1954
3 Norman Rockwell, painter, 1894
4 Rosa Parks, civil rights activist, 1913
5 Cristiano Ronaldo, soccer player, 1985
6 Babe Ruth, baseball player, 1895
7 Charles Dickens, author, 1812
8 Seth Green, actor, 1974
9 Alice Walker, author, 1944
10 George Stephanopoulos, TV news personality, 1961
11 Thomas Edison, inventor, 1847
12 Abraham Lincoln, president, 1809
13 Chuck Yeager, test pilot, 1923
14 Jack Benny, radio and TV entertainer, 1894
15 Susan B. Anthony, suffragist and civil rights leader, 1820
16 Ice-T, rap musician and actor, 1958
17 Michael Jordan, basketball player, 1963
18 John Travolta, actor, 1954
19 Jeff Daniels, actor, 1955
20 Gloria Vanderbilt, fashion designer, 1924
21 W. H. Auden, poet, 1907
22 Edward Kennedy, U.S. senator, 1932
23 Dakota Fanning, actor, 1994
24 Steve Jobs, cofounder of Apple Computers, 1955
25 Sean Astin, actor, 1971
26 Johnny Cash, singer and songwriter, 1932
27 Chelsea Clinton, U.S presidential daughter, 1980
28 Frank O. Gehry, architect, 1929
29 Jimmy Dorsey, orchestra leader, 1904

March

1 Ron Howard, actor and director, 1954
2 Dr. Seuss (Theodor Geisel), author, 1904
3 Jackie Joyner-Kersee, track star, 1962
4 Knute Rockne, football star, 1888
5 Eva Mendes, actor, 1974
6 Michelangelo, painter, 1475
7 Rachel Weisz, actor, 1970
8 Freddie Prinze Jr., actor, 1976
9 Juliette Binoche, actor, 1964
10 Shannon Miller, gymnast, 1977
11 Terrence Howard, actor, 1969
12 Amelia Earhart, aviator, 1897
13 Abigail Fillmore, U.S. First Lady, 1798
14 Billy Crystal, actor, 1948
15 Ruth Bader Ginsberg, Supreme Court justice, 1933
16 Jerry Lewis, entertainer, 1926
17 Mia Hamm, soccer player, 1972
18 Queen Latifah, entertainer, 1970
19 Wyatt Earp, U.S. western lawman, 1848
20 Lois Lowry, author, 1937
21 Matthew Broderick, actor, 1962
22 Bob Costas, sportscaster, 1952
23 Jason Kidd, basketball player, 1973
24 Peyton Manning, football player, 1976
25 Gloria Steinem, feminist and author, 1934
26 Sandra Day O'Connor, U.S. Supreme Court justice, 1930
27 Sarah Vaughan, singer, 1924
28 Lady Gaga, singer, 1986
29 Jennifer Capriati, tennis player, 1976
30 Vincent van Gogh, painter, 1853
31 René Descartes, philosopher, 1596

Birthdays

April

1 Susan Boyle, singer, 1961
2 Dana Carvey, entertainer, 1955
3 Jane Goodall, anthropologist, 1934
4 Maya Angelou, poet, 1928
5 Booker T. Washington, inventor, 1856
6 Zach Braff, actor, 1975
7 Jackie Chan, actor, 1954
8 Kofi Atta Annan, UN attorney general, 1938
9 Cynthia Nixon, actor, 1966
10 Frances Perkins, first female member of U.S. Presidential Cabinet (Secretary of Labor), 1880
11 Joss Stone, singer, 1987
12 Tom Clancy, author, 1947
13 Samuel Beckett, playwright, 1906
14 Adrien Brody, actor, 1973
15 Emma Watson, actor, 1990
16 Wilbur Wright, aviator, 1867
17 John Pierpoint Morgan, industrialist, 1837
18 Conan O'Brien, TV personality, 1963
19 Kate Hudson, actor, 1979
20 Don Mattingly, baseball player, 1961
21 John Muir, environmentalist, 1838
22 Jack Nicholson, actor, 1937
23 William Shakespeare, poet and playwright, 1564
24 Kelly Clarkson, singer, 1982
25 Renée Zellweger, actor, 1969
26 John James Audubon, naturalist, 1785
27 Ulysses S. Grant, U.S. President, 1822
28 Jay Leno, TV personality, 1950
29 Duke Ellington, jazz musician, 1899
30 Kirsten Dunst, actor, 1982

May

1 Tim McGraw, country singer, 1967
2 David Beckham, soccer player, 1975
3 James Brown, singer and songwriter, 1933
4 Will Arnett, actor, 1970
5 Tammy Wynette, country singer, 1942
6 Willie Mays, baseball player, 1931
7 Tim Russert, TV news personality, 1950
8 Bobby Labonte, NASCAR driver, 1964
9 Candice Bergen, actor, 1946
10 Fred Astaire, actor, 1899
11 Salvador Dali, painter, 1904
12 Yogi Berra, baseball player, 1925
13 Robert Pattinson, actor, 1986
14 Gabriel Daniel Fahrenheit, scientist, 1686
15 Emmitt Smith, football player, 1969
16 Olga Korbut, gymnast, 1955
17 Craig Ferguson, TV personality, 1962
18 Tina Fey, TV personality, 1970
19 Nora Ephron, author and director, 1941
20 Bono, musician, 1960
21 Al Franken, entertainer and U.S. senator, 1951
22 Apolo Anton Ohno, speed skater, 1982
23 Jewel, singer and songwriter, 1974
24 Victoria, Queen of England, 1819
25 Mike Myers, actor, 1963
26 Sally Ride, astronaut, 1951
27 Henry Kissinger, U.S. diplomat, 1923
28 Kylie Minogue, singer, 1968
29 Carmelo Anthony, basketball player, 1984
30 Wynonna Judd, country singer and songwriter, 1964
31 Clint Eastwood, actor and director, 1930

June

1 Marilyn Monroe, actress, 1926
2 Martha Washington, First U.S. First Lady, 1731
3 Rafael Nadal, tennis player, 1986
4 Evan Lysacek, ice skater, 1985
5 Mark Wahlberg, actor, 1971
6 Alexander Pushkin, author, 1799
7 Dean Martin, singer and actor, 1917
8 Frank Lloyd Wright, architect, 1867
9 Johnny Depp, actor, 1963
10 Maurice Sendak, author, 1928
11 Shia LaBeouf, actor, 1986
12 Anne Frank, Holocaust diarist, 1929
13 Ashley and Mary-Kate Olsen, actors, 1986
14 Donald Trump, businessman, 1946
15 Courtney Cox Arquette, actor, 1971
16 Joyce Carol Oates, author, 1938
17 Venus Williams, tennis player, 1981
18 Paul McCartney, musician, 1942
19 Guy Lombardo, band leader, 1902
20 Shefali Chowdhury, actor, 1988
21 Prince William of Wales, British royal, 1982
22 John Dillinger, bank robber, 1903
23 Randy Jackson, TV personality, 1956
24 Mick Fleetwood, musician, 1942
25 Sonia Sotomayor, U.S. Supreme Court justice, 1954
26 Babe Didrikson Zaharias, athlete, 1911
27 Khloé Kardashian Odom, TV personality, 1984
28 John Cusack, actor, 1966
29 George Washington Goethals, chief engineer of the Panama Canal, 1858
30 Michael Phelps, swimmer, 1985

July

1 Benjamin Oliver Davis, first African American general in the U.S. Army, 1877
2 Lindsay Lohan, actor, 1986
3 Tom Cruise, actor, 1962
4 George Steinbrenner, New York Yankees owner, 1930
5 P. T. Barnum, showman and entertainer, 1810
6 50 Cent, rap musician, 1976
7 Michelle Kwan, ice skater, 1980
8 Anna Quindlen, author, 1952
9 Tom Hanks, actor, 1956
10 Jessica Simpson, actor and singer, 1980
11 Sela Ward, actor, 1956
12 Henry David Thoreau, author and philosopher, 1817
13 Harrison Ford, actor, 1942
14 Crown Princess Victoria, Swedish monarch, 1977
15 Rembrandt, painter, 1606
16 Will Ferrell, actor, 1967
17 Phyllis Diller, comedian, 1917
18 Nelson Mandela, South African political leader, 1918
19 Edgar Degas, painter, 1834
20 Gisele Bundchen, model, 1980
21 Brandi Chastain, soccer player, 1968
22 Oscar de la Renta, fashion designer, 1932
23 Daniel Radcliffe, actor, 1989
24 Jennifer Lopez, actor and singer, 1969
25 Matt LeBlanc, actor, 1967
26 Sandra Bullock, actor, 1964
27 Alex Rodriguez, baseball player, 1975
28 Beatrix Potter, author, 1866
29 Martina McBride, country singer, 1966
30 Emily Brontë, novelist, 1818
31 J. K. Rowling, author, 1965

August

1 Francis Scott Key, writer of "The Star-Spangled Banner"
2 James Baldwin, author, 1924
3 Martha Stewart, lifestyle spokesperson and TV personality, 1941
4 Jeff Gordon, NASCAR driver, 1971
5 Neil Armstrong, astronaut, 1930
6 Lucille Ball, actor, 1911
7 Sidney Crosby, hockey player, 1987
8 Roger Federer, tennis player, 1981
9 John Dryden, poet, 1631
10 Betsey Johnson, fashion designer, 1942
11 Hulk Hogan, wrestler, 1953
12 Pete Sampras, tennis player, 1971
13 Annie Oakley, Wild West entertainer, 1860
14 Robyn Smith, jockey, 1944
15 Napoleon Bonaparte, emperor, 1769
16 Angela Bassett, actor, 1958
17 Davy Crockett, frontiersman, 1786
18 Roberto Clemente, baseball player, 1934
19 Gene Rodenberry, creator of *Star Trek*, 1921
20 Al Roker, TV meteorologist, 1954
21 Wilt Chamberlain, basketball player, 1936
22 Tori Amos, musician, 1963
23 Kobe Bryant, basketball player, 1978
24 Chad Michael Murray, actor, 1981
25 Leonard Bernstein, conductor and composer, 1918
26 Branford Marsalis, musician, 1960
27 Mother Teresa, nun and humanitarian, 1910
28 Shania Twain, country singer, 1965
29 Michael Jackson, musician and performer, 1958
30 Mary Shelley, author of *Frankenstein*, 1797
31 Richard Gere, actor, 1949

September

1 Gloria Estefan, singer, 1957
2 Keanu Reeves, actor, 1964
3 Shaun White, snowboarder, 1986
4 Beyoncé Knowles, singer and actress, 1981
5 Kim Yu-Na, figure skater, 1990
6 John Dalton, scientist, 1766
7 Michael DeBakey, pioneer heart surgeon, 1908
8 Pink, singer, 1979
9 Adam Sandler, actor, 1966
10 Colin Firth, actor, 1960
11 William Sydney Porter, better known as O. Henry, short story writer, 1862
12 Yao Ming, basketball player, 1980
13 Milton Hershey, chocolate magnate, 1857
14 Kimberly Williams-Paisley, actor, 1971
15 Prince Henry ("Harry") of Wales, British royal, 1984
16 Alexis Bledel, actor, 1981
17 William Carlos Williams, poet, 1883
18 Lance Armstrong, bicycle racer, 1971
19 Trisha Yearwood, country singer, 1964
20 Sophia Loren, actor, 1934
21 Stephen King, author, 1947
22 Joan Jett, singer, 1960
23 Bruce Springsteen, musician, 1949
24 Jim Henson, creator of the Muppets, 1936
25 Will Smith, actor, 1968
26 Serena Williams, tennis player, 1981
27 Avril Lavigne, singer, 1984
28 Caravaggio, painter, 1571
29 Enrico Fermi, physicist and atom bomb developer, 1901
30 Elie Wiesel, author and Holocaust survivor, 1928

October

1 Vladimir Horowitz, pianist, 1904
2 Groucho Marx, comedian, 1890
3 Gwen Stefani, singer, 1969
4 Alicia Silverstone, actor, 1976
5 Maya Lin, architect, 1959
6 George Westinghouse, inventor, 1846
7 Yo-Yo Ma, cellist, 1955
8 Rev. Jesse Jackson, African American leader, 1941
9 Annika Sorenstam, tennis player, 1970
10 Brett Favre, football player, 1969
11 Eleanor Roosevelt, U.S. First Lady and diplomat, 1884
12 Bode Miller, skier, 1977
13 Margaret Thatcher, British prime minister, 1925
14 Usher, rap singer, 1979
15 Emeril Lagasse, chef, 1959
16 John Mayer, singer, 1977
17 Mae Jemison, first African American female astronaut, 1956
18 Lindsey Vonn, skier, 1984
19 Peter Max, artist, 1937
20 Bela Lugosi, actor who played Dracula, 1882
21 Alfred Nobel, scientist, 1883
22 Deepak Chopra, self-help writer, 1946
23 Pelé, soccer player, 1940
24 Kevin Kline, actor, 1947
25 Pablo Picasso, artist, 1881
26 Hilary Rodham Clinton, U.S. First Lady, U.S. senator, and Secretary of State, 1947
27 Captain James Cook, explorer, 1728
28 Bill Gates, Microsoft founder, 1955
29 Gabrielle Union, actor, 1972
30 Nastia Liukin, gymnast, 1989
31 Chiang Kai-Shek, Nationalist Chinese leader, 1887

November

1 Toni Collette, actor, 1972
2 Daniel Boone, U.S. frontiersman, 1734
3 Vincenzo Bellini, composer, 1801
4 Walter Cronkite, newscaster, 1916
5 Roy Rogers, TV cowboy, 1911
6 James A. Naismith, inventor of basketball, 1861
7 Marie Curie, chemist, 1867
8 Margaret Mitchell, author, 1900
9 Carl Sagan, scientist, 1934
10 Sinbad, entertainer, 1956
11 Leonardo DiCaprio, actor, 1974
12 Elizabeth Cady Stanton, suffragist, 1815
13 Louis Brandeis, U.S. Supreme Court justice, 1856
14 Georgia O'Keeffe, painter, 1887
15 Kevin Eubanks, musician and TV personality, 1957
16 Trevor Pinick, musician and singer, 1979
17 Danny DeVito, actor, 1944
18 Wilma Mankiller, first female Chief of the Cherokee Nation, 1945
19 Calvin Klein, fashion designer, 1942
20 Edwin Hubble, scientist, 1889
21 Ken Griffey Jr., boxer, 1969
22 Mark Ruffalo, actor, 1967
23 Miley Cyrus, singer, 1992
24 Scott Joplin, composer, 1868
25 Andrew Carnegie, industrialist, 1883
26 Charles Schulz, cartoonist, 1922
27 Anders Celsius, scientist, 1701
28 Jon Stewart, TV personality, 1965
29 Mariano Rivera, baseball player, 1969
30 Mark Twain, author, 1835

December

1 Woody Allen, actor and director, 1935
2 Britney Spears, singer, 1981
3 Ozzy Osbourne, musician and performer, 1948
4 Thomas Carlyle, author, 1795
5 Walt Disney, producer and animator, 1901
6 Ira Gershwin, lyricist, 1896
7 Willa Cather, author, 1873
8 Eli Whitney, inventor, 1765
9 Clarence Birdseye, frozen food pioneer, 1886
10 Emily Dickinson, poet, 1830
11 Mo'Nique, actor, 1967
12 Frank Sinatra, singer and actor, 1915
13 Taylor Swift, singer, 1989
14 Vanessa Hudgens, actor, 1988
15 Gustave Eiffel, designer of the Eiffel Tower, 1832
16 Jane Austen, author, 1775
17 Milla Jovovich, actor, 1975
18 Steven Spielberg, director, 1946
19 Edith Piaf, singer, 1915
20 Harvey Samuel Firestone, tire manufacturer, 1868
21 Kiefer Sutherland, actor, 1966
22 Diane Sawyer, TV news anchor, 1945
23 Madame C. J. Walker, inventor and businesswoman, 1867
24 Stephenie Meyer, author, 1973
25 Clara Barton, founder, American Red Cross, 1821
26 Chris Daughtry, musician, 1979
27 Louis Pasteur, chemist, 1822
28 Denzel Washington, actor, 1954
29 Charles Goodyear, inventor, 1800
30 Meredith Vieira, TV news anchor, 1953
31 Henri Matisse, painter, 1869

Books & Literature

Horror Is Still Hot

In 2009, kids' favorite books were pretty much a repeat of their favorites the year before, topped by superselling author Stephenie Meyer's Twilight series. Other horror series like The Vampire Diaries and Night World were big hits, too. But it's nothing new that kids love scary stories. From *Frankenstein* to *Dracula* to *Dr. Jekyll and Mr. Hyde*, horror stories have always been a superpopular genre of literature with kids and adults alike.

The Facts on Fiction

The Twilight series and *Frankenstein* are works of fiction. They come from an author's imagination. Besides horror, other genres of fiction are fairy tales, humor, mystery, myths and legends, historical fiction, and fantasy and science fiction. The Harry Potter books are fantasy. The new Percy Jackson series is based on myths about gods like Hades and Zeus.

True or False?

Fiction is made up, but nonfiction is fact. Nonfiction books give us information about the world and tell about real people and events. Biographies like *Anne Frank: The Diary of a Young Girl* and reference books like this almanac are examples of nonfiction. What's your favorite kind of book?

Wimps Rule—

Vampires rule with kids, but so do wimps! The Diary of a Wimpy Kid series sold millions of copies in 2009. This series uses cartoons to tell a story. More and more, pictures are becoming an important

So Do Pictures

part of young adult fiction. In The Invention of Hugo Cabret, hundreds of pictures help tell the exciting, mysterious story. You can enjoy favorite series such as the Baby-sitters Club and the Boxcar Children as graphic novels.

TAKE a LOOK

Books have traditionally been printed on paper, but that's changing. E-books, or electronic books, that you download from websites are becoming common. Some people say e-books are good because they're lightweight, easy to carry, and better for the environment because they save trees. Others prefer the old-fashioned kind of book. Would you rather read your favorite series on a screen or on a printed page?

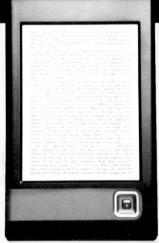

CHECK IT OUT !

Ready for takeoff, Muggles? When this almanac went to press, a new theme park called the Wizarding World of Harry Potter was scheduled to open on June 18, 2010, at Universal Resort Orlando in Orlando, Florida. The featured attractions include a twisting, looping, midair dragon chase and a ride that uses robotics and projection technology to make visitors feel like they're flying over Hogwarts Castle.

Ten Top-Selling Young Adult Books of 2009

Title	Author
New Moon	Stephenie Meyer
Breaking Dawn	Stephenie Meyer
Eclipse (hardcover)	Stephenie Meyer
Twilight	Stephenie Meyer
The Last Straw	Jeff Kinney
Dog Days	Jeff Kinney
Diary of a Wimpy Kid	Jeff Kinney
The Last Olympian	Rick Riordan
Eclipse (paperback)	Stephenie Meyer
Diary of a Wimpy Kid Do-It-Yourself	Jeff Kinney

Top-Selling Young Adult Series of 2009

Title	Author
Twilight	Stephenie Meyer
Diary of a Wimpy Kid	Jeff Kinney
House of Night	PC and Kristin Cast
Percy Jackson and the Olympians	Rick Riordan
The Immortals	Alyson Noël
Alex Rider	James Patterson
Daniel X	James Patterson and Ned Rust
The 39 Clues	Peter Lerangis
Vampire Academies	Richelle Mead
The Mortal Instruments	Cassandra Clare

2010 Children's Book Award Winners

Caldecott Medal: *The Lion and the Mouse*, Jerry Pinkney

Newbery Award: *When You Reach Me*, Rebecca Stead

National Book Award: *Claudette Colvin: Twice Toward Justice*, Phillip Hoose*

Printz Award: *Going Bovine*, Libba Bray

Coretta Scott King Award: *Bad News for Outlaws: The Remarkable Life of Bass Reeves*, Vaunda Micheaux Nelson

Scott O'Dell Award for Historical Fiction: *The Storm in the Barn*, Matt Phelan

Teen Choice Book of the Year: *Catching Fire*, Suzanne Collins

*2009 winner

2010 Nickelodeon Kids' Choice Awards Book Winner

Favorite Book: *Diary of a Wimpy Kid*

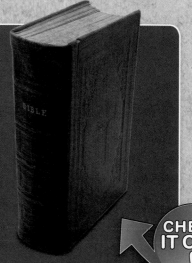

The Twilight saga has sold 80 million books. The Harry Potter series has sold over 350 million. However, the Bible beats them all. With over one billion copies sold, the Bible is the bestselling book of all time. The number one author? According to several sources, it's a tie between playwright/poet William Shakespeare and mystery writer Agatha Christie. Both are estimated to have sold between two and four billion books.

CHECK IT OUT!

Buildings & Landmarks

The Face of a Place

Humans have been building remarkable structures out of a variety of materials since ancient times. In fact, buildings are probably the clearest symbols of civilization. Different cities have unique buildings and landmarks that set them apart from one another. The skyline of Manhattan cannot be confused with that of any other city on Earth. The Golden Gate Bridge says San Francisco the same way the Space Needle says Seattle. And the Great Pyramids and Sphinx can only mean Egypt.

A Big Buildup

Why do we build the things we do? Bridges, roads, and tunnels are practical pathways for people to travel over, on, and through. Dams hold water back to create new space, harness power, and control waterways. Buildings provide shelter, spaces to work, and places to gather and worship.

In this section you'll see what kinds of buildings people have been making through time. How can a building reflect a culture's personality?

SUPER SKYSCRAPERS

Churches and castles were once the biggest, most impressive buildings around. Created out of stone, wood, and metal, these structures were a symbol of power and provided focus to a culture. Nowadays the biggest buildings in many cities are skyscrapers. These towering buildings—crafted from modern materials like steel, wire, concrete, and glass—can contain residences, shops, banks, offices, schools, hospitals, museums, and more.

TAKE a LOOK

The Pyramids at Giza were built around 2600 to 2500 BCE as elaborate royal tombs. Created without the use of modern machinery or iron tools, they are the only "Wonder of the Ancient World" still standing. How do modern "wonders" differ from the ancient ones? (See pages 46 and 47.)

CHECK IT OUT!

At one time, a landmark was something in the natural landscape, like a mountain or river, that could be used to guide explorers. Now a landmark can be any recognizable human-built or natural structure. What kinds of landmarks are in your town? Have you ever used one to find your way?

Milestones in Modern Architecture Timeline

First modern metal-frame skyscraper, Chicago's ten-story Home Insurance Company Building, is designed by U.S. architect William Jenney (1832–1907). It features a metal skeleton of cast-iron columns and nonsupporting curtain walls, which become characteristic of modern design.

1884

U.S. architect Frank Lloyd Wright (1867–1959) becomes famous for designing houses in the Prairie style, characterized by low, horizontal lines and use of natural earth colors. Wright believes buildings should complement settings.

1900

Walter Gropius (1883–1969) founds Bauhaus, a German school of design, to combine art and architecture with modern industrial technology. Bauhaus styles are notable for geometric lines and use of steel, glass, and concrete.

1919

Noted American architect (Richard) Buckminster Fuller (1895–1983) designs a self-contained "4-D" prefabricated house. Fuller becomes known for his "Dymaxion" principle of trying to get the most from the least amount of material and energy.

1928

1937

Ludwig Mies van der Rohe (1886–1969) emigrates to the United States and becomes a leader in glass-and-steel architecture. He pioneers rectangular lines in design, including cubelike brick structures, uncovered steel columns, and large areas of tinted glass.

1948

Petronas Twin Towers in Kuala Lumpur, Malaysia, are built and become the world's tallest buildings at a height of 1,483 feet (452 m). In 2003, the towers lose their title to the Taipei 101 Tower in Taiwan. Taipei 101 measures 1,674 feet (508 m) tall.

Finnish-born American architect Eero Saarinen (1910–1961) becomes known for innovative designs for various buildings in the United States. His sweeping style features soaring rooflines, extensive use of glass, and curved lines.

1996

2009

Taipei 101's title falls to Burj Khalifa in Dubai, United Arab Emirates, 2,717 feet (828 m) tall.

Construction of Important Earthworks, Dams, and Canals Timeline

Elaborate system of earthen levees is built along the Mississippi River at New Orleans, Lousiana, to control floodwaters.

1718

United States opens New York's Erie Canal, linking the Great Lakes with New York City by way of the Hudson River. The canal leads to increased development of western New York State.

1825

Suez Canal, 101 miles (163 km) long, is completed, built by French engineer Ferdinand de Lesseps (1805–1894) to connect the Mediterranean and Red seas. It is enlarged in 1980 to enable passage of supertankers.

1869

Aswan Dam is built on the Nile River in Egypt. Considered one of the finest dams of all time, it has a record-setting length of 6,400 feet (1,951 m).

1902

Panama Canal, dug across Isthmus of Panama, connects the Atlantic and Pacific oceans. It is built by U.S. military engineers on land leased from the Republic of Panama. The Canal Zone is returned to Panama in 1979.

1904–1914

Grand Coulee Dam, built for electric generation and irrigation, is completed on the Columbia River in Washington State. At 550 feet (168 m) high and 5,223 feet (1,592 m) long, it is the world's largest concrete structure.

1942

World's longest tunnel, Delaware Aqueduct, is complete. It is 105 miles (169 km) long and supplies water to New York City.

1944

United States and Canada complete construction of the St. Lawrence Seaway. It provides access to Lake Ontario for oceangoing traffic by way of the St. Lawrence River.

1959

Aswan High Dam, on the Nile River in Egypt, is completed. The dam is 364 feet (111 m) high and 12,562 feet (3,829 m) long.

1970

Construction on the world's longest railroad tunnel is completed in Japan. Almost 33.4 miles (54 km) long, the Seikan Tunnel connects the islands of Hokkaido and Honshu.

1988

2000

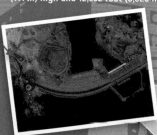

Laerdal-Aurland Tunnel, the world's longest road tunnel, opens in Norway. This 15.2-mile (24.5 km) tunnel connects Oslo to the port of Bergen.

The Seven Wonders of the Modern World

Wonder/Location		Description
Channel Tunnel England and France		The 31-mile (50 km) Channel Tunnel (Chunnel) is actually three concrete tubes, each 5 feet (2 m) thick, which burrow through the English Channel. They enter the earth at Coquelles, France, and reemerge at Folkstone, England, behind the white cliffs of Dover.
CN Tower Toronto		The world's third-tallest freestanding structure soars 1,815 feet (553 m) above Toronto, Canada. The CN Tower was designed to withstand 260-mph (418 kph) gusts.
Empire State Building New York City		At 1,250 feet (381 m), the Empire State Building is the best-known skyscraper in the world. For more than 40 years it was the tallest building in the world. Construction took only one year and 45 days.
Netherlands North Sea Protection Works Netherlands		This is not just one structure but a complex system of dams, floodgates, storm surge barriers, and other engineered works that protect the country against destructive floods.
Golden Gate Bridge San Francisco		Once the world's tallest suspension bridge, the Golden Gate Bridge hangs from two 746-foot (227 m) towers and is supported by enough cable to circle the earth three times.
Itaipu Dam Brazil and Paraguay		Five miles (8 km) wide and as high as a 65-story building, the main dam is made of concrete while the flanking wings are earth and rock fill. The dam generates enough energy to power most of California.
Panama Canal Panama		To build the Panama Canal, 42,000 workers dredged, blasted, and excavated from Colón to Balboa. They moved enough earth and rubble to bury the island of Manhattan to a depth of 12 feet (4 m)—or enough to open a 16-foot (5 m) tunnel to the center of the earth.

The Seven Wonders of the Ancient World

Wonder/Location	Description
Colossus of Rhodes Harbor of Rhodes, in Aegean Sea, off coast of Turkey	This huge bronze statue of the sun god, Helios, took 12 years to build and stood about 105 feet (32 m) tall. It was destroyed by an earthquake in 225 BCE.
Hanging Gardens of Babylon Ancient city of Babylon (now near Baghdad, Iraq)	The hanging gardens were a series of landscaped terraces along the banks of the Euphrates River, planted with trees, flowers, and shrubs. The gardens were probably built by King Nebuchadnezzar II for his wife.
Pharos (lighthouse) Pharos Island, off coast of Alexandria, Egypt	Built around 270 BCE, this was the world's first important lighthouse. It stood in the harbor for 1,000 years until it was destroyed by an earthquake. It served as a prototype for all other lighthouses built by the Roman Empire.
Mausoleum of Halicarnassus Ancient city of Halicarnassus, now Turkish town of Bodrum	This monumental marble tomb was built by the widow of Mausolus, king of Anatolia, in 353 BCE.
Statue of Zeus Olympia, Greece	This huge, ornate statue of the god on his throne was almost 60 feet (18 m) tall.
Pyramids of Egypt Giza, Egypt	The oldest pyramid was built with more than two million limestone blocks and stands more than 480 feet (146 m) high. This is the only one of the ancient wonders still in existence.
Temple of Artemis Ancient Greek city of Ephesus, now in Turkey near Selçuk	Built in the sixth century BCE to honor the goddess Artemis, this was one of the largest Greek temples ever built. It was famous for the artistic decoration and use of marble.

World's Tallest Dams

Name/Location	Completed	Height above lowest formation
Rogun Vakhsh River, Tajikistan	*	1,099 ft. (335 m)
Nurek Vakhsh River, Tajikistan	1980	984 ft. (300 m)
Xiaowan Lancang River, China	*	958 ft. (292 m)
Grande Dixence Dixence River, Switzerland	1961	935 ft. (285 m)
Inguri Inguri River, Georgia	1980	892 ft. (272 m)
Vaiont Vaiont River, Italy	1961	859 ft. (262 m)
Manuel M. Torres Grijalva River, Mexico	1980	856 ft. (261 m)
Tehri Bhagirathi, India	*	856 ft. (261 m)
Alvaro Obregon Mextiquic, Mexico	1946	853 ft. (260 m)
Mauvoisin Drance de Bagnes, Switzerland	1957	820 ft. (250 m)

*Planned or under construction

47

Top 10 Longest Suspension Bridges in North America

Name/Location	Completed	Length of main span
Verrazano-Narrows Lower New York Bay, NY	1964	4,260 ft. (1,298 m)
Golden Gate San Francisco Bay, CA	1937	4,200 ft. (1,280 m)
Mackinac Lakes Michigan and Huron, MI	1957	3,800 ft. (1,158 m)
George Washington Hudson River at New York City, NY	1931	3,500 ft. (1,067 m)
Tacoma Narrows II Puget Sound at Tacoma, WA	1950, 2007	2,800 ft. (853 m)
Carquinez Carquinez Strait, CA	2003	2,388 ft. (728 m)
San Francisco—Oakland Bay San Francisco Bay, CA	1936	2,310 ft. (704 m)
Bronx—Whitestone East River, New York City, NY	1939	2,300 ft. (701 m)
Pierre Laporte Quebec City, QC	1970	2,190 ft. (668 m)
Delaware Memorial (twin) Delaware River near Wilmington, DE	1951, 1968	2,150 ft. (655 m)

Top 10 Longest Road Tunnels in the World

Name/Location	Completed	Tunnel length
Laerdal-Aurland Norway	2000	15.2 mi. (24.5 km)
Zhongnanshan China	2007	11.2 mi. (18 km)
St. Gotthard Switzerland	1980	10.5 mi. (16.9 km)
Arlberg Austria	1978	8.7 mi. (14.0 km)
Fréjus France/Italy	1980	8.0 mi. (12.9 km)
Hsuehshan Taiwan	2007	8.0 mi. (12.9 km)
Mont Blanc France/Italy	1965	7.3 mi. (11.7 km)
Gudvanga Norway	1991	7.1 mi. (11.4 km)
Folgefonn Norway	2001	7.0 mi. (11.2 km)
Kanetsu Japan	1991	6.9 mi. (11.1 km)

Top 10 "Tallest" Cities in the World

City	Towers 700–999 ft. (213–304.5 m)	Towers 1000+ ft. (304.8 m)
New York, New York, United States	31	4
Hong Kong, China	25	5
Dubai, United Arab Emirates	17	8
Shanghai, China	18	3
Chicago, Illinois, United States	12	5
Shenzhen, China	12	1
Tokyo, Japan	11	0
Houston, Texas, United States	9	1
Singapore	10	0
Los Angeles, California, United States	7	1

Top 10 Tallest Buildings in the World

Name/Location	Height
Burj Khalifa Dubai, United Arab Emirates	2,717 ft. (828 m)
Taipei 101 Taipei, Taiwan	1,670 ft. (508 m)
Shanghai World Financial Center Shanghai, China	1,614 ft. (492 m)
International Commerce Centre Hong Kong, China	1,585 ft. (483 m)
Petronas Tower 1 Kuala Lumpur, Malaysia	1,483 ft. (452 m)
Petronas Tower 2 Kuala Lumpur, Malaysia	1,483 ft. (452 m)
Nanjing Greenland Financial Center Nanjing, China	1,476 ft. (450 m)
Willis (formerly Sears) Tower Chicago, Illinois, United States	1,451 ft. (442 m)
Trump International Hotel & Tower Chicago, Illinois, United States	1,389 ft. (423 m)
Jin Mao Building Shanghai, China	1,381 ft. (421 m)

Exploring Museums

Museums are buildings that preserve and display important pieces of history, culture, and human knowledge. They let us explore everything from Renaissance paintings to baseball cards, from mummies to lightning. Read about these famous museums and learn a little of what's inside each one. Visit them online if you can't get there in person.

British Museum

Location: London, England

What's Inside: This London landmark holds seven million objects representing civilizations and cultures from prehistory to modern times. World-famous exhibits include the Rosetta Stone, an ancient (196 BCE) Egyptian tablet that helped us understand Egyptian hieroglyphics.

Website: www.britishmuseum.org

The Exploratorium

Location: San Francisco, California, United States

What's Inside: "Don't touch" is definitely NOT the rule here. This hands-on museum has hundreds and hundreds of interactive exhibits to let visitors explore sound, light, motion, electricity, perception, the weather, and so much more up close.

Website: www.exploratorium.edu

Guggenheim Museum Bilbao

Location: Bilbao, Spain

What's Inside: This museum has an impressive collection of art from all over the world, mostly from the last half of the twentieth century. However, equally impressive is the spectacular titanium and glass building itself, designed by famous architect Frank Gehry.

Website: www.guggenheim.org/bilbao

The Louvre

Location: Paris, France

What's Inside: The most-visited museum in the world, the Louvre is home to 35,000 art objects dating from ancient times to the 19th century. Visitors flock to da Vinci's *Mona Lisa* and the famous sculptures *Winged Victory* and *Venus de Milo*.

Website: www.louvre.fr

Buildings & Landmarks

Metropolitan Museum of Art

Location: New York, New York, United States

What's Inside: "The Met" is so gigantic that its Egyptian art section contains an entire temple, which was shipped to America as a gift. The massive museum contains art from every period in history and every part of the world. In the Newbery Award-winning novel *From the Mixed-Up Files of Mrs. Basil E. Frankweiler*, two kids hide out at the Met for days after running away from home.

Website: www.metmuseum.org

Museum of Modern Art

Location: New York, New York, United States

What's Inside: This New York City landmark holds one of the world's best collections of modern art, including van Gogh's *Starry Night*, Monet's *Water Lilies*, and Warhol's *Campbell's Soup Cans*.

Website: www.moma.org

National Baseball Hall of Fame and Museum

Location: Cooperstown, New York, United States

What's Inside: This popular upstate New York attraction is the center of the world of baseball, past and present. There are thousands of clippings, photos, and baseball cards and special displays to Babe Ruth, Jackie Robinson, and women's baseball. Thirty glass-enclosed lockers, one for each Major League team, contain team jerseys and other items.

Website: www.baseballhall.org

Smithsonian Institution

Location: Washington, DC, United States

What's Inside: The Smithsonian is the largest museum complex in the world, composed of 19 different museums and the National Zoo. Within the complex you can check out Dorothy's red slippers from *The Wizard of Oz*, the lunar landing "dune buggy" from the Apollo moon missions—and millions of other items and displays.

Website: www.si.edu

Until recently the most famous resident of the National Zoo was the panda Tai Shan. Returned to his native China in 2009, Tai Shan will be part of a new breeding program to produce more pandas, whose worldwide population has shrunk to about 1,600.

NEWSworthy

Calendars & Holidays

Mark Your Calendar!

We use calendars to keep track of all the things we need to do in our busy days, weeks, months, and years. But in one way or another, human beings have always been creating calendars. Ever since people first noticed the passing of time, they have figured out interesting ways to measure and record it. They used sticks in the ground to show how shadows changed throughout a day. They made marks on a wall to show how many nights passed until the Moon became full again.

Luna-tics!

The Moon was an essential tool in creating early calendars. Ancient Egyptians noticed that the Nile flooded every 12 moons, leaving rich soils for growing crops. This was an important event to plan for. They figured out that it took about 365 days for these 12 moons to pass and for the floods to begin again.

The Spin Is In

Ancient peoples understood that time never stands still. Earth is constantly in motion, rotating on its axis while it makes its slow orbit around the Sun. A day is 24 hours—the time it takes for Earth to make one rotation. A year is the time it takes for Earth to revolve around the Sun—365¼ days. Every four years we have to add a day to make the math right, resulting in what we call a leap year.

WHEN IN ROME

There are several kinds of calendars in use around the world today. The months in the calendar used most often, called the Gregorian calendar, were originally named by the Romans after rulers and gods. July is named for Roman ruler Julius Caesar. March is named for Mars, the god of war. Some days of the week were also named after gods. The French word for "Tuesday" is *mardi*, after the same god of war.

TAKE a LOOK

In this chapter, read about holidays and special occasions celebrated around the world. If you were in charge, what event or events would you want celebrated with a special day? (Besides your birthday, of course!)

CHECK IT OUT !

Every day of the year, there's something to celebrate or honor:

JAN	MAY	JUNE	SEPT	OCT
21	**1**	**6**	**19**	**9**
National Hugging Day	Save the Rhino Day	National Yo-Yo Day	National Butterscotch Pudding Day	Moldy Cheese Day

Periods of Time

MAY **9**

MAY **1**

JULY **10**

NOV **5**

annual	yearly
biannual	twice a year
bicentennial	marking a period of 200 years
biennial	marking a period of 2 years
bimonthly	every 2 months; twice a month
biweekly	every 2 weeks; twice a week
centennial	marking a period of 100 years
decennial	marking a period of 10 years
diurnal	daily; of a day
duodecennial	marking a period of 12 years
millennial	marking a period of 1,000 years
novennial	marking a period of 9 years
octennial	marking a period of 8 years
perennial	occurring year after year
quadrennial	marking a period of 4 years
quadricentennial	marking a period of 400 years
quincentennial	marking a period of 500 years
quindecennial	marking a period of 15 years
quinquennial	marking a period of 5 years
semiannual	twice a year
semicentennial	marking a period of 50 years
semidiurnal	twice a day
semiweekly	twice a week
septennial	marking a period of 7 years
sesquicentennial	marking a period of 150 years
sexennial	marking a period of 6 years
thrice weekly	3 times a week
tricennial	marking a period of 30 years
triennial	marking a period of 3 years
trimonthly	every 3 months
triweekly	every 3 weeks; 3 times a week
undecennial	marking a period of 11 years
vicennial	marking a period of 20 years

Months of the Year in Different Calendars

Gregorian	Jewish	Hindu	Muslim
January	Shevat	Magha	Muharram
February	Adar	Phalgun	Safar
March	Nisan	Cait	Rabi I
April	Iyar	Baisakh	Rabi II
May	Sivan	Jyeshtha	Jumada I
June	Tammuz	Asarh	Jumada II
July	Av	Sravan	Rajab
August	Elul	Bhadon	Sha'ban
September	Tishrei	Asvin	Ramadan
October	Cheshvan	Kartik	Shawwal
November	Kislev	Margasira	Dhu'l-Qa'dah
December	Tevet	Pus	Dhu'l-Hijja

Wedding Anniversary Gift Chart

Anniversary	Traditional	Modern
1st	paper	clocks
2nd	cotton	china
3rd	leather	crystal
4th	fruit/flowers	linen/silk
5th	wood	silverware
6th	iron	wood
7th	wool	desk sets
8th	bronze	linen
9th	pottery	leather
10th	tin	diamond jewelry
11th	steel	fashion jewelry
12th	silk/linen	pearls
13th	lace	textiles
14th	ivory	gold jewelry
15th	crystal	watches
20th	china	platinum
25th	silver	silver
30th	pearls	diamonds
35th	coral	jade
40th	rubies	rubies
45th	sapphires	sapphires
50th	gold	gold
55th	emeralds	emeralds
60th	diamonds	diamonds

Chinese Years, 1900–2019

Rat	Ox	Tiger	Hare (Rabbit)	Dragon	Snake
1900	1901	1902	1903	1904	1905
1912	1913	1914	1915	1916	1917
1924	1925	1926	1927	1928	1929
1936	1937	1938	1939	1940	1941
1948	1949	1950	1951	1952	1953
1960	1961	1962	1963	1964	1965
1972	1973	1974	1975	1976	1977
1984	1985	1986	1987	1988	1989
1996	1997	1998	1999	2000	2001
2008	2009	2010	2011	2012	2013

Horse	Sheep (Goat)	Monkey	Rooster	Dog	Pig
1906	1907	1908	1909	1910	1911
1918	1919	1920	1921	1922	1923
1930	1931	1932	1933	1934	1935
1942	1943	1944	1945	1946	1947
1954	1955	1956	1957	1958	1959
1966	1967	1968	1969	1970	1971
1978	1979	1980	1981	1982	1983
1990	1991	1992	1993	1994	1995
2002	2003	2004	2005	2006	2007
2014	2015	2016	2017	2018	2019

Perpetual Calendar, 1775–2050

A perpetual calendar lets you find the day of the week for any date in any year. The number next to each year below corresponds to one of the 14 calendars that follow.

Year	#	Year	#	Year	#	Year	#	Year	#	Year	#
1775	1	1821	2	1867	3	1913	4	1959	5	2005	7
1776	9	1822	3	1868	11	1914	5	1960	13	2006	1
1777	4	1823	4	1869	6	1915	6	1961	1	2007	2
1778	5	1824	12	1870	7	1916	14	1962	2	2008	10
1779	6	1825	7	1871	1	1917	2	1963	3	2009	5
1780	14	1826	1	1872	9	1918	3	1964	11	2010	6
1781	2	1827	2	1873	4	1919	4	1965	6	2011	7
1782	3	1828	10	1874	5	1920	12	1966	7	2012	8
1783	4	1829	5	1875	6	1921	7	1967	1	2013	3
1784	12	1830	6	1876	14	1922	1	1968	9	2014	4
1785	7	1831	7	1877	2	1923	2	1969	4	2015	5
1786	1	1832	8	1878	3	1924	10	1970	5	2016	13
1787	2	1833	3	1879	4	1925	5	1971	6	2017	1
1788	10	1834	4	1880	12	1926	6	1972	14	2018	2
1789	5	1835	5	1881	7	1927	7	1973	2	2019	3
1790	6	1836	13	1882	1	1928	8	1974	3	2020	11
1791	7	1837	1	1883	2	1929	3	1975	4	2021	6
1792	8	1838	2	1884	10	1930	4	1976	12	2022	7
1793	3	1839	3	1885	5	1931	5	1977	7	2023	1
1794	4	1840	11	1886	6	1932	13	1978	1	2024	9
1795	5	1841	6	1887	7	1933	1	1979	2	2025	4
1796	13	1842	7	1888	8	1934	2	1980	10	2026	5
1797	1	1843	1	1889	3	1935	3	1981	5	2027	6
1798	2	1844	9	1890	4	1936	11	1982	6	2028	14
1799	3	1845	4	1891	5	1937	6	1983	7	2029	2
1800	4	1846	5	1892	13	1938	7	1984	8	2030	3
1801	5	1847	6	1893	1	1939	1	1985	3	2031	4
1802	6	1848	14	1894	2	1940	9	1986	4	2032	12
1803	7	1849	2	1895	3	1941	4	1987	5	2033	7
1804	8	1850	3	1896	11	1942	5	1988	13	2034	1
1805	3	1851	4	1897	6	1943	6	1989	1	2035	2
1806	4	1852	12	1898	7	1944	14	1990	2	2036	10
1807	5	1853	7	1899	1	1945	2	1991	3	2037	5
1808	13	1854	1	1900	2	1946	3	1992	11	2038	6
1809	1	1855	2	1901	4	1947	4	1993	6	2039	7
1810	2	1856	10	1902	4	1948	12	1994	7	2040	8
1811	3	1857	5	1903	5	1949	7	1995	1	2041	3
1812	11	1858	6	1904	13	1950	1	1996	9	2042	4
1813	6	1859	7	1905	1	1951	2	1997	4	2043	5
1814	8	1860	8	1906	2	1952	10	1998	5	2044	13
1815	1	1861	3	1907	7	1953	5	1999	6	2045	1
1816	9	1862	4	1908	11	1954	6	2000	14	2046	2
1817	4	1863	5	1909	6	1955	7	2001	2	2047	3
1818	5	1864	13	1910	7	1956	8	2002	3	2048	11
1819	6	1865	1	1911	1	1957	3	2003	4	2049	6
1820	14	1866	2	1912	9	1958	4	2004	12	2050	7

Calendar 1

Calendar 2

3

```
JANUARY                FEBRUARY               MARCH
S  M  T  W  T  F  S     S  M  T  W  T  F  S     S  M  T  W  T  F  S
      1  2  3  4  5                 1  2                  1  2
 6  7  8  9 10 11 12     3  4  5  6  7  8  9     3  4  5  6  7  8  9
13 14 15 16 17 18 19    10 11 12 13 14 15 16    10 11 12 13 14 15 16
20 21 22 23 24 25 26    17 18 19 20 21 22 23    17 18 19 20 21 22 23
27 28 29 30 31          24 25 26 27 28          24 25 26 27 28 29 30
                                                31

APRIL                  MAY                    JUNE
S  M  T  W  T  F  S     S  M  T  W  T  F  S     S  M  T  W  T  F  S
    1  2  3  4  5  6              1  2  3  4                       1
 7  8  9 10 11 12 13     5  6  7  8  9 10 11     2  3  4  5  6  7  8
14 15 16 17 18 19 20    12 13 14 15 16 17 18     9 10 11 12 13 14 15
21 22 23 24 25 26 27    19 20 21 22 23 24 25    16 17 18 19 20 21 22
28 29 30                26 27 28 29 30 31       23 24 25 26 27 28 29
                                                30

JULY                   AUGUST                 SEPTEMBER
S  M  T  W  T  F  S     S  M  T  W  T  F  S     S  M  T  W  T  F  S
    1  2  3  4  5  6              1  2  3        1  2  3  4  5  6  7
 7  8  9 10 11 12 13     4  5  6  7  8  9 10     8  9 10 11 12 13 14
14 15 16 17 18 19 20    11 12 13 14 15 16 17    15 16 17 18 19 20 21
21 22 23 24 25 26 27    18 19 20 21 22 23 24    22 23 24 25 26 27 28
28 29 30 31             25 26 27 28 29 30 31    29 30

OCTOBER                NOVEMBER               DECEMBER
S  M  T  W  T  F  S     S  M  T  W  T  F  S     S  M  T  W  T  F  S
       1  2  3  4  5                 1  2        1  2  3  4  5  6  7
 6  7  8  9 10 11 12     3  4  5  6  7  8  9     8  9 10 11 12 13 14
13 14 15 16 17 18 19    10 11 12 13 14 15 16    15 16 17 18 19 20 21
20 21 22 23 24 25 26    17 18 19 20 21 22 23    22 23 24 25 26 27 28
27 28 29 30 31          24 25 26 27 28 29 30    29 30 31
```

4

```
JANUARY                FEBRUARY               MARCH
S  M  T  W  T  F  S     S  M  T  W  T  F  S     S  M  T  W  T  F  S
          1  2  3  4                       1                       1
 5  6  7  8  9 10 11     2  3  4  5  6  7  8     2  3  4  5  6  7  8
12 13 14 15 16 17 18     9 10 11 12 13 14 15     9 10 11 12 13 14 15
19 20 21 22 23 24 25    16 17 18 19 20 21 22    16 17 18 19 20 21 22
26 27 28 29 30 31       23 24 25 26 27 28       23 24 25 26 27 28 29
                                                30 31

APRIL                  MAY                    JUNE
S  M  T  W  T  F  S     S  M  T  W  T  F  S     S  M  T  W  T  F  S
       1  2  3  4  5              1  2  3        1  2  3  4  5  6  7
 6  7  8  9 10 11 12     4  5  6  7  8  9 10     8  9 10 11 12 13 14
13 14 15 16 17 18 19    11 12 13 14 15 16 17    15 16 17 18 19 20 21
20 21 22 23 24 25 26    18 19 20 21 22 23 24    22 23 24 25 26 27 28
27 28 29 30             25 26 27 28 29 30 31    29 30

JULY                   AUGUST                 SEPTEMBER
S  M  T  W  T  F  S     S  M  T  W  T  F  S     S  M  T  W  T  F  S
       1  2  3  4  5                 1  2        1  2  3  4  5  6
 6  7  8  9 10 11 12     3  4  5  6  7  8  9     7  8  9 10 11 12 13
13 14 15 16 17 18 19    10 11 12 13 14 15 16    14 15 16 17 18 19 20
20 21 22 23 24 25 26    17 18 19 20 21 22 23    21 22 23 24 25 26 27
27 28 29 30 31          24 25 26 27 28 29 30    28 29 30
                        31

OCTOBER                NOVEMBER               DECEMBER
S  M  T  W  T  F  S     S  M  T  W  T  F  S     S  M  T  W  T  F  S
          1  2  3  4                       1        1  2  3  4  5  6
 5  6  7  8  9 10 11     2  3  4  5  6  7  8     7  8  9 10 11 12 13
12 13 14 15 16 17 18     9 10 11 12 13 14 15    14 15 16 17 18 19 20
19 20 21 22 23 24 25    16 17 18 19 20 21 22    21 22 23 24 25 26 27
26 27 28 29 30 31       23 24 25 26 27 28 29    28 29 30 31
                        30
```

5

```
JANUARY                FEBRUARY               MARCH
S  M  T  W  T  F  S     S  M  T  W  T  F  S     S  M  T  W  T  F  S
             1  2  3     1  2  3  4  5  6  7     1  2  3  4  5  6  7
 4  5  6  7  8  9 10     8  9 10 11 12 13 14     8  9 10 11 12 13 14
11 12 13 14 15 16 17    15 16 17 18 19 20 21    15 16 17 18 19 20 21
18 19 20 21 22 23 24    22 23 24 25 26 27 28    22 23 24 25 26 27 28
25 26 27 28 29 30 31                            29 30 31

APRIL                  MAY                    JUNE
S  M  T  W  T  F  S     S  M  T  W  T  F  S     S  M  T  W  T  F  S
          1  2  3  4                    1  2        1  2  3  4  5  6
 5  6  7  8  9 10 11     3  4  5  6  7  8  9     7  8  9 10 11 12 13
12 13 14 15 16 17 18    10 11 12 13 14 15 16    14 15 16 17 18 19 20
19 20 21 22 23 24 25    17 18 19 20 21 22 23    21 22 23 24 25 26 27
26 27 28 29 30          24 25 26 27 28 29 30    28 29 30
                        31

JULY                   AUGUST                 SEPTEMBER
S  M  T  W  T  F  S     S  M  T  W  T  F  S     S  M  T  W  T  F  S
          1  2  3  4                       1        1  2  3  4  5
 5  6  7  8  9 10 11     2  3  4  5  6  7  8     6  7  8  9 10 11 12
12 13 14 15 16 17 18     9 10 11 12 13 14 15    13 14 15 16 17 18 19
19 20 21 22 23 24 25    16 17 18 19 20 21 22    20 21 22 23 24 25 26
26 27 28 29 30 31       23 24 25 26 27 28 29    27 28 29 30
                        30 31

OCTOBER                NOVEMBER               DECEMBER
S  M  T  W  T  F  S     S  M  T  W  T  F  S     S  M  T  W  T  F  S
             1  2  3     1  2  3  4  5  6  7        1  2  3  4  5
 4  5  6  7  8  9 10     8  9 10 11 12 13 14     6  7  8  9 10 11 12
11 12 13 14 15 16 17    15 16 17 18 19 20 21    13 14 15 16 17 18 19
18 19 20 21 22 23 24    22 23 24 25 26 27 28    20 21 22 23 24 25 26
25 26 27 28 29 30 31    29 30                   27 28 29 30 31
```

6

```
JANUARY                FEBRUARY               MARCH
S  M  T  W  T  F  S     S  M  T  W  T  F  S     S  M  T  W  T  F  S
                1  2        1  2  3  4  5  6        1  2  3  4  5  6
 3  4  5  6  7  8  9     7  8  9 10 11 12 13     7  8  9 10 11 12 13
10 11 12 13 14 15 16    14 15 16 17 18 19 20    14 15 16 17 18 19 20
17 18 19 20 21 22 23    21 22 23 24 25 26 27    21 22 23 24 25 26 27
24 25 26 27 28 29 30    28                      28 29 30 31
31

APRIL                  MAY                    JUNE
S  M  T  W  T  F  S     S  M  T  W  T  F  S     S  M  T  W  T  F  S
             1  2  3                       1        1  2  3  4  5
 4  5  6  7  8  9 10     2  3  4  5  6  7  8     6  7  8  9 10 11 12
11 12 13 14 15 16 17     9 10 11 12 13 14 15    13 14 15 16 17 18 19
18 19 20 21 22 23 24    16 17 18 19 20 21 22    20 21 22 23 24 25 26
25 26 27 28 29 30       23 24 25 26 27 28 29    27 28 29 30
                        30 31

JULY                   AUGUST                 SEPTEMBER
S  M  T  W  T  F  S     S  M  T  W  T  F  S     S  M  T  W  T  F  S
             1  2  3     1  2  3  4  5  6  7           1  2  3  4
 4  5  6  7  8  9 10     8  9 10 11 12 13 14     5  6  7  8  9 10 11
11 12 13 14 15 16 17    15 16 17 18 19 20 21    12 13 14 15 16 17 18
18 19 20 21 22 23 24    22 23 24 25 26 27 28    19 20 21 22 23 24 25
25 26 27 28 29 30 31    29 30 31                26 27 28 29 30

OCTOBER                NOVEMBER               DECEMBER
S  M  T  W  T  F  S     S  M  T  W  T  F  S     S  M  T  W  T  F  S
                1  2        1  2  3  4  5  6           1  2  3  4
 3  4  5  6  7  8  9     7  8  9 10 11 12 13     5  6  7  8  9 10 11
10 11 12 13 14 15 16    14 15 16 17 18 19 20    12 13 14 15 16 17 18
17 18 19 20 21 22 23    21 22 23 24 25 26 27    19 20 21 22 23 24 25
24 25 26 27 28 29 30    28 29 30                26 27 28 29 30 31
31
```

7

```
JANUARY                FEBRUARY               MARCH
S  M  T  W  T  F  S     S  M  T  W  T  F  S     S  M  T  W  T  F  S
                   1        1  2  3  4  5        1  2  3  4  5
 2  3  4  5  6  7  8     6  7  8  9 10 11 12     6  7  8  9 10 11 12
 9 10 11 12 13 14 15    13 14 15 16 17 18 19    13 14 15 16 17 18 19
16 17 18 19 20 21 22    20 21 22 23 24 25 26    20 21 22 23 24 25 26
23 24 25 26 27 28 29    27 28                   27 28 29 30 31
30 31

APRIL                  MAY                    JUNE
S  M  T  W  T  F  S     S  M  T  W  T  F  S     S  M  T  W  T  F  S
                1  2     1  2  3  4  5  6  7           1  2  3  4
 3  4  5  6  7  8  9     8  9 10 11 12 13 14     5  6  7  8  9 10 11
10 11 12 13 14 15 16    15 16 17 18 19 20 21    12 13 14 15 16 17 18
17 18 19 20 21 22 23    22 23 24 25 26 27 28    19 20 21 22 23 24 25
24 25 26 27 28 29 30    29 30 31                26 27 28 29 30

JULY                   AUGUST                 SEPTEMBER
S  M  T  W  T  F  S     S  M  T  W  T  F  S     S  M  T  W  T  F  S
                1  2        1  2  3  4  5  6           1  2  3
 3  4  5  6  7  8  9     7  8  9 10 11 12 13     4  5  6  7  8  9 10
10 11 12 13 14 15 16    14 15 16 17 18 19 20    11 12 13 14 15 16 17
17 18 19 20 21 22 23    21 22 23 24 25 26 27    18 19 20 21 22 23 24
24 25 26 27 28 29 30    28 29 30 31             25 26 27 28 29 30
31

OCTOBER                NOVEMBER               DECEMBER
S  M  T  W  T  F  S     S  M  T  W  T  F  S     S  M  T  W  T  F  S
                   1        1  2  3  4  5        1  2  3
 2  3  4  5  6  7  8     6  7  8  9 10 11 12     4  5  6  7  8  9 10
 9 10 11 12 13 14 15    13 14 15 16 17 18 19    11 12 13 14 15 16 17
16 17 18 19 20 21 22    20 21 22 23 24 25 26    18 19 20 21 22 23 24
23 24 25 26 27 28 29    27 28 29 30             25 26 27 28 29 30 31
30 31
```

8

```
JANUARY                FEBRUARY               MARCH
S  M  T  W  T  F  S     S  M  T  W  T  F  S     S  M  T  W  T  F  S
 1  2  3  4  5  6  7           1  2  3  4              1  2  3
 8  9 10 11 12 13 14     5  6  7  8  9 10 11     4  5  6  7  8  9 10
15 16 17 18 19 20 21    12 13 14 15 16 17 18    11 12 13 14 15 16 17
22 23 24 25 26 27 28    19 20 21 22 23 24 25    18 19 20 21 22 23 24
29 30 31                26 27 28 29             25 26 27 28 29 30 31

APRIL                  MAY                    JUNE
S  M  T  W  T  F  S     S  M  T  W  T  F  S     S  M  T  W  T  F  S
 1  2  3  4  5  6  7           1  2  3  4  5                 1  2
 8  9 10 11 12 13 14     6  7  8  9 10 11 12     3  4  5  6  7  8  9
15 16 17 18 19 20 21    13 14 15 16 17 18 19    10 11 12 13 14 15 16
22 23 24 25 26 27 28    20 21 22 23 24 25 26    17 18 19 20 21 22 23
29 30                   27 28 29 30 31          24 25 26 27 28 29 30

JULY                   AUGUST                 SEPTEMBER
S  M  T  W  T  F  S     S  M  T  W  T  F  S     S  M  T  W  T  F  S
 1  2  3  4  5  6  7           1  2  3  4                       1
 8  9 10 11 12 13 14     5  6  7  8  9 10 11     2  3  4  5  6  7  8
15 16 17 18 19 20 21    12 13 14 15 16 17 18     9 10 11 12 13 14 15
22 23 24 25 26 27 28    19 20 21 22 23 24 25    16 17 18 19 20 21 22
29 30 31                26 27 28 29 30 31       23 24 25 26 27 28 29
                                                30

OCTOBER                NOVEMBER               DECEMBER
S  M  T  W  T  F  S     S  M  T  W  T  F  S     S  M  T  W  T  F  S
 1  2  3  4  5  6                 1  2  3                       1
 7  8  9 10 11 12 13     4  5  6  7  8  9 10     2  3  4  5  6  7  8
14 15 16 17 18 19 20    11 12 13 14 15 16 17     9 10 11 12 13 14 15
21 22 23 24 25 26 27    18 19 20 21 22 23 24    16 17 18 19 20 21 22
28 29 30 31             25 26 27 28 29 30       23 24 25 26 27 28 29
                                                30 31
```

Calendar 9

JANUARY
S M T W T F S
  1 2 3 4 5 6
7 8 9 10 11 12 13
14 15 16 17 18 19 20
21 22 23 24 25 26 27
28 29 30 31

FEBRUARY
S M T W T F S
      1 2 3
4 5 6 7 8 9 10
11 12 13 14 15 16 17
18 19 20 21 22 23 24
25 26 27 28 29

MARCH
S M T W T F S
      1 2
3 4 5 6 7 8 9
10 11 12 13 14 15 16
17 18 19 20 21 22 23
24 25 26 27 28 29 30
31

APRIL
S M T W T F S
1 2 3 4 5 6
7 8 9 10 11 12 13
14 15 16 17 18 19 20
21 22 23 24 25 26 27
28 29 30

MAY
S M T W T F S
    1 2 3 4
5 6 7 8 9 10 11
12 13 14 15 16 17 18
19 20 21 22 23 24 25
26 27 28 29 30 31

JUNE
S M T W T F S
        1
2 3 4 5 6 7 8
9 10 11 12 13 14 15
16 17 18 19 20 21 22
23 24 25 26 27 28 29
30

JULY
S M T W T F S
1 2 3 4 5 6
7 8 9 10 11 12 13
14 15 16 17 18 19 20
21 22 23 24 25 26 27
28 29 30 31

AUGUST
S M T W T F S
     1 2 3
4 5 6 7 8 9 10
11 12 13 14 15 16 17
18 19 20 21 22 23 24
25 26 27 28 29 30 31

SEPTEMBER
S M T W T F S
1 2 3 4 5 6 7
8 9 10 11 12 13 14
15 16 17 18 19 20 21
22 23 24 25 26 27 28
29 30

OCTOBER
S M T W T F S
    1 2 3 4 5
6 7 8 9 10 11 12
13 14 15 16 17 18 19
20 21 22 23 24 25 26
27 28 29 30 31

NOVEMBER
S M T W T F S
      1 2
3 4 5 6 7 8 9
10 11 12 13 14 15 16
17 18 19 20 21 22 23
24 25 26 27 28 29 30

DECEMBER
S M T W T F S
1 2 3 4 5 6 7
8 9 10 11 12 13 14
15 16 17 18 19 20 21
22 23 24 25 26 27 28
29 30 31

Calendar 10

JANUARY
S M T W T F S
1 2 3 4 5
6 7 8 9 10 11 12
13 14 15 16 17 18 19
20 21 22 23 24 25 26
27 28 29 30 31

FEBRUARY
S M T W T F S
1 2
3 4 5 6 7 8 9
10 11 12 13 14 15 16
17 18 19 20 21 22 23
24 25 26 27 28

MARCH
S M T W T F S
1
2 3 4 5 6 7 8
9 10 11 12 13 14 15
16 17 18 19 20 21 22
23 24 25 26 27 28 29
30 31

APRIL
S M T W T F S
1 2 3 4 5
6 7 8 9 10 11 12
13 14 15 16 17 18 19
20 21 22 23 24 25 26
27 28 29 30

MAY
S M T W T F S
1 2 3
4 5 6 7 8 9 10
11 12 13 14 15 16 17
18 19 20 21 22 23 24
25 26 27 28 29 30 31

JUNE
S M T W T F S
1 2 3 4 5 6 7
8 9 10 11 12 13 14
15 16 17 18 19 20 21
22 23 24 25 26 27 28
29 30

JULY
S M T W T F S
1 2 3 4 5
6 7 8 9 10 11 12
13 14 15 16 17 18 19
20 21 22 23 24 25 26
27 28 29 30 31

AUGUST
S M T W T F S
1 2
3 4 5 6 7 8 9
10 11 12 13 14 15 16
17 18 19 20 21 22 23
24 25 26 27 28 29 30
31

SEPTEMBER
S M T W T F S
1 2 3 4 5 6
7 8 9 10 11 12 13
14 15 16 17 18 19 20
21 22 23 24 25 26 27
28 29 30

OCTOBER
S M T W T F S
1 2 3 4
5 6 7 8 9 10 11
12 13 14 15 16 17 18
19 20 21 22 23 24 25
26 27 28 29 30 31

NOVEMBER
S M T W T F S
1
2 3 4 5 6 7 8
9 10 11 12 13 14 15
16 17 18 19 20 21 22
23 24 25 26 27 28 29
30

DECEMBER
S M T W T F S
1 2 3 4 5 6
7 8 9 10 11 12 13
14 15 16 17 18 19 20
21 22 23 24 25 26 27
28 29 30 31

Calendar 11

JANUARY
S M T W T F S
1 2 3 4
5 6 7 8 9 10 11
12 13 14 15 16 17 18
19 20 21 22 23 24 25
26 27 28 29 30 31

FEBRUARY
S M T W T F S
1
2 3 4 5 6 7 8
9 10 11 12 13 14 15
16 17 18 19 20 21 22
23 24 25 26 27 28

MARCH
S M T W T F S
1
2 3 4 5 6 7 8
9 10 11 12 13 14 15
16 17 18 19 20 21 22
23 24 25 26 27 28 29
30 31

APRIL
S M T W T F S
1 2 3 4 5
6 7 8 9 10 11 12
13 14 15 16 17 18 19
20 21 22 23 24 25 26
27 28 29 30

MAY
S M T W T F S
1 2 3
4 5 6 7 8 9 10
11 12 13 14 15 16 17
18 19 20 21 22 23 24
25 26 27 28 29 30 31

JUNE
S M T W T F S
1 2 3 4 5 6
7 8 9 10 11 12 13
14 15 16 17 18 19 20
21 22 23 24 25 26 27
28 29 30

JULY
S M T W T F S
1 2 3 4
5 6 7 8 9 10 11
12 13 14 15 16 17 18
19 20 21 22 23 24 25
26 27 28 29 30 31

AUGUST
S M T W T F S
1
2 3 4 5 6 7 8
9 10 11 12 13 14 15
16 17 18 19 20 21 22
23 24 25 26 27 28 29
30 31

SEPTEMBER
S M T W T F S
1 2 3 4 5
6 7 8 9 10 11 12
13 14 15 16 17 18 19
20 21 22 23 24 25 26
27 28 29 30

OCTOBER
S M T W T F S
1 2 3
4 5 6 7 8 9 10
11 12 13 14 15 16 17
18 19 20 21 22 23 24
25 26 27 28 29 30 31

NOVEMBER
S M T W T F S
1 2 3 4 5 6 7
8 9 10 11 12 13 14
15 16 17 18 19 20 21
22 23 24 25 26 27 28
29 30

DECEMBER
S M T W T F S
1 2 3 4 5
6 7 8 9 10 11 12
13 14 15 16 17 18 19
20 21 22 23 24 25 26
27 28 29 30 31

Calendar 12

JANUARY
S M T W T F S
1 2 3
4 5 6 7 8 9 10
11 12 13 14 15 16 17
18 19 20 21 22 23 24
25 26 27 28 29 30 31

FEBRUARY
S M T W T F S
1 2 3 4 5 6 7
8 9 10 11 12 13 14
15 16 17 18 19 20 21
22 23 24 25 26 27 28

MARCH
S M T W T F S
1 2 3 4 5 6 7
8 9 10 11 12 13 14
15 16 17 18 19 20 21
22 23 24 25 26 27 28
29 30 31

APRIL
S M T W T F S
1 2 3
4 5 6 7 8 9 10
11 12 13 14 15 16 17
18 19 20 21 22 23 24
25 26 27 28 29 30

MAY
S M T W T F S
1
2 3 4 5 6 7 8
9 10 11 12 13 14 15
16 17 18 19 20 21 22
23 24 25 26 27 28 29
30 31

JUNE
S M T W T F S
1 2 3 4 5
6 7 8 9 10 11 12
13 14 15 16 17 18 19
20 21 22 23 24 25 26
27 28 29 30

JULY
S M T W T F S
1 2 3
4 5 6 7 8 9 10
11 12 13 14 15 16 17
18 19 20 21 22 23 24
25 26 27 28 29 30 31

AUGUST
S M T W T F S
1 2 3 4 5 6 7
8 9 10 11 12 13 14
15 16 17 18 19 20 21
22 23 24 25 26 27 28
29 30 31

SEPTEMBER
S M T W T F S
1 2 3 4
5 6 7 8 9 10 11
12 13 14 15 16 17 18
19 20 21 22 23 24 25
26 27 28 29 30

OCTOBER
S M T W T F S
1 2
3 4 5 6 7 8 9
10 11 12 13 14 15 16
17 18 19 20 21 22 23
24 25 26 27 28 29 30
31

NOVEMBER
S M T W T F S
1 2 3 4 5 6
7 8 9 10 11 12 13
14 15 16 17 18 19 20
21 22 23 24 25 26 27
28 29 30

DECEMBER
S M T W T F S
1 2 3 4
5 6 7 8 9 10 11
12 13 14 15 16 17 18
19 20 21 22 23 24 25
26 27 28 29 30 31

Calendar 13

JANUARY
S M T W T F S
1 2
3 4 5 6 7 8 9
10 11 12 13 14 15 16
17 18 19 20 21 22 23
24 25 26 27 28 29 30
31

FEBRUARY
S M T W T F S
1 2 3 4 5 6
7 8 9 10 11 12 13
14 15 16 17 18 19 20
21 22 23 24 25 26 27
28 29

MARCH
S M T W T F S
1 2 3 4 5
6 7 8 9 10 11 12
13 14 15 16 17 18 19
20 21 22 23 24 25 26
27 28 29 30 31

APRIL
S M T W T F S
1 2
3 4 5 6 7 8 9
10 11 12 13 14 15 16
17 18 19 20 21 22 23
24 25 26 27 28 29 30

MAY
S M T W T F S
1 2 3 4 5 6 7
8 9 10 11 12 13 14
15 16 17 18 19 20 21
22 23 24 25 26 27 28
29 30 31

JUNE
S M T W T F S
1 2 3 4
5 6 7 8 9 10 11
12 13 14 15 16 17 18
19 20 21 22 23 24 25
26 27 28 29 30

JULY
S M T W T F S
1 2
3 4 5 6 7 8 9
10 11 12 13 14 15 16
17 18 19 20 21 22 23
24 25 26 27 28 29 30
31

AUGUST
S M T W T F S
1 2 3 4 5 6
7 8 9 10 11 12 13
14 15 16 17 18 19 20
21 22 23 24 25 26 27
28 29 30 31

SEPTEMBER
S M T W T F S
1 2 3
4 5 6 7 8 9 10
11 12 13 14 15 16 17
18 19 20 21 22 23 24
25 26 27 28 29 30

OCTOBER
S M T W T F S
1
2 3 4 5 6 7 8
9 10 11 12 13 14 15
16 17 18 19 20 21 22
23 24 25 26 27 28 29
30 31

NOVEMBER
S M T W T F S
1 2 3 4 5
6 7 8 9 10 11 12
13 14 15 16 17 18 19
20 21 22 23 24 25 26
27 28 29 30

DECEMBER
S M T W T F S
1 2 3
4 5 6 7 8 9 10
11 12 13 14 15 16 17
18 19 20 21 22 23 24
25 26 27 28 29 30 31

Calendar 14

JANUARY
S M T W T F S
1
2 3 4 5 6 7 8
9 10 11 12 13 14 15
16 17 18 19 20 21 22
23 24 25 26 27 28 29
30 31

FEBRUARY
S M T W T F S
1 2 3 4 5
6 7 8 9 10 11 12
13 14 15 16 17 18 19
20 21 22 23 24 25 26
27 28 29

MARCH
S M T W T F S
1 2 3 4 5
6 7 8 9 10 11 12
13 14 15 16 17 18 19
20 21 22 23 24 25 26
27 28 29 30 31

APRIL
S M T W T F S
1 2
3 4 5 6 7 8 9
10 11 12 13 14 15 16
17 18 19 20 21 22 23
24 25 26 27 28 29 30

MAY
S M T W T F S
1 2 3 4
8 9 10 11 12 13 14
15 16 17 18 19 20 21
22 23 24 25 26 27 28
29 30 31

JUNE
S M T W T F S
1 2 3
4 5 6 7 8 9 10
11 12 13 14 15 16 17
18 19 20 21 22 23 24
25 26 27 28 29 30

JULY
S M T W T F S
1
2 3 4 5 6 7 8
9 10 11 12 13 14 15
16 17 18 19 20 21 22
23 24 25 26 27 28 29
30 31

AUGUST
S M T W T F S
1 2 3 4 5
6 7 8 9 10 11 12
13 14 15 16 17 18 19
20 21 22 23 24 25 26
27 28 29 30 31

SEPTEMBER
S M T W T F S
1 2
3 4 5 6 7 8 9
10 11 12 13 14 15 16
17 18 19 20 21 22 23
24 25 26 27 28 29 30

OCTOBER
S M T W T F S
1 2 3 4 5 6 7
8 9 10 11 12 13 14
15 16 17 18 19 20 21
22 23 24 25 26 27 28
29 30 31

NOVEMBER
S M T W T F S
1 2 3 4
5 6 7 8 9 10 11
12 13 14 15 16 17 18
19 20 21 22 23 24 25
26 27 28 29 30

DECEMBER
S M T W T F S
1 2
3 4 5 6 7 8 9
10 11 12 13 14 15 16
17 18 19 20 21 22 23
24 25 26 27 28 29 30
31

Fixed Dates

These events are celebrated on the same date every year, regardless of where the date falls in the week.

Event	Date
New Year's Day[1]	January 1
Groundhog Day	February 2
Abraham Lincoln's Birthday	February 12
Valentine's Day	February 14
Susan B. Anthony Day	February 15
George Washington's Birthday	February 22
St. Patrick's Day	March 17
April Fools' Day	April 1
Earth Day	April 22
National Maritime Day	May 22
Flag Day	June 14
Canada Day[2]	July 1
Independence Day[1]	July 4
Citizenship Day	September 17
United Nations Day	October 24
Halloween	October 31
Veterans Day[1,3]	November 11
Remembrance Day[2]	November 11
Christmas	December 25
Boxing Day[2]	December 26
New Year's Eve	December 31

Changing Dates

These events are celebrated on different dates every year, but are always on a certain day of a certain week of a certain month.

Event	Day
Martin Luther King Jr. Day[1]	third Monday in January
Presidents' Day[1]	third Monday in February
Daylight saving time begins	second Sunday in March
Arbor Day	last Friday in April
National Teacher Day	Tuesday of the first full week in May
Mother's Day	second Sunday in May
Armed Forces Day	third Saturday in May
Victoria Day[2]	Monday on or before May 24
Memorial Day[1]	last Monday in May
Father's Day	third Sunday in June
Labor Day[1,2]	first Monday in September
Columbus Day[1]	second Monday in October
Thanksgiving Day (Canada)[2]	second Monday in October
Daylight saving time ends	first Sunday in November
Thanksgiving Day (United States)	fourth Thursday in November

Calendars & Holidays

1. Federal holiday in United States   2. Federal holiday in Canada   3. Also known as Armistice Day

Why we celebrate . . .

New Year's Day

The first record of a new year festival is from about 2,000 BCE in Mesopotamia. The festival took place not in January but in mid-March, with the new moon after the spring equinox.

Martin Luther King Jr. Day

This holiday honors the birthday of the slain civil rights leader who preached nonviolence and led the March on Washington in 1963. Dr. King's most famous speech is entitled "I Have a Dream."

Groundhog Day

According to legend, if a groundhog in Punxsutawney, Pennsylvania, peeks his head out of his burrow and sees his shadow, he'll return to his hole and there will be six more weeks of winter.

Lincoln's Birthday

This holiday honors the 16th president of the United States, who led the nation through the Civil War (1861—1865) and was then assassinated. It was first formally observed in Washington, DC, in 1866, when both houses of Congress gathered to pay tribute to the slain president.

Valentine's Day

This holiday of love originated as a festival for several martyrs from the third century, all named St. Valentine. The holiday's association with romance may have come from an ancient belief that birds mate on this day.

Presidents' Day

This official government holiday was created in observance of both Washington's and Lincoln's birthdays.

Washington's Birthday

This holiday honors the first president of the United States, known as the Father of Our Country. It was first officially observed in America in 1879.

St. Patrick's Day

This holiday honors the patron saint of Ireland. Most often celebrated in the United States with parties and special dinners, the most famous event is the annual St. Patrick's Day parade on Fifth Avenue in New York City.

Mother's Day

First proposed by Anna Jarvis of Philadelphia in 1907, this holiday has become a national time for family gatherings and showing appreciation for mothers.

Memorial Day

Also known as Decoration Day, this legal holiday was created in 1868 by order of General John A. Logan as a day on which the graves of Civil War soldiers would be decorated. Since that time, the day has been set aside to honor all American soldiers who have given their lives for their country.

Flag Day

This holiday was set aside to commemorate the adoption of the Stars and Stripes by the Continental Congress on June 14, 1777. It is a legal holiday only in Pennsylvania but is generally acknowledged and observed in many states each year.

Father's Day

This holiday honors the role of the father in the American family, as Mother's Day honors the role of the mother.

Independence Day

This holiday celebrates the signing of the Declaration of Independence, on July 4, 1776. It has been celebrated nationwide since 1777, the first anniversary of the signing.

Labor Day

First proposed by Peter J. McGuire in New York in 1882, this holiday was created to honor the labor unions and workers who built the nation.

Columbus Day

This holiday commemorates the discovery of the New World by Italian explorer Christopher Columbus in 1492. Even though the land was already populated by Native Americans when Columbus arrived, this discovery marks the beginning of European influence in America.

United Nations Day

This holiday marks the founding of the United Nations, which began in its present capacity in 1945 but had already been in operation as the League of Nations.

Halloween

Also known as All Hallows' Eve, this holiday has its origins in ancient Celtic rituals that marked the beginning of winter with bonfires, masquerades, and dressing in costume to frighten away spirits.

Election Day

Since Congress declared it an official holiday in 1845, this has been the day for presidential elections every four years. Most statewide elections are also held on this day, but election years vary according to state.

Veterans Day

Originally called Armistice Day, this holiday was created to celebrate the end of World War I in 1918. In June 1954, Congress changed the name of the holiday to Veterans Day and declared that the day would honor all men and women who have served in America's armed forces.

Thanksgiving

President Lincoln was the first president to proclaim Thanksgiving a national holiday, in 1863. Most people believe the tradition of reserving a day of thanks began with an order given by Governor Bradford of Plymouth Colony in New England in 1621.

January 1 New Year's Day throughout the Western world and in India, Indonesia, Japan, Korea, the Philippines, Singapore, Taiwan, and Thailand; Founding Day of Republic of China (Taiwan)

January 2 Berchtoldstag in Switzerland

January 3 Genshi-Sai (First Beginning) in Japan

January 5 Twelfth Night (Wassail Eve or Eve of Epiphany) in England

January 6 Epiphany, observed by Catholics throughout Europe and Latin America

Mid-January Martin Luther King Jr.'s Birthday on the third Monday in the Virgin Islands

January 15 Adults' Day in Japan

January 20 St. Agnes Eve in Great Britain

January 26 Republic Day in India; Australia Day in Australia

January–February Chinese New Year and Vietnamese New Year (Tet)

February 3 Setsubun (Bean-throwing Festival) in Japan

February 5 Promulgation of the Constitution Day in Mexico

February 11 National Foundation Day in Japan

February 27 Independence Day in the Dominican Republic

March 1 Independence Movement Day in Korea

March 8 International Women's Day in China, Russia, Great Britain, and the United States

March 17 St. Patrick's Day in Ireland and Northern Ireland

March 19 St. Joseph's Day in Colombia, Costa Rica, Italy, and Spain

March 21 Benito Juarez's Birthday in Mexico

March 22 Arab League Day in Arab League countries

March 23 Pakistan Day in Pakistan

March 25 Independence Day in Greece; Lady Day (Quarter Day) in Great Britain

March 26 Fiesta del Arbol (Arbor Day) in Spain

March 29 Youth and Martyr's Day in Taiwan

March 30 Muslim New Year in Indonesia

March–April Carnival/Lent/Easter: The pre-Lenten celebration of Carnival (Mardi Gras) and the post-Lenten celebration of Easter are movable feasts widely observed in Christian countries

April 1 April Fools' Day (All Fools' Day) in Great Britain and the United States

April 5 Arbor Day in Korea

April 7 World Health Day in UN member nations

April 8 Buddha's Birthday in Korea and Japan; Hana Matsuri (Flower Festival) in Japan

April 14 Pan American Day in the Americas

April 19 Declaration of Independence Day in Venezuela

April 22 Queen Isabella Day in Spain

April 23 St. George's Day in England

April 25 Liberation Day in Italy; ANZAC Day in Australia and New Zealand

April 30 Queen's Birthday in the Netherlands; Walpurgis Night in Germany and Scandinavia

May 3 Constitution Day in Japan

May 1 May Day (Labor Day) in Russia and most of Europe and Latin America

May 5 Children's Day in Japan and Korea; Cinco de Mayo in Mexico; Liberation Day in the Netherlands

May 8 V-E Day in Europe

May 9 Victory over Fascism Day in Russia

Late May Victoria Day on Monday before May 25 in Canada

June 2 Founding of the Republic Day in Italy

June 5 Constitution Day in Denmark

June 6 Memorial Day in Korea; Flag Day in Sweden

June 10 Portugal Day in Portugal

June 12 Independence Day in the Philippines

Mid-June Queen's Official Birthday on second Saturday in Great Britain

June 16 Soweto Day in UN member nations

June 20 Flag Day in Argentina

June 24 Midsummer's Day in Great Britain

June 29 Feasts of Saints Peter and Paul in Chile, Colombia, Italy, Peru, Spain, and Venezuela

July 1 Canada Day in Canada; Half-year Holiday in Hong Kong; Bank Holiday in Taiwan

July 5 Independence Day in Venezuela

July 9 Independence Day in Argentina

July 12 Orangemen's Day in Northern Ireland

July 14 Bastille Day in France

Mid-July Feria de San Fermin during second week in Spain

July 17 Constitution Day in Korea

July 20 Independence Day in Colombia

July 21 National Holiday in Belgium

July 22 National Liberation Day in Poland

July 24 Simon Bolivar's Birthday in Ecuador and Venezuela

July 25 St. James Day in Spain

JAN
20

MAY
9

JUNE
20

Calendars & Holidays

July 28 Independence Day in Peru

August Holiday on first Monday in Grenada, Guyana, and Ireland

August 1 Lammas Day in England; National Day in Switzerland

August 6 Independence Day in Jamaica

August 9 National Day in Singapore

August 10 Independence Day in Ecuador

August 12 Queen's Birthday in Thailand

August 14 Independence Day in Pakistan

August 15 Independence Day in India and Korea; Assumption Day in Catholic countries

August 16 National Restoration Day in the Dominican Republic

August 17 Independence Day in Indonesia

August 31 Independence Day in Trinidad and Tobago

September Respect for the Aged Day in Japan on third Monday

September 7 Independence Day in Brazil

September 9 Choxo-no-Sekku (Chrysanthemum Day) in Japan

September 14 Battle of San Jacinto Day in Nicaragua

Mid-September Sherry Wine Harvest in Spain

September 15 Independence Day in Costa Rica, Guatemala, and Nicaragua

September 16 Independence Day in Mexico and Papua New Guinea

September 18–19 Independence Day in Chile; St. Gennaro Day in Italy

September 28 Confucius's Birthday in Taiwan

October 1 National Day in People's Republic of China; Armed Forces Day in Korea; National Holiday in Nigeria

October 2 Mahatma Gandhi's Birthday in India

October 3 National Foundation Day in Korea; Day of German Unity in Germany

October 5 Proclamation of the Portuguese Republic Day in Portugal

October 9 Korean Alphabet Day in Korea

October 10 Kruger Day in South Africa; Founding Day of the Republic of China in Taiwan

October 12 Columbus Day in Spain and widely throughout Mexico, and Central and South America

October 20 Revolution Day in Guatemala; Kenyatta Day in Kenya

October 24 United Nations Day in UN member nations

October 26 National Holiday in Austria

October 28 Greek National Day in Greece

November 1 All Saints' Day, observed by Catholics in most countries

November 2 All Souls' Day in Ecuador, El Salvador, Luxembourg, Macao, Mexico (Day of the Dead), San Marino, Uruguay, and Vatican City

November 4 National Unity Day in Italy

November 5 Guy Fawkes Day in Great Britain

November 7–8 October Revolution Day in Russia

November 11 Armistice Day in Belgium, France, French Guiana, and Tahiti; Remembrance Day in Canada

November 12 Sun Yat-sen's Birthday in Taiwan

November 15 Proclamation of the Republic Day in Brazil

November 17 Day of Penance in Federal Republic of Germany

November 19 National Holiday in Monaco

November 20 Anniversary of the Revolution in Mexico

November 23 Kinro-Kansha-no-Hi (Labor Thanksgiving Day) in Japan

November 30 Bonifacio Day in the Philippines

December 5 Discovery by Columbus Day in Haiti; Constitution Day in Russia

December 6 Independence Day in Finland

December 8 Feast of the Immaculate Conception, widely observed in Catholic countries

December 10 Constitution Day in Thailand; Human Rights Day in UN member nations

December 12 Jamhuri Day in Kenya; Guadalupe Day in Mexico

Mid-December Nine Days of Posada during third week in Mexico

December 25 Christmas Day, widely observed in all Christian countries

December 26 St. Stephen's Day in Christian countries; Boxing Day in Canada, Australia, and Great Britain

December 26–January 1 Kwanzaa in the United States

December 31 New Year's Eve throughout the world; Omisoka (Grand Last Day) in Japan; Hogmanay Day in Scotland

NOV
5

DEC
5

WHAT'S YOUR SIGN?

The original zodiac signs are thought to have originated in Mesopotamia as far back as 2000 BCE. The Greeks later picked up some of the symbols from the Babylonians and then passed them on to other ancient cultures. Some other societies that developed their own zodiac charts based on these early ideas include the Egyptians, the Chinese, and the Aztecs.

The positions of the Sun, Moon, and planets in the zodiac on the day you are born determine your astrological sign. **What's yours?**

Aries, the Ram

March 21–April 19

Planet: Mars
Element: Fire
Personality Traits: Independent, enthusiastic, bold, impulsive, confident

Taurus, the Bull

April 20–May 20

Planet: Venus
Element: Earth
Personality Traits: Decisive, determined, stubborn, stable

Gemini, the Twins

May 21–June 21

Planet: Mercury
Element: Air
Personality Traits: Curious, sociable, ambitious, alert, intelligent, temperamental

Cancer, the Crab

June 22–July 22

Planet (Celestial Object): Moon
Element: Water
Personality Traits: Organized, busy, moody, sensitive, supportive

Leo, the Lion

July 23–August 22

Planet (Celestial Object): Sun
Element: Fire
Personality Traits: Born leader, bold, noble, generous, enthusiastic, sympathetic

Virgo, the Virgin

August 23–September 22

Planet: Mercury
Element: Earth
Personality Traits: Analytical, critical, intellectual, clever

Libra, the Scales

September 23–October 23

Planet: Venus
Element: Air
Personality Traits: Affectionate, thoughtful, sympathetic, orderly, persuasive

Scorpio, the Scorpion

October 24–November 21

Planet: Mars
Element: Water
Personality Traits: Intense, fearless, loyal, willful

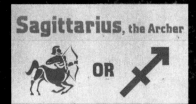

Sagittarius, the Archer

November 22–December 21

Planet: Jupiter
Element: Fire
Personality Traits: Energetic, good-natured, practical, clever

Capricorn, the Goat

December 22–January 19

Planet: Saturn
Element: Earth
Personality Traits: Serious, domineering, ambitious, blunt, loyal, persistent

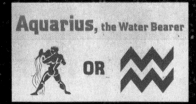

Aquarius, the Water Bearer

January 20–February 18

Planet: Uranus
Element: Air
Personality Traits: Independent, unselfish, generous, idealistic

Pisces, the Fishes

February 19–March 20

Planet: Neptune
Element: Water
Personality Traits: Compassionate, sympathetic, sensitive, timid, methodical

Crime

It's a Crime

A crime is the act of breaking a law. Stealing something, hurting someone, or destroying the property of others are all crimes because there are laws in our society forbidding us to do these things. Laws protect people. However, as long as there are laws, there will be people who break them. In 2002, the FBI reported that there was a crime committed in the United States every 2.7 seconds. That adds up to 11,680,000 crimes a year—and lots of criminals to catch.

Fingerprints Point the Finger

To identify suspects and establish guilt, law enforcement officers use a variety of crime-solving techniques. One of the oldest identification techniques is fingerprinting. In eighth-century Japan, a thumbprint was a legal substitute for a signature. Even earlier, a murder in ancient Rome was supposedly solved by matching a bloody handprint at the crime scene with a suspect's.

Today, computer technology has turned an ancient technique into a high-tech tool. Prints are digitally scanned into a massive crime scene database called Automated Fingerprinting Identification System (AFIS), which contains the prints and criminal history of 65 million people.

DNA: Living Proof

A thoroughly modern crime-solving technique is the analysis of DNA, a molecule found in every cell of every living creature. Investigators collect traces of DNA in saliva, sweat, blood, and skin cells left behind at a crime scene. They create a DNA profile, which they scan into another huge database called CODIS, short for Combined DNA Index System, in an effort to find a match.

TAKE a LOOK

Edward Henry, of England's famous Scotland Yard, identified the four basic patterns in fingerprints in the late nineteenth century. Which patterns are in your fingerprints? How about your relatives' and friends' prints? Use a magnifying glass for the best view.

Arch   Whorl   Loop   Composite

CHECK IT OUT!

No two humans have the same DNA, except for identical twins. That's why DNA found at a crime scene can prove guilt. And DNA *not* found at a crime scene can prove innocence. As of November 2009, DNA has played a key part in establishing the innocence of 17 people awaiting execution for crimes they did not commit.

Cases Not Yet Cracked

Not every crime can be solved. In these famous cases, the criminals were either never caught or never identified.

1888   Jack the Ripper   London, England
The real identity of one of history's most famous serial killers has never been proved, although there have been many suspects—including Prince Albert Victor, the grandson of Queen Victoria. The killer named himself Jack the Ripper in letters to the police.

1971   D. B. Cooper   Between Seattle, WA, and Portland, OR
After hijacking a plane and receiving $200,000 in ransom money, Cooper boarded another plane and parachuted out a rear door with 20 pounds of cash strapped to his body. Some of the money was later found, and a parachute turned up in 2008, but there has been no trace of Cooper.

1982   Unknown   Chicago, IL
Seven people died after swallowing Tylenol pain-relieving pills that someone had laced with cyanide, a deadly poison. The criminal was never caught, but the incident led to the institution of tamper-proof seals on medicines.

1990   Unknown   Boston, MA
Two men slashed 13 paintings worth $300 million out of their frames at the Gardner Museum in Boston, Massachusetts, and walked out with them. Security guards had let the men in because they were wearing police uniforms.

Innocent Until Proven Guilty

Even if you are suspected of committing a crime, as a citizen of the United States you have rights. You're protected by the 14th amendment of the U.S. Constitution:

> "Nor shall any state deprive any person of life, liberty, or property, without due process of law."

In other words, anyone accused of committing a crime is considered legally innocent until proven guilty. In certain other countries, it's the other way around: You're presumed guilty and have to prove your innocence.

How Due Process Works

Criminal cases are heard in a state or federal court of law, where both sides are represented.

The **defendant** is the person accused of the crime.

The **defense attorney** represents the defendant and presents his or her side of the case.

The **prosecutor** represents the state or federal government in trying to prove the defendant's guilt.

The **judge** presides over the courtroom and determines the sentence.

All the information and evidence is presented to a **jury**, citizens chosen to decide whether or not the defendant has been proven guilty. Their decision is called the **verdict**.

Miranda Rights

The Miranda rights are named for Ernesto Miranda, whose 1963 conviction on kidnapping and assault charges was reversed by the U.S. Supreme Court because his confession was obtained without providing him access to a lawyer. Since that court decision, police officers are required to give some form of the following warning to any person being arrested:

"You have the right to remain silent. Anything you say can and will be used against you in a court of law. You have the right to an attorney. If you cannot afford an attorney, one will be appointed to you. Do you understand these rights as they have been read to you?"

Disasters

"What a Disaster!"

How often have you said those words, or thought them? You spill ink all over your favorite jeans. You study the wrong chapter for a test. These things seem disastrous at the time, but in the long run they won't permanently affect your life. That's not true with real disasters.

Destruction and Death

A disaster causes destruction, usually on a large scale, and usually causes injuries and loss of life. Disasters can be natural events such as earthquakes, tornadoes, and hurricanes. They can also be the result of mechanical failures, human error, or terrorism, such as the plane crashes in the United States on September 11, 2001.

Geography Matters

Not every extreme natural event has to turn into a disaster. It's the location of the event that often makes the difference. Quakes that strike unpopulated areas can't kill people or knock down buildings that aren't there. Quakes that strike densely populated areas, such as the one that struck Haiti on January 12, 2010, have the most potential for destruction. The earthquake hit a few miles from Port-au-Prince, Haiti's populous capital, destroying an estimated 280,000 buildings, injuring at least 300,000 people, and causing more than 220,000 deaths.

BEING PREPARED

On February 27, 2010, an earthquake several hundred times larger than the one in Haiti struck Chile. It caused damage and loss of life that were terrible, but much less than what Haiti suffered. Why the difference? For one thing, Chile's earthquake struck a less populated area. For another, powerful earthquakes occur more frequently in Chile, so its buildings are built to withstand the violent shaking.

TAKE a LOOK

What does a tsunami have to do with an earthquake? What are the deadliest volcanic eruptions in history? See page 73.

Ash from the April 2010 eruption of a volcano in Iceland disrupted international air travel for days. Ash from the eruption of Mount Tambora in 1815 changed weather patterns for more than a year. Mary Shelley came up with the idea for *Frankenstein* in the summer of 1816, when she was staying in Switzerland with friends. The cold, dreary weather kept everyone indoors, where they amused themselves by telling ghost stories. Shelley later turned hers into a novel.

CHECK IT OUT !

What Makes an Earthquake?

At certain places, there are breaks in the rocks that make up Earth's surface. These places are called faults. An earthquake is a shock wave that occurs when the tectonic plates beneath a fault rub or crash together. The U.S. Geological Survey estimates that there are several million earthquakes a year. Most are too small to be detected.

10 Deadliest Earthquakes

Date	Place	Number of Deaths
Jan. 23, 1556	Shaanxi, China	830,000
Oct. 11, 1737	Calcutta, India	300,000
July 27, 1976	Tangshan, China	255,000
May 20, 526 CE	Antioch, Syria	250,000
Aug. 9, 1138	Aleppo, Syria	230,000
Dec. 26, 2004	Near Sumatra, Indonesia	227,898
Jan. 12, 2010	Near Port-au-Prince, Haiti	222,570
Dec. 22, 856 CE	Damghan, Iran	200,000
Dec. 16, 1920	Gansu, China	200,000
May 22, 1927	Tsinghai, China	200,000

NEWSworthy

In an earthquake or other disaster, the water supply often becomes contaminated with sewage, causing widespread disease and even death. But U.S. corporate giant Procter & Gamble has come up with a lifesaving product: a water purifier called PUR. One small packet of PUR can remove dirt and bacteria from 2.6 gallons (10 L) of water, making it safe to drink. Two hundred million packets of PUR have been distributed in 57 countries, including Haiti, providing 528,344,104.7 gallons (2 billion L) of clean water.

What Makes a Volcano?

A volcano is an opening in Earth's surface that allows hot melted rock, called magma, to escape from below the surface. Scientists say there are about 550 historically active volcanoes.

Gently curved shield volcanoes build up over thousands of years. Mauna Loa is a shield volcano on the island of Hawaii. It rises about 56,000 feet (17 km) above the ocean floor.

Some of the most famous volcanoes in the world are stratovolcanoes, including Mt. Vesuvius, Krakatau, and Mt. Mayon, the most active volcano in the Philippines.

10 Deadliest Volcanic Eruptions

Date	Volcano	Number of Deaths
April 10–12, 1815	Mt. Tambora, Indonesia	92,000
Aug. 26–28, 1883	Krakatau, Indonesia	36,000
May 8, 1902	Mt. Pelee, Martinique	28,000
Nov. 13, 1985	Nevado del Ruiz, Colombia	23,000
Aug. 24, 79 CE	Mt. Vesuvius, Italy	16,000
May 21, 1792	Mt. Unzen, Japan	14,500
1586 (month and day unknown)	Kelut, Indonesia	10,000
June 8, 1783	Laki, Iceland	9,350
May 19, 1919	Mt. Kelut, Indonesia	5,000
Dec. 15, 1631	Mt. Vesuvius, Italy	4,000

What Makes a Tsunami?

A tsunami is a wave that is often caused by an underwater earthquake. The wave travels across the ocean at speeds up to 600 miles per hour (970 kph), then crashes on shore with devastating power. A massive tsunami triggered by an earthquake in the Indian Ocean struck parts of Asia and Africa in December 2004, causing about 225,000 people to lose their lives.

Wild Windstorms

Hurricanes

Hurricanes are huge storms with winds over 74 mph (119 kph) blowing around a center, or eye. Most hurricanes form over the mild waters of the southern Atlantic Ocean, the Caribbean Sea, or the Gulf of Mexico. Equally powerful storms that form over the western Pacific Ocean are called typhoons. If they form over the Indian Ocean, they're called cyclones.

Hurricane Katrina, which hit the Gulf Coast in 2005, was the costliest natural disaster in U.S. history and the third-deadliest hurricane, causing $81 billion in damages and 1,833 deaths.

Tornadoes

Tornadoes are powerful storms with funnels of furious wind spinning from 40 mph (64 kph) to more than 300 mph (482.8 kph). The funnels touch down and rip paths of destruction on land. About 1,500 tornadoes hit the United States every year.

A group of tornadoes is called an outbreak. On April 3, 1974, a group of 148 tornadoes swept through 13 states and parts of Canada in the 1974 Super Outbreak. The storm's path on the ground covered almost 2,500 miles (4,023 km).

Major U.S. Natural Disasters

Earthquake
When: April 18, 1906
Where: San Francisco, California
An earthquake accompanied by a fire destroyed more than 4 square miles (10 sq km) and left at least 3,000 dead or missing.

Hurricane
When: August 27–September 15, 1900
Where: Galveston, Texas
More than 6,000 died from the devastating combination of high winds and tidal waves.

Tornado
When: March 18, 1925
Where: Missouri, Illinois, and Indiana
Called the Great Tri-State Tornado, this twister caused 695 deaths and ripped along a path of 219 miles (352 km) after touching down near Ellington, Missouri.

Blizzard
When: March 11–14, 1888
Where: East Coast
Four hundred people died, and 40–50 inches (101.6–127 cm) of snow fell in the Blizzard of '88. Damage was estimated at $20 million.

Major U.S. Disasters Caused by Humans

Aircraft
When: September 11, 2001
Where: New York, New York; Arlington, Virginia; Shanksville, Pennsylvania
Hijacked planes crashed into the World Trade Center, the Pentagon, and a field in Pennsylvania, causing nearly 3,000 deaths.

Fire
When: March 25, 1911
Where: New York, New York
The Triangle Shirtwaist Factory caught fire, trapping workers inside and causing 146 deaths.

Passenger Train
When: July 9, 1918
Where: Nashville, Tennessee
An inbound and an outbound train collided in a crash that witnesses heard miles away and took more than 100 lives. The crash was caused by errors and misunderstandings by both train crews.

Environmental
When: April 20, 2010
Where: Gulf of Mexico, 42 miles off the Louisiana coast
The Deepwater Horizon oil rig exploded, killing 11 workers and letting loose an underwater gush of oil of up to 798,000 gallons (about 3,000,000 L) a day. The massive oil spill has been called the worst environmental disaster in U.S. history, threatening wildlife, ecosystems, and industry along the Gulf Coast. As of June 1, 2010, efforts to plug the leak had been unsuccessful.

Environment

A Place to Call Home

From deserts to oceans, our planet offers a wide variety of environments. Environments are made up of living and nonliving things. Water, sunlight, soil, and climate are the nonliving elements of an environment. Plants and animals (including humans) are the living part.

Power Trip

All living things need energy to survive, but energy is not all the same. The energy that comes from the Sun, wind, and ocean tides is renewable. There is an unlimited supply in nature. However, some energy sources, such as petroleum, coal, and other fossil fuels, are nonrenewable. In time we could use up every last one of them.

Don't Be a (Carbon) Bigfoot

Using fossil fuels, such as gasoline, to power our cars, and burning oil and coal to heat our homes releases harmful gases into the atmosphere. These gases, known as greenhouse gases, include methane and carbon dioxide, and they can increase the temperature and change the weather on Earth. The amount of carbon dioxide humans create through activities and energy choices is called their carbon footprint.

The Three Rs

Three key things we can do to protect our planet are: reduce, reuse, and recycle. Reduce trash production by buying only what you need. Be creative and see how many new uses you can find for things you ordinarily toss out after one use. Recycle plastic, glass, and paper. For more tips, see pages 82–83.

TAKE a LOOK

Trash Talk

Reducing the amount of trash we produce every day can have a significant impact in protecting our environment. The average American creates about 4.5 pounds (2 kg) of trash per day. That adds up to more than 1,640 pounds (743 kg) every year. Recycling makes a huge difference. Each ton of recycled paper can save 17 trees, 380 gallons (1,440 L) of oil, 3 cubic yards (2.3 cu m) of landfill space, 4,000 kilowatts of energy, and 7,000 gallons (26,500 L) of water! (See page 78 for examples of what's in the average landfill.)

CHECK IT OUT!

In the 1970s, Americans were fighting against pollution—oil spills, raw sewage, and pesticides. On April 22, 1970, about 20 million Americans celebrated the first Earth Day to raise environmental awareness. That same year, the Environmental Protection Agency was created to enforce environmental standards. Every year millions of people in the United States still celebrate environmental awareness on Earth Day.

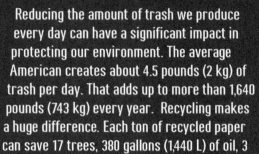

EARTH DAY

What's Filling Up U.S. Landfills?
(in millions of tons)

Rubber, leather, textiles
19.78

Wood
16.39

Metals
20.85

Plastics
30.05

Glass
12.15

Food scraps
31.79

Other materials
and wastes
8.28

Yard trimmings
32.60

Paper and paperboard
77.42

Total amount of trash =
249.6 million tons

How Much Is Recycled?

Material	Percent recycled yearly
Yard trimmings	64.7
Paper and paperboard	55.5
Metals	34.6
Rubber, leather, textiles	29.6
Glass	23.1
Wood	9.6
Plastics	7.1
Food scraps	2.5
Other	25.6

Top 5 Paper Recycling Countries

For every 1,000 people in the United States, about 160 tons of paper are recycled every year. That's a lot, but these other countries recycle even more.

Country	Amount recycled (per 1,000 people)
Sweden	186 tons
Austria	182 tons
Switzerland	179 tons
Germany	176 tons
The Netherlands	162 tons

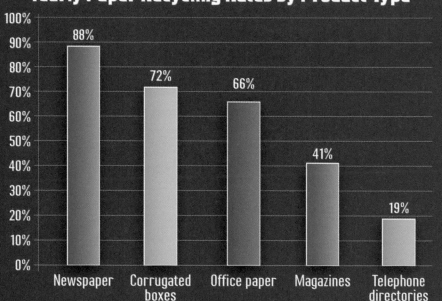

Yearly Paper Recycling Rates by Product Type

- Newspaper: 88%
- Corrugated boxes: 72%
- Office paper: 66%
- Magazines: 41%
- Telephone directories: 19%

CHECK IT OUT!

More than 5,000 different products can be made from recycled paper, including lampshades, money, and bandages.

Rising Carbon Dioxide Levels

The amount of the main greenhouse gas, carbon dioxide (CO_2), in the atmosphere has been steadily rising for more than a century. Experts say the increase comes mostly from the burning of fossil fuels for energy.

Carbon Dioxide in the Atmosphere, 1903–2009

Year	CO_2 (parts per million)
1903	295
1915	301
1927	306
1943	308
1960	317
1970	326
1980	339
1990	354
2000	367
2005	377
2006	379
2007	381
2008	385.6
2009	387.4

10 Worst Carbon Dioxide–Producing Countries

Country	Millions of Metric Tons Produced Annually
China	6,017.69
United States	5,902.75
Russia	1,704.35
India	1,293.17
Japan	1,246.76
Germany	857.60
Canada	614.33
United Kingdom	585.71
South Korea	514.53
Iran	471.48

Environment

Something's in the Air

There are six common air pollutants: ground-level ozone, carbon monoxide, sulfur and nitrogen oxides, lead, and particulate matter such as soot and smoke. The charts on this page show the urban areas that lead in two of these categories. Find out more at www.epa.gov.

10 U.S. Urban Areas with the Worst Ozone Levels

Rank	City
1	Los Angeles, CA
2	Bakersfield, CA
3	Visalia-Porterville, CA
4	Fresno-Madera, CA
5	Houston, TX
6	Sacramento, CA
7	Dallas, TX
8	Charlotte, NC
9	Phoenix, AZ
10	El Centro, CA

10 U.S. Urban Areas with the Highest Number of Soot Particulates

Rank	City
1	Bakersfield, CA
2	Pittsburgh, PA
3	Visalia, CA
4	Birmingham, AL
5	Hanford, CA
6	Fresno, CA
7	Cincinnati, OH
8	Detroit, MI
9	Los Angeles, CA
10	Cleveland, OH

Going G-R-R-R-E-E-N!

You won't find green spelled that way in any dictionary, but if we all remember the environmental 3 Rs—Reduce, Reuse, Recycle—we can improve the health and life of our planet. Here are simple things everyone can do.

REDUCE

Five Reducing Tips

1. Buy less. Try to purchase only what you need.

2. Use less. For instance, instead of buying two notepads and using only one side of the paper, buy one and use both sides.

3. Buy with minimum packaging in mind. Suggest that your family buy large sizes of cereal, toothpaste, and other things you use all the time to eliminate multiple boxes.

4. Buy longer-lasting products. Compact fluorescent lightbulbs make the same amount of light and use only one-fourth the amount of electricity that incandescent ones use.

5. Make things last longer. Fix your old bike rather than asking for a new one.

What a Waste!

Municipal solid waste (MSW) is trash—the stuff that we dump in landfills by millions of tons every year. What's the best way to reduce waste? Don't make it in the first place!

REUSE

Second Chance

You may be surprised at how many things can be reused. Think before tossing!

Five Reusing Tips

1. Pack your lunch in reusable containers instead of plastic or paper bags. If 25 percent of American homes used 10 fewer plastic bags a month, it would keep 2.5 billion bags out of landfills every year.

2. Use washable cups, travel mugs, and reusable sports bottles for beverages on the go. If you have to use plastic cups or plates, wash and reuse them.

3. Use a sponge to wipe up spills instead of reaching for paper towels.

4. Save wrapping paper and ribbon from gifts and reuse them.

5. Use rechargeable batteries whenever you can. Americans use approximately 2 billion unrechargeable batteries every year, which can release harmful metals into landfills.

RECYCLE

Around We Go

In the United States, we recycle about 32 percent of our MSW. More than 30 percent of the raw material used in glass production comes from recycled glass. That's good news, but we can do better. Even recycling a tiny amount makes a huge difference:

Five Recycling Stats

1. Recycling one glass bottle saves enough energy to light a 100-watt lightbulb for four hours.
2. If every American household recycled the Sunday newspaper, more than half a million trees would be saved—every week!
3. Recycling one aluminum can saves enough energy to run a TV for three hours.
4. Manufacturing one ton of recycled paper takes about 60 percent of the energy to make a ton of paper from raw pulp.
5. In California in 2004, 12 billion bottles and cans were recycled—enough to power as many as 522,000 homes.

Always Recycle These Items

Acid batteries
Aluminum cans
Appliances
Building materials
Cardboard
Chemicals

Electronic equipment
Glass (particularly bottles and jars)
Lead
Magazines
Metal

Newspaper
Oil
Paint
Paper
Plastic bags
Plastic bottles

Steel cans
Tires
Wood
Writing/copy paper
Yard waste

Some of these items have special rules for handling or disposal. Look in your phone book for your local recycling office. Check out the Environmental Protection Agency (EPA) website at www.epa.gov for a state-by-state list of locations and other helpful information.

Don't turn Earth into a pigSTY! Avoid Styrofoam. It will stay in landfills forever.

CHECK IT OUT !

Tips to Save Energy and Natural Resources

Close It Up

Close fireplace dampers when there's no fire burning. An open fireplace damper can let 8 percent of the heat from your furnace escape. Close the refrigerator door to keep the cold air inside.

Turn It Up

When it's warm outside, set your home thermostat at 78°F (25.5°C). When no one's home, set it at 85°F (29.4°C). (Check with an adult first.)

Turn It Down

When it's cold, set the thermostat at 68°F (20°C) or lower during the day. Turn it down to 55°F (12.7°C) or turn it off at night. (Again, check with an adult before changing household routines.)

Turn It Off

Save up to 20,000 gallons of water a year by not leaving the faucet running when brushing teeth, washing dishes, or washing the car. Turn off lights, the TV, your computer, radios, and stereos if the room is going to be empty for more than five minutes.

CHECK IT OUT!

Trees, please! If every American family planted just one tree, more than a billion pounds of greenhouse gases would be removed from the atmosphere every year.

Environment

Bike It or Hike It!

Every time you travel, you have choices about how you impact the environment. When you go, go green!

Skateboard, walk, or ride your bike whenever safety and weather permit. These are the greenest ways to travel, and they're great for your health.

Take the bus. A bus carrying 40 passengers takes one-sixth the energy of one car carrying one passenger, while replacing six city blocks' worth of cars.

Suggest that the adults in your family drive less, or carpool. Driving 25 fewer miles (40 km) every week can eliminate 1,500 pounds (680 km) of carbon dioxide from the air. Riding with two or more people two days a week can eliminate 1,590 pounds (721 kg) from the air.

NEWSworthy

Can going green win you gold? It did for Great Britain's Nicole Cooke! When Nicole was 11, her dad encouraged her to ride her bike to school instead of taking the bus. It was the beginning of training that would win her a gold medal in cycling at the 2008 Beijing Olympics.

Shrink Your Carbon Footprint

You can't control the size of your sneakers, but you can control the size of your carbon footprint. Go to www.globalwarming.house.gov/getinvolved to measure your impact on the environment and learn ways to shrink it.

Countries of the
World

There are 195 independent countries in the world. Each one has its own traditions, history, culture, foods, and more. Each country has different challenges, too, like weather and natural disasters. But in two ways every country is the same as every other one: Its citizens are all part of the same human race. And every country has its own unique national flag.

Some flags show a country's religious beliefs with symbols:

An ancient symbol of the Jewish people called the Star of David appears on the flag of Israel.

Flying Colors

Strictly speaking, a country's flag is a piece of cloth. But it's so much more than that. Every color, pattern, shape, and image on a flag stands for something about the country—its land, history, geography, people, government, or beliefs. The flag is a country's most important source of pride, and countries demand that their flags be respected. Most countries have strict rules about how to treat their flag, such as never allowing it to touch the ground or to be made into clothing.

Most national flags use these colors: red, white, blue, green, yellow, black, and orange. The South African flag uses six colors, the most of any nation. The Libyan flag uses the fewest. Its flag is solid green, the traditional color of Islam.

★ SEEING STARS ★

The number of stars on a country's flag may show how many states form that country. The flag of Cape Verde has ten stars, each one standing for an island state.

A constellation called the Southern Cross, which can be seen in the Southern Hemisphere's night sky, is shown on four flags, including the flag of Australia (above).

A cross, symbolizing Christianity, appears on the flags of many Christian nations.

The crescent and star in the flags of many Muslim countries are symbols of peace and life.

CHECK IT OUT !

Countries and nations are the same things, right? Nope. A nation is a large group of people with the same language, government, history, or culture. A country is a type of nation with definite borders.

TAKE a LOOK

As you look through this section, try to find the three other flags that show the Southern Cross. (Answers are on page 350.)

Notice other crosses, stars, shapes, colors, and symbols. See if you can guess what they mean about the country—then do some research to see if you guessed right.

Countries of the World

ARCTIC OCEAN

75°N

GREENLAND
(Denmark)

Arctic Circl

ICELAND

CANADA

IRELAND

UN
KIN

45°N

UNITED STATES

ATLANTIC OCEAN

AZORES
(Portugal)

PORTUGAL

SPA

30°N

MOROCC

MEXICO

BAHAMAS

CANARY ISLANDS
(Spain)

WESTERN
SAHARA

Tropic of Cancer

CUBA

DOMINICAN
REPUBLIC

HAITI

MAURITANIA

15°N

BELIZE

JAMAICA

CAPE VERDE

GUATEMALA

HONDURAS

SENEGAL

EL SALVADOR

NICARAGUA

GAMBIA

COSTA RICA

PANAMA

GUINEA-BISSAU

GUINEA

PACIFIC OCEAN

VENEZUELA

SURINAME

SIERRA LEONE

CÔTE
D'IVOIRE

GUYANA

FRENCH
GUIANA
(France)

LIBERIA

0°

Equator

COLOMBIA

"Equator

SÃO

ECUADOR

FRENCH POLYNESIA
(France)

15°S

PERU

B R A Z I L

BOLIVIA

Tropic of Capricorn

PARAGUAY

30°S

CHILE

URUGUAY

0	1,000	2,000 Miles
0	1,000	2,000 Kilometers

ARGENTINA

ATLANTIC OCEAN

45°S

FALKLAND ISLANDS
(U.K.)

SOUTH GEORGIA
(U.K.)

60°S

165°W   150°W   135°W   120°W   105°W   90°W   75°W   60°W   45°W   30°W   15°W

Antarctic Circle

ARCTIC OCEAN

ARCTIC OCEAN

FINLAND

RUSSIA

ESTONIA
LATVIA
LITHUANIA
BELARUS
ND
VAKIA
UKRAINE
MOLDOVA
ROMANIA
ICAN REP.
BULGARIA
GREECE
TURKEY
CYPRUS
LEBANON
ISRAEL
SYRIA
JORDAN
GEORGIA
ARMENIA
AZERBAIJAN
IRAQ
KUWAIT
IRAN
BAHRAIN
QATAR
U.A.E.

KAZAKHSTAN

MONGOLIA

UZBEKISTAN
KYRGYZSTAN
TURKMENISTAN
TAJIKISTAN
AFGHANISTAN

CHINA

NORTH
KOREA
SOUTH
KOREA

JAPAN

PACIFIC OCEAN

EGYPT

SAUDI ARABIA

OMAN

PAKISTAN

NEPAL

BHUTAN

INDIA

MYANMAR

Tropic of Cancer

SUDAN

ERITREA

YEMEN

BANGLADESH

LAOS

THAILAND

VIETNAM

NORTHERN
MARIANA ISLANDS
(U.S.)

DJIBOUTI

ETHIOPIA

SOMALIA

CAMBODIA

PHILIPPINES

FEDERATED STATES
OF MICRONESIA

MARSHALL
ISLANDS

CENTRAL
ICAN REP.

MALDIVES

SRI
LANKA

BRUNEI

PALAU

DEMOCRATIC
REPUBLIC OF
THE CONGO
UGANDA
KENYA

MALAYSIA

Equator

RWANDA
BURUNDI
TANZANIA

INDONESIA

PAPUA
NEW GUINEA

SOLOMON
ISLANDS

KIRIBATI

ZAMBIA

MALAWI

COMOROS

TIMOR-LESTE

TUVALU

SAMOA

ZIMBABWE
MOZAMBIQUE

MADAGASCAR

INDIAN OCEAN

Tropic of Capricorn

AUSTRALIA

NEW CALEDONIA
(France)

VANUATU

FIJI

TONGA

BOTSWANA

SOUTH
AFRICA

SWAZILAND

LESOTHO

NEW
ZEALAND

N
W   E
S

30°E   45°E   60°E   75°E   90°E   105°E   120°E   135°E   150°E   165°E   180°

ANTARCTICA

AFGHANISTAN

Capital: Kabul
Population: 33,609,937
Area: 250,001 sq. mi. (647,500 sq km)
Language: Dari (Afghan Persian), Pashto
Money: Afghani
Government: Islamic republic

⬆ CHECK IT OUT

Kite running is a popular sport in Afghanistan. Kids fly kites, cut them loose, and then race to recover them.

ALBANIA

Capital: Tirana
Population: 3,639,453
Area: 11,100 sq. mi. (28,748 sq km)
Language: Albanian, Greek
Money: Lek
Government: Republic

⬆ CHECK IT OUT

The Adriatic and Ionian Seas border the western coast of Albania.

ALGERIA

Capital: Algiers
Population: 34,178,188
Area: 919,595 sq. mi. (2,381,740 sq km)
Language: Arabic, Berber, French
Money: Dinar
Government: Republic

⬆ CHECK IT OUT

Algeria is the second-largest country in Africa.

ANDORRA

Capital: Andorra la Vella
Population: 83,888
Area: 180 sq. mi. (468 sq km)
Language: Catalan, French, Castillan, Portuguese
Money: Euro
Government: Parliamentary democracy

⬆ CHECK IT OUT

Andorra is about half the size of New York City. For 700 years, until 1993, this little country had two rulers: France and Spain.

ANGOLA

Capital: Luanda
Population: 12,799,293
Area: 481,400 sq. mi. (1,246,700 sq km)
Language: Portuguese, Bantu, others
Money: Kwanza
Government: Republic

⬆ CHECK IT OUT

Eighty-five percent of the country's revenue (GDP) comes from oil production.

ANTIGUA AND BARBUDA

Capital: St. John's
Population: 85,632
Area: 171 sq. mi. (443 sq km)
Language: English
Money: Dollar
Government: Parliamentary democracy; independent sovereign state within the Commonwealth

⬆ CHECK IT OUT

Thousands of frigate birds live in a sanctuary on Barbuda. A frigate bird's wingspan can reach nearly eight feet (2.4 m).

ARGENTINA

Capital: Buenos Aires
Population: 40,913,584
Area: 1,068,302 sq. mi.
(2,766,890 sq km)
Language: Spanish, Italian,
English, German, French
Money: Peso
Government: Republic

CHECK IT OUT

The Andes mountains run along
the western edge of Argentina,
on the border with Chile.

ARMENIA

Capital: Yerevan
Population: 2,967,004
Area: 11,484 sq. mi. (29,743 sq km)
Language: Armenian, Yezidi,
Russian
Money: Dram
Government: Republic

CHECK IT OUT

Armenia was the first nation to
formally adopt Christianity (in the
early fourth century).

AUSTRALIA

Capital: Canberra
Population: 21,262,641
Area: 2,967,909 sq. mi.
(7,686,850 sq km)
Language: English, Chinese,
Italian, aboriginal languages
Money: Dollar
Government: Constitutional
monarchy; democratic, federal-
state system recognizing British
monarchy as sovereign

CHECK IT OUT

The Great Barrier Reef, off the
coast of Australia, is larger than
the Great Wall of China.

AUSTRIA

Capital: Vienna
Population: 8,210,281
Area: 32,382 sq. mi. (83,870 sq km)
Language: German
Money: Euro
Government: Federal
parliamentary democracy

CHECK IT OUT

The Habsburg family ruled
Austria for nearly 750 years,
until the Treaty of St. Germain
in 1919 established the Republic
of Austria.

AZERBAIJAN

Capital: Baku
Population: 8,238,672
Area: 33,436 sq. mi. (86,600 sq km)
Language: Azerbaijani, Russian,
Armenian, others
Money: Manat
Government: Republic

CHECK IT OUT

The country's name is thought to
come from the ancient Persian
phrase that means "Land of Fire."

THE BAHAMAS

Capital: Nassau
Population: 309,156
Area: 5,382 sq. mi. (13,940 sq km)
Language: English, Creole
Money: Dollar
Government: Constitutional
parliamentary democracy

CHECK IT OUT

More than eight out of ten
Bahamians are of African
heritage.

BAHRAIN

Capital: Manama
Population: 727,785
Area: 257 sq. mi. (665 sq km)
Language: Arabic, English,
Farsi, Urdu
Money: Dinar
Government: Constitutional
monarchy

CHECK IT OUT

The land area of Bahrain is only
three and a half times the size of
Washington, DC.

BANGLADESH

Capital: Dhaka
Population: 156,050,883
Area: 55,599 sq. mi. (144,000 sq km)
Language: Bengali, Chakma, Bagh
Money: Taka
Government: Parliamentary
democracy

CHECK IT OUT

The Bengal tiger is the national
animal of Bangladesh.

BARBADOS

Capital: Bridgetown
Population: 284,589
Area: 166 sq. mi. (431 sq km)
Language: English
Money: Dollar
Government: Parliamentary
democracy

CHECK IT OUT

The British settled Barbados in
1627. When they arrived, there
was no one living there.

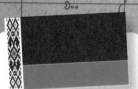

BELARUS

Capital: Minsk
Population: 9,648,533
Area: 80,155 sq. mi.
(207,600 sq km)
Language: Belarusian, Russian
Money: Ruble
Government: Republic

CHECK IT OUT

The name of this Eastern
European country means "White
Russia."

BELGIUM

Capital: Brussels
Population: 10,414,336
Area: 11,787 sq. mi. (30,528 sq km)
Language: Dutch, French,
German
Money: Euro
Government: Parliamentary
democracy under a constitutional
monarchy

CHECK IT OUT

Many people call Belgium the
chocolate capital of the world.
Hundreds of thousands of tons
of the sweet stuff are produced
here yearly.

BELIZE

Capital: Belmopan
Population: 307,899
Area: 8,867 sq. mi. (22,966 sq km)
Language: English, Creole,
Spanish, Mayan dialects
Money: Dollar
Government: Parliamentary
democracy

CHECK IT OUT

The mahogany industry was
central to Belize's economy
hundreds of years ago. That's
why a mahogany tree is pictured
on the country's flag.

BENIN

Capital: Porto-Novo
Population: 8,791,832
Area: 43,483 sq. mi.
(112,620 sq km)
Language: French, Fon, Yoruba in the south; Nagot, Bariba, Dendi in the north
Money: CFA franc
Government: Republic under multiparty democratic rule

CHECK IT OUT

Benin is only 215 miles across (about 325 km) at its widest point. It's eight times smaller than Nigeria, its neighbor.

BHUTAN

Capital: Thimphu
Population: 691,141
Area: 18,147 sq. mi. (47,000 sq km)
Language: Dzongkha, Nepali, Tibetan
Money: Ngultrum
Government: Constitutional monarchy

CHECK IT OUT

The Great Himalaya Range, the highest mountain system in the world, runs through northern Bhutan.

BOLIVIA

Capital: La Paz
Population: 9,775,246
Area: 424,164 sq. mi.
(1,098,580 sq km)
Language: Spanish, Quecha, Aymara, Guarani
Money: Boliviano
Government: Republic

CHECK IT OUT

Bolivia is named after independence fighter Simón Bolívar.

BOSNIA AND HERZEGOVINA

Capital: Sarajevo
Population: 4,613,414
Area: 19,772 sq. mi. (51,209 sq km)
Language: Bosnian, Serbian, Croatian
Money: Convertible marka
Government: Federal democratic republic

CHECK IT OUT

Sarajevo, the country's capital, hosted the 1984 Winter Olympics.

BOTSWANA

Capital: Gaborone
Population: 1,990,876
Area: 231,804 sq. mi.
(600,370 sq km)
Language: English, Setswana, Kalanga
Money: Pula
Government: Parliamentary republic

CHECK IT OUT

Botswana has one of the healthiest economies in Africa. About 70—80 percent of its export revenues come from diamond mining.

BRAZIL

Capital: Brasilia
Population: 198,739,269
Area: 3,286,488 sq. mi.
(8,511,965 sq km)
Language: Portuguese
Money: Real
Government: Federative republic

CHECK IT OUT

Brazil has the largest population in Latin America and the fifth-largest in the world.

BRUNEI

Capital: Bandar Seri Begawan
Population: 388,190
Area: 2,228 sq. mi. (5,770 sq km)
Language: Malay, English, Chinese
Money: Dollar
Government: Constitutional sultanate

CHECK IT OUT

For more than six centuries, the same royal family has ruled Brunei.

BULGARIA

Capital: Sofia
Population: 7,204,687
Area: 42,823 sq. mi. (110,910 sq km)
Language: Bulgarian, Turkish, Roma
Money: Lev
Government: Parliamentary democracy

CHECK IT OUT

One of Bulgaria's sweetest exports is rose oil, which is used throughout the world to make perfume.

BURKINA FASO

Capital: Ouagadougou
Population: 15,746,232
Area: 105,869 sq. mi. (274,200 sq km)
Language: French
Money: CFA franc
Government: Republic

CHECK IT OUT

Burkina Faso has western Africa's largest elephant population.

BURMA

Capital: Yangon (Rangoon)
Population: 48,137,741
Area: 261,970 sq. mi. (678,500 sq km)
Language: Burmese, many ethnic languages
Money: Kyat
Government: Military junta

CHECK IT OUT

The military junta ruling the nation changed Burma's name to Myanmar in 1989, but several countries, including the United States, refused to acknowledge the change. Others recognize Myanmar as the official name.

BURUNDI

Capital: Bujumbura
Population: 8,988,091
Area: 10,745 sq. mi. (27,830 sq km)
Language: Kirundi, French, Swahili
Money: Franc
Government: Republic

CHECK IT OUT

Burundi is on the shoreline of Lake Tanganyika, the second-deepest lake in the world.

CAMBODIA

Capital: Phnom Penh
Population: 14,494,293
Area: 69,900 sq. mi. (181,040 sq km)
Language: Khmer, French, English
Money: Riel
Government: Multiparty democracy under a constitutional monarchy

CHECK IT OUT

The Mekong River system, which runs through Cambodia, is the home of the giant catfish. These fish can reach 10 feet (3 m) in length and weigh up to 650 pounds (295 kg).

CAMEROON

Capital: Yaoundé
Population: 18,879,301
Area: 183,568 sq. mi. (475,440 sq km)
Language: French, English, 24 major African language groups
Money: CFA franc
Government: Republic

CHECK IT OUT

Mount Cameroon, the highest mountain in sub-Saharan west Africa, is an active volcano that last erupted in 2000.

CANADA

Capital: Ottawa
Population: 33,487,208
Area: 3,855,103 sq. mi.
(9,984,670 sq km)
Language: English, French
Money: Dollar
Government: Confederation
with parliamentary democracy
and constitutional monarchy

CHECK IT OUT

In land area, Canada is the second-largest country in the world. In population, it ranks only 39.

CAPE VERDE

Capital: Praia
Population: 429,474
Area: 1,557 sq. mi. (4,033 sq km)
Language: Portuguese, Crioulo
Money: Escudo
Government: Republic

CHECK IT OUT

The group of islands that make up Cape Verde was uninhabited until the Portuguese discovered it in 1460.

CENTRAL AFRICAN REPUBLIC

Capital: Bangui
Population: 4,511,488
Area: 240,535 sq. mi.
(622,984 sq km)
Language: Sangho, French,
tribal languages
Money: CFA franc
Government: Republic

CHECK IT OUT

There are more than 80 ethnic groups in the Central African Republic. Each group speaks its own language.

CHAD

Capital: N'Djaména
Population: 10,329,208
Area: 495,755 sq. mi.
(1,284,000 sq km)
Language: French, Arabic,
more than 120 others
Money: CFA franc
Government: Republic

CHECK IT OUT

Chad is about three times the size of California.

CHILE

Capital: Santiago
Population: 16,601,707
Area: 292,260 sq. mi.
(756,950 sq km)
Language: Spanish
Money: Peso
Government: Republic

CHECK IT OUT

The blue in Chile's flag stands for the sky and the white for the snow of the Andes mountains on its eastern border.

CHINA

Capital: Beijing
Population: 1,338,612,968
Area: 3,705,407 sq. mi.
(9,596,960 sq km)
Language: Mandarin, Yue,
Wu, Minhel, Minnan, Xiang, Gan,
Hakka dialects, others
Money: Yuan
Government: Communist
Party—led state

CHECK IT OUT

The name *China* comes from the Qin (or Ch'in) Dynasty, under which China was unified in 221 BCE.

COLOMBIA

Capital: Bogotá
Population: 45,644,023
Area: 439,736 sq. mi.
(1,138,910 sq km)
Language: Spanish
Money: Peso
Government: Republic

🔵CHECK IT OUT

Historically Colombia has been the world's top producer of emeralds.

COMOROS

Capital: Moroni
Population: 752,438
Area: 838 sq. mi. (2,170 sq km)
Language: Arabic, French, Shikomoro
Money: Franc
Government: Republic

🔵CHECK IT OUT

The three islands that make up Comoros are sometimes called the Perfume Islands. The country is the world's leading producer of essence of ylang-ylang, a flower oil used to make perfumes and soaps.

CONGO, Democratic Republic of the

Capital: Kinshasa
Population: 68,692,542
Area: 905,588 sq. mi.
(2,345,410 sq km)
Language: French, Lingala, Swahili, Kikongo, Tshiluba
Money: CFA franc
Government: Republic

🔵CHECK IT OUT

This country's enormous land area is equal to the United States east of the Mississippi River, or all of western Europe.

CONGO, Republic of the

Capital: Brazzaville
Population: 4,012,809
Area: 132,047 sq. mi. (342,000 sq km)
Language: French, Lingala, Monokutuba, Kikongo
Money: CFA franc
Government: Republic

🔵CHECK IT OUT

Oil is the country's largest revenue-generating industry.

COSTA RICA

Capital: San José
Population: 4,253,877
Area: 19,730 sq. mi. (51,100 sq km)
Language: Spanish, English
Money: Colón
Government: Democratic republic

🔵CHECK IT OUT

For a bird's-eye view of the rain forest, tourists in Costa Rica swing through the canopy on pulleys attached to treetops.

CÔTE d'IVOIRE (Ivory Coast)

Capital: Yamoussoukro
Population: 20,617,068
Area: 124,503 sq. mi.
(322,460 sq km)
Language: French, Dioula, 59 other native dialects
Money: CFA franc
Government: Republic with multiparty presidential regime

🔵CHECK IT OUT

Côte d'Ivoire is home to more than 60 ethnic groups.

CROATIA

Capital: Zagreb
Population: 4,489,409
Area: 21,831 sq. mi. (56,542 sq km)
Language: Croatian, Serbian
Money: Kuna
Government: Parliamentary democracy

CHECK IT OUT

Civil war ended in Croatia in 1998. Now tourists flock to its beautiful islands and national parks.

CUBA

Capital: Havana
Population: 11,451,652
Area: 42,803 sq. mi. (110,860 sq km)
Language: Spanish
Money: Peso
Government: Communist state

CHECK IT OUT

Cuba was controlled by the same leader, Fidel Castro, for nearly 50 years.

CYPRUS

Capital: Nicosia
Population: 796,740
Area: 3,571 sq. mi. (9,250 sq km)
Language: Greek, Turkish, English
Money: Euro
Government: Republic

CHECK IT OUT

Mythology says the goddess Aphrodite arose from the waves at a rock formation in Cyprus called *Petra tou Romiou*.

CZECH REPUBLIC

Capital: Prague
Population: 10,211,904
Area: 30,450 sq. mi. (78,866 sq km)
Language: Czech, Slovak
Money: Koruna
Government: Parliamentary democracy

CHECK IT OUT

In the country's capital is Prague Castle, the world's largest medieval castle.

DENMARK

Capital: Copenhagen
Population: 5,500,510
Area: 16,639 sq. mi. (43,094 sq km)
Language: Danish, Faroese, Greenlandic, English
Money: Krone
Government: Constitutional monarchy

CHECK IT OUT

Lego blocks were invented in Denmark. The name comes from the Danish words *leg* and *godt*, which mean "play well."

DJIBOUTI

Capital: Djibouti
Population: 516,055
Area: 8,880 sq. mi. (23,000 sq km)
Language: French, Arabic, Afar, Somali
Money: Franc
Government: Republic

CHECK IT OUT

The Djibouti countryside features dramatic limestone chimneys created by deposits of calcium carbonate from hot springs.

DOMINICA

Capital: Roseau
Population: 72,660
Area: 291 sq. mi. (754 sq km)
Language: English, French patois
Money: Dollar
Government: Parliamentary democracy

CHECK IT OUT

Parts of Dominica can receive as much as 300 inches (762 cm) of rain every year.

DOMINICAN REPUBLIC

Capital: Santo Domingo
Population: 9,650,054
Area: 18,815 sq. mi. (48,730 sq km)
Language: Spanish
Money: Peso
Government: Democratic republic

CHECK IT OUT

The Dominican Republic is the second-largest country in the West Indies.

ECUADOR

Capital: Quito
Population: 14,573,101
Area: 109,483 sq. mi. (283,560 sq km)
Language: Spanish, Quechua, Jivaroan
Money: Dollar
Government: Republic

CHECK IT OUT

The Galápagos Islands, off Ecuador's coast, are home to the Galápagos tortoise. These ancient creatures can weigh up to 475 pounds (215 kg) and live more than 100 years.

EGYPT

Capital: Cairo
Population: 83,082,869
Area: 386,662 sq. mi. (1,001,450 sq km)
Language: Arabic, English, French
Money: Pound
Government: Republic

CHECK IT OUT

The Great Pyramid of Khufu (Cheops) is 480 feet (146 m) high—about the height of a 48-story building.

EL SALVADOR

Capital: San Salvador
Population: 7,185,218
Area: 8,124 sq. mi. (21,040 sq km)
Language: Spanish, Nahua
Money: Colón
Government: Republic

CHECK IT OUT

El Salvador is the smallest and most densely populated country in Central America.

EQUATORIAL GUINEA

Capital: Malabo
Population: 633,441
Area: 10,831 sq. mi. (28,051 sq km)
Language: Spanish, French, Fang, Bubi
Money: CFA franc
Government: Republic

CHECK IT OUT

Scientists come to Bioko Island, where this country's capital is located, to study unique species of plants and animals, including a rare monkey called a drill.

ERITREA

Capital: Asmara
Population: 5,647,168
Area: 46,842 sq. mi. (121,320 sq km)
Language: Afar, Arabic, Tigre, Kunama
Money: Nakfa
Government: In transition

CHECK IT OUT

Many Eritreans wear a traditional shawl known as a *gabbi*.

ESTONIA

Capital: Tallinn
Population: 1,299,371
Area: 17,462 sq. mi. (45,226 sq km)
Language: Estonian, Russian, Latvian
Money: Kroon
Government: Parliamentary republic

CHECK IT OUT

Estonia is home to Old Town Tallinn, one of Europe's best-preserved medieval communities. It has 26 watchtowers and cobblestone streets.

ETHIOPIA

Capital: Addis Ababa
Population: 85,237,338
Area: 435,186 sq. mi. (1,127,127 sq km)
Language: Amarigna, Oromigna, Tigrigna, Somaligna, English
Money: Birr
Government: Federal republic

CHECK IT OUT

The Blue Nile river runs for more than 500 miles (800 km) through Ethiopia and carries the runoff from the highlands to the desert.

FIJI

Capital: Suva
Population: 944,720
Area: 7,054 sq. mi. (18,270 sq km)
Language: English, Fijian, Hindustani
Money: Dollar
Government: Republic

CHECK IT OUT

Fiji is composed of 333 different islands in the South Pacific, but most people live on the largest one—Viti Levu.

FINLAND

Capital: Helsinki
Population: 5,250,275
Area: 130,559 sq. mi. (338,145 sq km)
Language: Finnish, Swedish
Money: Euro
Government: Constitutional republic

CHECK IT OUT

One-fourth of Finland is north of the Arctic Circle, making winters there long and very cold.

FRANCE

Capital: Paris
Population: 64,057,792
Area: 248,429 sq. mi. (643,427 sq km)
Language: French
Money: Euro
Government: Republic

CHECK IT OUT

The TGV train, France's high-speed rail service, runs at speeds of up to 200 miles per hour (322 kph).

GABON

Capital: Libreville
Population: 1,514,993
Area: 103,347 sq. mi.
(267,667 sq km)
Language: French, Fang, others
Money: CFA franc
Government: Republic

CHECK IT OUT

The Kongou Falls, located in
Gabon's Invindo National Park, is
2 miles (3.2 km) wide.

THE GAMBIA

Capital: Banjul
Population: 1,782,893
Area: 4,363 sq. mi. (11,300 sq km)
Language: English, Mandinka,
Wolof, Fula, others
Money: Dalasi
Government: Republic

CHECK IT OUT

The Gambia is the smallest
country on the African continent.

GEORGIA

Capital: Tbilisi
Population: 4,615,807
Area: 26,911 sq. mi. (69,700 sq km)
Language: Georgian, Russian,
Abkhaz
Money: Lari
Government: Republic

CHECK IT OUT

Krubera Cave, in Georgia's
Caucasus Mountains, is said to
be the deepest cave in the world.
It has been explored to depths of
7,185 feet (2,190 m).

GERMANY

Capital: Berlin
Population: 82,329,758
Area: 137,847 sq. mi.
(357,021 sq km)
Language: German
Money: Euro
Government: Federal republic

CHECK IT OUT

The spires of the Cologne
Cathedral are an amazing 515
feet (157 m) high—taller than a
50-story building.

GHANA

Capital: Accra
Population: 23,832,495
Area: 92,456 sq. mi. (239,460 sq km)
Language: English, Asante, Ewe,
Fante
Money: Cedi
Government: Constitutional
democracy

CHECK IT OUT

Until 1957 Ghana was known as
the Gold Coast because of the
vast amounts of gold Portuguese
explorers found there.

GREECE

Capital: Athens
Population: 10,737,428
Area: 50,942 sq. mi. (131,940 sq km)
Language: Greek, Turkish,
English
Money: Euro
Government: Parliamentary
republic

CHECK IT OUT

The Parthenon, in Athens, is one
of the oldest and most famous
buildings in the world. The
ancient temple was built to honor
the Greek goddess Athena almost
2,500 years ago.

GRENADA

Capital: St. George's
Population: 90,739
Area: 133 sq. mi. (344 sq km)
Language: English, French patois
Money: Dollar
Government: Parliamentary
democracy

CHECK IT OUT

Grenada is known as the Spice
of the Caribbean. The country
produces one-third of the
world's nutmeg.

GUATEMALA

Capital: Guatemala City
Population: 13,276,517
Area: 42,043 sq. mi.
(108,890 sq km)
Language: Spanish, 23
Amerindian dialects
Money: Quetzal
Government: Constitutional
democratic republic

CHECK IT OUT

More than one-half of
Guatemalans are descended from
the Mayas. The Mayan Indian
civilization developed a calendar
with a 365-day year, among many
other achievements.

GUINEA

Capital: Conakry
Population: 10,057,975
Area: 94,926 sq. mi.
(245,857 sq km)
Language: French, Peul,
Malinke, Soussou
Money: Franc
Government: Republic

CHECK IT OUT

Despite its name, the guinea pig
does not come from Guinea. It is
native to South America. (And it's
not a pig!)

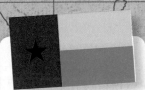

GUINEA-BISSAU

Capital: Bissau
Population: 1,533,964
Area: 13,946 sq. mi. (36,120 sq km)
Language: Portuguese, Creole,
French, others
Money: CFA franc
Government: Republic

CHECK IT OUT

Guinea-Bissau's main export crop
is cashew nuts.

GUYANA

Capital: Georgetown
Population: 772,298
Area: 83,000 sq. mi. (214,970 sq km)
Language: English, Guyanese,
Creole
Money: Dollar
Government: Republic

CHECK IT OUT

Guyana's Kaieteur Falls is five
times as tall as Niagara Falls.

HAITI

Capital: Port-au-Prince
Population: 9,035,536
Area: 10,714 sq. mi. (27,750 sq km)
Language: French, Creole
Money: Gourde
Government: Republic

CHECK IT OUT

On January 12, 2010, a
devastating earthquake struck
Haiti, killing or injuring hundreds
of thousands in the Port-au-
Prince area.

THE HOLY SEE
(VATICAN CITY)

Capital: Vatican City
Population: 826
Area: 0.17 sq. mi. (0.44 sq km)
Language: Italian, Latin, French, various others
Money: Euro
Government: Ecclesiastical

CHECK IT OUT

Vatican City, the seat of the Roman Catholic Church, is the world's smallest independent nation.

HONDURAS

Capital: Tegucigalpa
Population: 7,792,854
Area: 43,278 sq. mi. (112,090 sq km)
Language: Spanish, Amerindian dialects
Money: Lempira
Government: Democratic constitutional republic

CHECK IT OUT

The word *honduras* means "depths" in Spanish. Christopher Columbus named the area after the deep water off its coast when he landed there in 1502.

HUNGARY

Capital: Budapest
Population: 9,905,596
Area: 35,919 sq. mi. (93,030 sq km)
Language: Hungarian
Money: Forint
Government: Parliamentary democracy

CHECK IT OUT

The Danube River splits the capital city into two sides: Buda and Pest.

ICELAND

Capital: Reykjavik
Population: 306,694
Area: 39,769 sq. mi. (103,000 sq km)
Language: Icelandic
Money: Krona
Government: Constitutional republic

CHECK IT OUT

Iceland's glaciers, geysers, and warm, mineral-rich pools attract more than a quarter of a million tourists every year.

INDIA

Capital: New Delhi
Population: 1,166,079,217
Area: 1,269,346 sq. mi. (3,287,590 sq km)
Language: Hindi, English, 21 others
Money: Rupee
Government: Federal republic

CHECK IT OUT

India's Taj Mahal is one of the wonders of the world. It was built in the 1600s by Shah Jahan for his wife, Mumtaz Mahal.

INDONESIA

Capital: Jakarta
Population: 240,271,522
Area: 741,100 sq. mi. (1,919,440 sq km)
Language: Bahasa Indonesia, English, Dutch, Javanese
Money: Rupiah
Government: Republic

CHECK IT OUT

The largest volcanic eruption in history happened on the Indonesian island of Sumbawa in 1815. Scientists say that the eruption of Mount Tambora sent a massive cloud of ash 30 miles (43 km) into the atmosphere—much higher than a plane can fly—and killed 100,000 people.

IRAN

Capital: Tehran
Population: 66,429,284
Area: 636,296 sq. mi. (1,648,000 sq km)
Language: Persian, Turkic, Kurdish, Arabic, others
Money: Rial
Government: Islamic republic

CHECK IT OUT

For most of its history, Iran was called Persia.

IRAQ

Capital: Baghdad
Population: 28,945,657
Area: 168,754 sq. mi.
(437,072 sq km)
Language: Arabic, Kurdish,
Turkoman, Assyrian, Armenian
Money: Dinar
Government: Parliamentary
democracy

CHECK IT OUT

Iraq contains more oil than any
country in the world, except for
Saudi Arabia and Canada.

IRELAND

Capital: Dublin
Population: 4,302,200
Area: 27,135 sq. mi. (70,280 sq km)
Language: English, Gaelic
Money: Euro
Government: Parliamentary
republic

CHECK IT OUT

Ireland is known as the Emerald
Isle because of its beautiful green
fields and hillsides.

ISRAEL

Capital: Jerusalem
Population: 7,233,701
Area: 8,019 sq. mi. (20,770 sq km)
Language: Hebrew, Arabic,
English
Money: New shekel
Government: Republic

CHECK IT OUT

The Western Wall in Jerusalem
is also called the Wailing Wall. It
is one of Judaism's holiest places
and most sacred symbols.

ITALY

Capital: Rome
Population: 58,126,212
Area: 116,306 sq. mi.
(301,230 sq km)
Language: Italian, German,
French, Slovene
Money: Euro
Government: Republic

CHECK IT OUT

Engineers successfully stopped
Italy's famous Leaning Tower of
Pisa from collapsing through a
construction project in 2001.

JAMAICA

Capital: Kingston
Population: 2,825,928
Area: 4,244 sq. mi. (10,991 sq km)
Language: English, English patois
Money: Dollar
Government: Constitutional
monarchy with parliamentary
system

CHECK IT OUT

The pirate known as Blackbeard
(Edward Teach) is said to have
operated out of Jamaica in the
1700s. Some stories say that he
went into battle with lit matches
stuck in his hat to make enemies
think his head was smoking.

JAPAN

Capital: Tokyo
Population: 127,078,679
Area: 145,883 sq. mi.
(337,835 sq km)
Language: Japanese
Money: Yen
Government: Constitutional
monarchy with parliamentary
democracy

CHECK IT OUT

Japan has four major islands—
Honshu, Hokkaido, Kyushu, and
Shikoku—and thousands of
smaller ones.

JORDAN

Capital: Amman
Population: 6,342,948
Area: 35,637 sq. mi. (92,300 sq km)
Language: Arabic, English
Money: Dinar
Government: Constitutional monarchy

CHECK IT OUT

The points of the star on Jordan's flag stand for the first seven verses of the Koran, the holy book of Islam.

KAZAKHSTAN

Capital: Astana
Population: 15,399,437
Area: 1,049,155 sq. mi. (2,717,300 sq km)
Language: Kazakh, Russian, German
Money: Tenge
Government: Republic

CHECK IT OUT

The Caspian Sea, which borders Kazakhstan, is the largest enclosed body of water on Earth.

KENYA

Capital: Nairobi
Population: 39,002,772
Area: 224,962 sq. mi. (582,650 sq km)
Language: Kiswahili, English, numerous indigenous languages
Money: Shilling
Government: Republic

CHECK IT OUT

In Kenya's Lake Turkana area, scientists discovered a fossil known as Kenya Man, thought to be over three million years old.

KIRIBATI

Capital: Tawara
Population: 112,850
Area: 313 sq. mi. (811 sq km)
Language: English, I-Kiribati
Money: Dollar
Government: Republic

CHECK IT OUT

Kiribati consists of three groups of islands surrounded by coral reefs, roughly halfway between Australia and Hawaii.

KOREA, NORTH

Capital: Pyongyang
Population: 22,665,345
Area: 46,541 sq. mi. (120,540 sq km)
Language: Korean
Money: Won
Government: Communist state

CHECK IT OUT

North Korea has the fourth-largest army in the world.

KOREA, SOUTH

Capital: Seoul
Population: 48,508,972
Area: 38,023 sq. mi. (98,480 sq km)
Language: Korean, English
Money: Won
Government: Republic

CHECK IT OUT

South Korea has more than twice as many people as North Korea, but much less land area. It's one of the mostly densely populated countries in the world.

KOSOVO

Capital: Pristina
Population: 1,804,838
Area: 4,203 sq. mi.
(10,887 sq km)
Language: Albanian, Serbian,
Bosnian, Turkish, Roma
Money: Euro
Government: Republic

CHECK IT OUT

Kosovo, a country in southeastern
Europe that is about the size
of Connecticut, declared its
independence from Serbia on
February 17, 2008.

KUWAIT

Capital: Kuwait City
Population: 2,691,158
Area: 6,880 sq. mi. (17,820 sq km)
Language: Arabic, English
Money: Dinar
Government: Constitutional
emirate

CHECK IT OUT

Summers in Kuwait are dry and
extremely hot, averaging
108—115°F (42—46°C).

KYRGYZSTAN

Capital: Bishkek
Population: 5,431,747
Area: 76,641 sq. mi.
(198,500 sq km)
Language: Kyrgyz, Russian, Uzbek
Money: Som
Government: Republic

CHECK IT OUT

Kyrgyzstan is one of 15
countries that became
independent with the collapse
of the Soviet Union in 1991.

LAOS

Capital: Vientiane
Population: 6,834,942
Area: 91,429 sq. mi.
(236,800 sq km)
Language: Lao, French,
English, other ethnic languages
Money: Kip
Government: Communist state

CHECK IT OUT

In 2008, cavers exploring the 6-
mile-long (almost 10 km) Xe Bang
Fai River cave in central Laos
found huge rooms and spiders
as big as dinner plates.

LATVIA

Capital: Riga
Population: 2,231,503
Area: 24,938 sq. mi.
(64,589 sq km)
Language: Latvian,
Lithuanian, Russian
Money: Lat
Government: Parliamentary
democracy

CHECK IT OUT

Latvia has a 100 percent
literacy rate.

LEBANON

Capital: Beirut
Population: 4,017,095
Area: 4,015 sq. mi.
(10,400 sq km)
Language: Arabic, English,
French, Armenian
Money: Pound
Government: Republic

CHECK IT OUT

Beirut is a lively pop music
center, with TV music
channels, yearly festivals,
and talent shows such
as *Star Academy* and
Superstar.

LESOTHO

Capital: Maseru
Population: 2,130,819
Area: 11,720 sq. mi.
(30,355 sq km)
Language: Sesotho,
English, Zulu, Xhosa
Government:
Parliamentary constitutional
monarchy

CHECK IT OUT

To visualize Lesotho, think
of a doughnut hole—a small
circle of land surrounded
by the much larger nation of
South Africa.

LIBERIA

Capital: Monrovia
Population: 3,441,790
Area: 43,000 sq. mi. (111,370 sq km)
Language: English, about 20 ethnic languages
Money: Dollar
Government: Republic

CHECK IT OUT

Many Liberians are descendants of American slaves who were advised to live there in freedom by a U.S. antislavery group in the 1800s.

LIBYA

Capital: Tripoli
Population: 6,310,434
Area: 679,362 sq. mi. (1,759,540 sq km)
Language: Arabic, Italian, English
Money: Dinar
Government: Jamahiriya ("state of the masses")

CHECK IT OUT

Libya has a young population. About one-third of all Libyans are under 15.

LIECHTENSTEIN

Capital: Vaduz
Population: 34,761
Area: 62 sq. mi. (160 sq km)
Language: German, Alemannic dialect
Money: Swiss franc
Government: Constitutional monarchy

CHECK IT OUT

Tiny Liechtenstein shares some services with neighboring Switzerland. Its residents use Swiss money, and Switzerland runs Liechtenstein's telephone and postal systems.

LITHUANIA

Capital: Vilnius
Population: 3,555,179
Area: 25,212 sq. mi. (65,300 sq km)
Language: Lithuanian, Russian, Polish
Money: Litas
Government: Parliamentary democracy

CHECK IT OUT

Lithuania is the largest of the Baltic states, three countries on the eastern edge of the Baltic Sea. The others are Estonia and Latvia.

LUXEMBOURG

Capital: Luxembourg-Ville
Population: 491,775
Area: 998 sq. mi. (2,586 sq km)
Language: Luxembourgish, German, French
Money: Euro
Government: Constitutional monarchy

CHECK IT OUT

Luxembourg is an industrial country known particularly for two products: steel and computers.

MACEDONIA

Capital: Skopje
Population: 2,066,718
Area: 9,781 sq. mi. (25,333 sq km)
Language: Macedonian, Albanian, Turkish
Money: Denar
Government: Parliamentary democracy

CHECK IT OUT

About 80 percent of Macedonia consists of hills and mountains, but more than half the population lives in cities.

Countries of the World

MADAGASCAR

Capital: Antananarivo
Population: 20,653,556
Area: 226,657 sq. mi.
(587,040 sq km)
Language: Malagasy, English,
French
Money: Ariary
Government: Republic

CHECK IT OUT

Madagascar is the world's fourth-largest island, after Greenland, New Guinea, and Borneo. It is home to a huge variety of unique plants and animals that evolved 165 million years ago.

MALAWI

Capital: Lilongwe
Population: 14,268,711
Area: 45,745 sq km (118,480 sq km)
Language: Chichewa, Chinyan'ji,
Chiyao, Chitumbka
Money: Kwacha
Government: Multiparty
democracy

CHECK IT OUT

Lake Malawi is nearly 9,000 square miles (23,310 sq km). It takes up about a fifth of the country's total area.

MALAYSIA

Capital: Kuala Lumpur
Population: 25,715,819
Area: 127,317 sq. mi. (329,750
sq km)
Language: Bahasa Malaysia,
English, Chinese dialects, Panjabi,
Thai
Money: Ringgit
Government: Constitutional
monarchy

CHECK IT OUT

Malaysia's capital is the home of the 1,483-foot (452 m) Petronas Twin Towers. They were the tallest buildings in the world from 1996 to 2003.

MALDIVES

Capital: Male
Population: 396,334
Area: 116 sq. mi. (300 sq km)
Language: Maldivian Dhivehi,
English
Money: Rufiyaa
Government: Republic

CHECK IT OUT

About a 1,000 of the 1,190 coral islands that make up Maldives, located south of India in the Indian Ocean, are uninhabited.

MALI

Capital: Bamako
Population: 12,666,987
Area: 478,767 sq. mi.
(1,240,000 sq km)
Language: French, Bambara,
numerous African languages
Money: CFA franc
Government: Republic

CHECK IT OUT

Most of Mali's people make their living farming or fishing around the Niger River.

MALTA

Capital: Valletta
Population: 405,165
Area: 122 sq. mi. (316 sq km)
Language: Maltese, English
Money: Euro
Government: Republic

CHECK IT OUT

This group of islands in the Mediterranean Sea south of Sicily has one of the world's healthiest populations. The average life expectancy is over 79 years.

MARSHALL ISLANDS

Capital: Majuro
Population: 64,522
Area: 70 sq. mi. (181 sq km)
Language: Marshallese, English
Money: U.S. dollar
Government: Constitutional government in free association with the United States

⟳ CHECK IT OUT

The first hydrogen bomb was exploded in the Marshall Islands in 1952. Radiation levels in some areas are still high, but improving through environmental cleanup programs.

MAURITANIA

Capital: Nouakchott
Population: 3,129,486
Area: 397,955 sq. mi. (1,030,700 sq km)
Language: Arabic, Pulaar, Soninke, Wolof, French
Money: Ouguiya
Government: Military junta

⟳ CHECK IT OUT

This western African nation has it together! It's a major producer of gum arabic, used to make glue.

MAURITIUS

Capital: Port Louis
Population: 1,284,264
Area: 788 sq. mi. (2,040 sq km)
Language: Creole, Bhojpuri, French
Money: Rupee
Government: Parliamentary democracy

⟳ CHECK IT OUT

Mauritius has the second-highest per-person income in Africa. Most of the country's money comes from sugarcane.

MEXICO

Capital: Mexico City
Population: 111,211,789
Area: 761,606 sq. mi. (1,972,550 sq km)
Language: Spanish, various Mayan, Nahuati, other regional indigenous dialects
Money: Peso
Government: Federal republic

⟳ CHECK IT OUT

Mexico has dozens of bullfighting rings, including one that holds 50,000 people—about the entire population of Biloxi, Mississippi.

MICRONESIA

Capital: Palikir
Population: 107,434
Area: 271 sq. mi. (702 sq km)
Language: English, Chuukese, Kosrean, Pohnpeian, Yapese
Money: U.S. dollar
Government: Constitutional government in free association with the United States

⟳ CHECK IT OUT

Micronesia's first settlers have been traced back more than 4,000 years.

MOLDOVA

Capital: Chisinau
Population: 4,320,748
Area: 13,067 sq. mi. (333,843 sq km)
Language: Moldovan, Russian, Gagauz
Money: Leu
Government: Republic

⟳ CHECK IT OUT

Moldova was the first former Soviet state to elect a Communist as president.

MONACO

Capital: Monaco
Population: 32,965
Area: 0.75 sq. mi. (1.95 sq km)
Language: French, English, Italian, Monegasque
Money: Euro
Government: Constitutional monarchy

CHECK IT OUT

Mini-sized Monaco covers about as much area as New York City's Central Park.

MONGOLIA

Capital: Ulan Bator
Population: 3,041,142
Area: 603,909 sq. mi. (1,564,116 sq km)
Language: Khalka Mongol, Turkic, Russian
Money: Togrog/Tughrik
Government: Mixed parliamentary/presidential

CHECK IT OUT

Mongolia's average population density is only 5 people per square mile (1.9 per sq km), although many people live in the cities.

MONTENEGRO

Capital: Podgorica
Population: 672,180
Area: 5,415 sq. mi. (14,026 sq km)
Language: Montenegrin, Serbian, Bosnian, Albanian, Croatian
Money: Euro
Government: Republic

CHECK IT OUT

Montenegro's name means "black mountain." The name comes from the dark forests on the mountains that once covered most of the country.

MOROCCO

Capital: Rabat
Population: 34,859,364
Area: 172,414 sq. mi. (446,550 sq km)
Language: Arabic, Berber dialects, French
Money: Dirham
Government: Constitutional monarchy

CHECK IT OUT

Morocco is a North African country about the size of California. Part of it is covered by the Sahara Desert, whose 3,500,000 square miles (9,064,958 sq km) make it the largest desert in the world.

MOZAMBIQUE

Capital: Maputo
Population: 21,669,278
Area: 309,496 sq. mi. (801,590 sq km)
Language: Portuguese, Emakhuwa, Xichangana, Elomwe, Cisena
Money: Metical
Government: Republic

CHECK IT OUT

Portuguese is the official language of Mozambique. However, most residents, who are of African descent, speak a form of Bantu.

NAMIBIA

Capital: Windhoek
Population: 2,108,665
Area: 318,696 sq. mi. (825,418 sq km)
Language: Afrikaans, German, English, other indigenous languages
Money: Dollar, South African rand
Government: Republic

CHECK IT OUT

Namibia's rich diamond deposits have made it one of the world's best sources of high-quality diamonds.

NAURU

Capital: Yaren
Population: 14,019
Area: 8 sq. mi. (21 sq km)
Language: Nauruan, English
Money: Australian dollar
Government: Republic

CHECK IT OUT

Nauru joined the United Nations in 1999 as the world's smallest independent republic.

NEPAL

Capital: Kathmandu
Population: 28,563,377
Area: 56,827 sq. mi. (147,181 sq km)
Language: Nepali, Maithali, English
Money: Rupee
Government: Federal democratic republic

CHECK IT OUT

Eight of the world's ten highest mountain peaks are in Nepal, including Mount Everest, the highest of them all—29,035 feet (8,850 m).

NETHERLANDS

Capital: Amsterdam
Population: 16,715,999
Area: 16,033 sq. mi. (41,526 sq km)
Language: Dutch, Frisian
Money: Euro
Government: Constitutional monarchy

CHECK IT OUT

Most Netherlanders dress in modern clothing, but many farmers say wooden shoes, known as *klompen*, keep feet drier.

NEW ZEALAND

Capital: Wellington
Population: 4,213,418
Area: 103,738 sq. mi. (268,680 sq km)
Language: English, Maori, sign language
Money: Dollar
Government: Parliamentary democracy

CHECK IT OUT

New Zealand was settled by the Polynesian Maori in 800 CE. Today Maori make up about 9.38 percent of the country's population.

NICARAGUA

Capital: Managua
Population: 5,891,199
Area: 49,998 sq. mi. (129,494 sq km)
Language: Spanish, English, indigenous languages on Atlantic coast
Money: Gold cordoba
Government: Republic

CHECK IT OUT

Nicaragua got its name from Nicarao, a tribal chief who lived and reigned here in the 16th century.

NIGER

Capital: Niamey
Population: 15,306,252
Area: 489,191 sq. mi.
(1,267,000 sq km)
Language: French, Hausa,
Djerma
Money: CFA franc
Government: Republic

CHECK IT OUT

Niger is known as the Frying Pan of the World. It can get hot enough to make raindrops evaporate before they hit the ground.

NIGERIA

Capital: Abuja
Population: 149,229,090
Area: 356,669 sq. mi.
(923,768 sq km)
Language: English, Hausa,
Yoruba, Igbo, Fulani
Money: Naira
Government: Federal republic

CHECK IT OUT

Nigeria is the most heavily populated country in Africa. More than half the continent's people live there.

NORWAY

Capital: Oslo
Population: 4,660,539
Area: 125,021 sq. mi.
(323,802 sq km)
Language: Bokmal Norwegian,
Nynorsk Norwegian, Sami
Money: Krone
Government: Constitutional monarchy

CHECK IT OUT

Moving glaciers during the Ice Age left Norway with a jagged coastline marked by long strips of water-filled fjords and thousands of islands.

OMAN

Capital: Muscat
Population: 3,418,085
Area: 82,031 sq. mi.
(212,460 sq km)
Language: Arabic, English,
Baluchi, Urdu, Indian dialects
Money: Rial
Government: Monarchy

CHECK IT OUT

Members of the Al Bu Said family have ruled Oman for more than 250 years.

PAKISTAN

Capital: Islamabad
Population: 176,242,949
Area: 310,403 sq. mi.
(803,940 sq km)
Language: English, Urdu,
Punjabi, Sindhi, Siraiki, Pashtu
Money: Rupee
Government: Federal republic

CHECK IT OUT

Pakistan is the sixth most heavily populated country in the world. The others, in order, are China, India, the United States, Indonesia, and Brazil.

PALAU

Capital: Melekeok
Population: 20,796
Area: 177 sq. mi. (458 sq km)
Language: English, Palauan,
various Asian languages
Money: U.S. dollar
Government: Constitutional
government in free association
with the United States

CHECK IT OUT

In March 2008, thousands of human bones, some of them ancient and very small, were found by scientists in Palau.

PANAMA

Capital: Panama City
Population: 3,360,474
Area: 30,193 sq. mi. (78,200 sq km)
Language: Spanish, English
Money: Balboa
Government: Constitutional democracy

CHECK IT OUT

Spain was the first country to think of cutting a canal across the Isthmus of Panama. The French started building the 51-mile-long (82 km) canal in 1881 and the United States finished it in 1914.

PAPUA NEW GUINEA

Capital: Port Moresby
Population: 6,057,263
Area: 178,704 sq. mi. (462,840 sq km)
Language: Melanesian Pidgin, English, 820 indigenous languages
Money: Kina
Government: Constitutional parliamentary democracy

CHECK IT OUT

Living in Papua New Guinea means coping with the constant threat of active volcanoes, frequent earthquakes, mud slides, and tsunamis.

PARAGUAY

Capital: Asuncíon
Population: 6,995,655
Area: 157,047 sq. mi. (406,750 sq km)
Language: Spanish, Guarani
Money: Guarani
Government: Constitutional republic

CHECK IT OUT

Paraguay's got the power! Hydroelectric dams, including the largest one in the world, keep the country well supplied with electricity.

PERU

Capital: Lima
Population: 29,546,963
Area: 496,226 sq. mi. (1,285,220 sq km)
Language: Spanish, Quechua, Aymara, numerous minor languages
Money: Nuevo sol
Government: Constitutional republic

CHECK IT OUT

The third-largest country in South America (after Brazil and Argentina), Peru is three times as big as California but has only two-thirds of that state's population.

Machu Picchu, Peru

PHILIPPINES

Capital: Manila
Population: 97,976,603
Area: 115,831 sq. mi. (300,000 sq km)
Language: Filipino, English, 8 major dialects
Money: Peso
Government: Republic

CHECK IT OUT

Almost half of all working Filipinos earn their living by farming, although the farmland itself is owned by a wealthy few.

POLAND

Capital: Warsaw
Population: 38,482,919
Area: 120,726 sq. mi. (312,679 sq km)
Language: Polish
Money: Zloty
Government: Republic

CHECK IT OUT

Physicist Marie Curie and composer Frederic Chopin are just two of the many world-famous people who came from Poland.

PORTUGAL

Capital: Lisbon
Population: 10,707,924
Area: 35,672 sq. mi. (92,391 sq km)
Language: Portuguese, Mirandese
Money: Euro
Government: Republic, parliamentary democracy

CHECK IT OUT

The national music of Portugal is called *fado*. The songs are often sad but can also be funny.

QATAR

Capital: Doha
Population: 833,285
Area: 4,416 sq. mi. (11,437 sq km)
Language: Arabic, English
Money: Rial
Government: Emirate

CHECK IT OUT

Qatar is only about as big as Los Angeles County, California, but it holds more than 15 percent of the world's gas reserves.

ROMANIA

Capital: Bucharest
Population: 22,215,421
Area: 91,699 sq. mi. (237,500 sq km)
Language: Romanian, Hungarian, Romany (Gypsy)
Money: New leu
Government: Republic

CHECK IT OUT

Cruel 15th-century Romanian prince Vlad Tepes was the model for the horror novel *Dracula*. One of Vlad's homes, Bran Castle, is Romania's most popular tourist attraction.

RUSSIA

Capital: Moscow
Population: 140,041,247
Area: 6,592,772 sq. mi. (17,075,200 sq km)
Language: Russian, many minority languages
Money: Ruble
Government: Federation

CHECK IT OUT

Russia is the largest country in the world and contains the ninth-largest population. It was formerly the center of the Union of Soviet Socialist Republics (USSR), which broke up into 15 separate states in 1991.

RWANDA

Capital: Kigali
Population: 10,473,282
Area: 10,169 sq. mi. (26,338 sq km)
Language: Kinyarwanda, French, English, Swahili
Money: Franc
Government: Republic, presidential-multiparty system

CHECK IT OUT

Rwanda leads the world in terms of female representation in its parliamentary body. Roughly half of its legislators are women.

SAINT KITTS and NEVIS

Capital: Basseterre
Population: 40,131
Area: 101 sq. mi. (261 sq km)
Language: English
Money: Dollar
Government: Parliamentary democracy

CHECK IT OUT

These two Caribbean islands have been a single state since 1983.

SAINT LUCIA

Capital: Castries
Population: 160,267
Area: 238 sq. mi. (616 sq km)
Language: English, French patois
Money: Dollar
Government: Parliamentary democracy

ⓘ CHECK IT OUT

This small Caribbean island changed hands between France and England 14 times before being given to the United Kingdom in 1814. It became independent in 1979.

SAINT VINCENT and the GRENADINES

Capital: Kingstown
Population: 104,574
Area: 150 sq. mi. (389 sq km)
Language: English, French patois
Money: Dollar
Government: Parliamentary democracy

ⓘ CHECK IT OUT

These islands are the world's leading suppliers of arrowroot, which is used to thicken fruit pie fillings and sauces.

SAMOA

Capital: Apia
Population: 219,998
Area: 1,137 sq. mi. (2,944 sq km)
Language: Samoan, English
Money: Tala
Government: Parliamentary democracy

ⓘ CHECK IT OUT

Author Robert Louis Stevenson (*Treasure Island, Kidnapped*) lived in Samoa from 1890 until he died in 1894. His Polynesian neighbors called him *Tusitala*, or "Storyteller."

SAN MARINO

Capital: San Marino
Population: 30,324
Area: 24 sq. mi. (61 sq km)
Language: Italian
Money: Euro
Government: Republic

ⓘ CHECK IT OUT

San Marino, in central Italy, is the third-smallest state in Europe. Some historians say it was founded in 301 CE, making it the world's oldest republic.

SÃO TOMÉ and PRINCIPE

Capital: São Tomé
Population: 212,679
Area: 387 sq. mi. (1,001 sq km)
Language: Portuguese
Money: Dobra
Government: Republic

ⓘ CHECK IT OUT

São Tomé and Principe are the two largest islands in an African island group in the Gulf of Guinea.

SAUDI ARABIA

Capital: Riyadh
Population: 28,686,633
Area: 830,000 sq. mi. (2,149,690 sq km)
Language: Arabic
Money: Riyal
Government: Monarchy

ⓘ CHECK IT OUT

Saudi Arabia is known as the birthplace of Islam.

SENEGAL

Capital: Dakar
Population: 13,711,597
Area: 75,749 sq. mi. (196,190 sq km)
Language: French, Wolof, Pulaar, Jola, Mandinka
Money: CFA Franc
Government: Republic

CHECK IT OUT

Senegal's economy depends on peanuts. In recent years the country has produced more than 800,000 tons of them, 95 percent for oil.

SERBIA

Capital: Belgrade
Population: 7,379,339
Area: 29,913 sq. mi. (77,474 sq km)
Language: Serbian, Hungarian
Money: Dinar
Government: Republic

CHECK IT OUT

Favorite foods in Serbia are *cevacici*, a grilled meatball sandwich with raw onions, and *burek*, a pastry layered with cheese, meat, or jam.

SEYCHELLES

Capital: Victoria
Population: 87,476
Area: 176 sq. mi. (455 sq km)
Language: Creole, English
Money: Rupee
Government: Republic

CHECK IT OUT

From the early 1500s to the 1700s, Seychelles was a popular pirate hideout.

SIERRA LEONE

Capital: Freetown
Population: 6,440,053
Area: 27,699 sq. mi. (71,740 sq km)
Language: English, Mende and Temne vernaculars, Krio (English-based Creole)
Money: Leone
Government: Constitutional democracy

CHECK IT OUT

Sierra Leone is one of the wettest places in western Africa. Rainfall can reach 195 inches (495 cm) a year.

SINGAPORE

Capital: Singapore
Population: 4,657,542
Area: 241 sq. mi. (693 sq km)
Language: Mandarin, English, Malay, Hokkien, Cantonese, Teochew
Money: Dollar
Government: Republic

CHECK IT OUT

Singapore is a city-state—an independent state made up of a city and the areas around it. It is an important international business center with one of the busiest harbors in the world.

SLOVAKIA

Capital: Bratislava
Population: 5,463,046
Area: 18,859 sq. mi. (48,845 sq km)
Language: Slovak, Hungarian
Money: Koruna
Government: Parliamentary democracy

CHECK IT OUT

Following World War I, Slovaks and Czechs were joined into a single nation: Czechoslovakia. But in 1993 Czechoslovakia redivided into Slovakia and the Czech Republic.

Countries of the World

SLOVENIA

Capital: Ljubljana
Population: 2,005,692
Area: 7,827 sq. mi. (20,273 sq km)
Language: Slovenian, Serbo-Croatian
Money: Euro
Government: Parliamentary democracy

ⓘ CHECK IT OUT

Big puddles and small lakes can appear and disappear suddenly in Slovenia because of underground caves and channels.

SOLOMON ISLANDS

Capital: Honiara
Population: 595,613
Area: 10,985 sq. mi. (28,450 sq km)
Language: English, Melanesian pidgin, 120 indigenous languages
Money: Dollar
Government: Parliamentary democracy

ⓘ CHECK IT OUT

On April 1, 2007, a massive underwater earthquake triggered a tsunami that caused widespread destruction in the Solomon Islands.

SOMALIA

Capital: Mogadishu
Population: 9,832,017
Area: 246,201 sq. mi. (637,657 sq km)
Language: English, Arabic, Italian
Money: Shilling
Government: In transition

ⓘ CHECK IT OUT

Each point of the flag's white star stands for a region of Somalia.

SOUTH AFRICA

Capital: Pretoria (administrative), Cape Town (legislative), Bloemfontein (judicial)
Population: 49,052,489
Area: 471,011 sq. mi. (1,219,912 sq km)
Language: IsiZulu, IsiXhosa, Afrikaans, English, Sepedi, Setswana, Sesotho
Money: Rand
Government: Republic

ⓘ CHECK IT OUT

South Africa is in a subtropical location—so how come penguins thrive there? The penguins' breeding grounds are cooled by Antarctic Ocean currents on the west coast.

SPAIN

Capital: Madrid
Population: 40,525,002
Area: 194,897 sq. mi. (504,782 sq km)
Language: Castilian Spanish, Catalan, Galician, Basque
Money: Euro
Government: Parliamentary monarchy

ⓘ CHECK IT OUT

Spain's capital city is in almost the exact center of the country.

SRI LANKA

Capital: Colombo
Population: 21,324,791
Area: 25,332 sq. mi. (65,610 sq km)
Language: Sinhala, Tamil, English
Money: Rupee
Government: Republic

ⓘ CHECK IT OUT

Once named Ceylon, Sri Lanka was an important port in the ancient world. Arab traders called it Serendip, the origin of the word *serendipity*, which means "a pleasing chance discovery."

SUDAN

Capital: Khartoum
Population: 41,087,825
Area: 967,499 sq. mi. (2,505,810 sq km)
Language: Arabic, Nubian, Ta Bedawie, Nilotic, Nilo-Hamitic, Sudanic dialects, English
Money: Pound
Government: Power sharing, with military dominant (elections in April 2010)

CHECK IT OUT

Sudan is the largest country in Africa. Two branches of the Nile River, the White Nile and the Blue Nile, meet in Khartoum to form the main Nile River corridor.

SURINAME

Capital: Paramaribo
Population: 481,267
Area: 63,039 sq. mi. (163,270 sq km)
Language: Dutch, English, Sranang Tongo, Caribbean Hindustani, Javanese
Money: Dollar
Government: Constitutional democracy

CHECK IT OUT

Suriname is the smallest independent country in South America. It could fit into Brazil, its massive neighbor to the south, 52 times.

SWAZILAND

Capital: Mbabane
Population: 1,123,913
Area: 6,704 sq. mi. (17,363 sq km)
Language: English, siSwati
Money: Lilangeni
Government: Monarchy

CHECK IT OUT

Other parts of southern Africa suffer from drought, but four major rivers—the Komati, the Umbuluzi, the Ingwavuma, and the Great Usutu—keep Swaziland's water supply healthy.

SWEDEN

Capital: Stockholm
Population: 9,059,651
Area: 173,732 sq. mi. (449,964 sq km)
Language: Swedish, Finnish, Sami
Money: Krona
Government: Constitutional monarchy

CHECK IT OUT

Sweden has an army, navy, and air force, but its military can only be used in peacekeeping actions, not wars.

SWITZERLAND

Capital: Bern
Population: 7,604,467
Area: 15,942 sq. mi. (41,290 sq km)
Language: German, French, Italian, Romansch
Money: Franc
Government: Federal republic-like confederation

CHECK IT OUT

Switzerland's famous flag comes in two shapes. A square version is flown on land and a rectangular flag (like the one above) is flown at sea.

SYRIA

Capital: Damascus
Population: 20,178,485
Area: 71,498 sq. mi. (185,180 sq km)
Language: Arabic, Kurdish, Armenian, Aramaic, Circassian
Money: Pound
Government: Republic (under military regime)

CHECK IT OUT

In 2008, archaeologists excavating in the Syrian desert dug up a camel jawbone they said could be a million years old.

TAIWAN

Capital: Taipei
Population: 22,974,347
Area: 13,892 sq. mi. (35,980 sq km)
Language: Mandarin,
Taiwanese, Hakka
Money: Dollar (yuan)
Government: Multiparty
democracy

CHECK IT OUT

Taiwan's Palace Museum's collection of Chinese bronze, jade, calligraphy, painting, and porcelain is so big that only 1 percent of it is displayed at any one time.

TAJIKISTAN

Capital: Dushanbe
Population: 7,349,145
Area: 55,251 sq. mi. (143,100 sq km)
Language: Tajik, Russian
Money: Somoni
Government: Republic

CHECK IT OUT

When mountainous Tajikistan became independent after the breakup of the Soviet Union, it inherited a mountain called Communism Peak. The Tajiks quickly changed the name to Imeni Ismail Samani Peak.

TANZANIA

Capital: Dodoma
Population: 41,048,532
Area: 364,900 sq. mi.
(945,087 sq km)
Language: Kiswahili, English,
Arabic, many local languages
Money: Shilling
Government: Republic

CHECK IT OUT

Africa's highest mountain, 19,340-foot-high (5,895 m) Mount Kilimanjaro, is in Tanzania. Lions, elephants, giraffes, and other animals roam free, protected by the government, in Serengeti Park.

THAILAND

Capital: Bangkok
Population: 65,905,410
Area: 198,457 sq. mi.
(514,000 sq km)
Language: Thai, English, other ethnic languages
Money: Baht
Government: Constitutional monarchy

CHECK IT OUT

Formerly Siam, this Southeast Asian country has contributed Thai food, kickboxing, and the musical *The King and I* to world culture—among many other things.

TIMOR-LESTE

Capital: Dili
Population: 1,131,612
Area: 5,794 sq. mi. (15,007 sq km)
Language: Tetum, Portuguese,
Indonesian, English
Money: U.S. dollar
Government: Republic

CHECK IT OUT

Timor-Leste is a really young nation. It became independent amid protests in 1999, and in 2007 it held largely peaceful presidential and parliamentary elections for the first time.

TOGO

Capital: Lomé
Population: 6,019,877
Area: 21,925 sq. mi. (56,785 sq km)
Language: French, Ewe, Mina,
Kabye, Dagomba
Money: CFA franc
Government: Republic
(under transition to multiparty democratic rule)

CHECK IT OUT

Watch your step! Poisonous vipers—cobras, pythons, and green and black mambas—are abundant here. So are scorpions and spiders.

Countries of the World

TONGA

Capital: Nuku'alofa
Population: 120,898
Area: 289 sq. mi. (748 sq km)
Language: Tongan, English
Money: Pa'anga
Government: Constitutional monarchy

CHECK IT OUT

Tonga, an archipelago of about 150 islands east of Australia, is the last remaining monarchy in the Pacific.

TRINIDAD and TOBAGO

Capital: Port of Spain
Population: 1,222,953
Area: 1,980 sq. mi. (5,128 sq km)
Language: English, Caribbean Hindustani, French, Spanish, Chinese
Money: Dollar
Government: Parliamentary democracy

CHECK IT OUT

Native animals include the quenck, a kind of wild hog, and the agouti, a rabbitlike rodent. Howler monkeys are also native, but increasing development has made them rare.

TUNISIA

Capital: Tunis
Population: 10,486,339
Area: 63,170 sq. mi. (163,610 sq km)
Language: Arabic, French
Money: Dinar
Government: Republic

CHECK IT OUT

Every Star Wars movie but one was filmed in Tunisia. So was *Indiana Jones: Raiders of the Lost Ark.*

TURKEY

Capital: Ankara
Population: 76,805,524
Area: 301,384 sq. mi. (780,580 sq km)
Language: Turkish, Kurdish, Dimli
Money: New lira
Government: Republican parliamentary democracy

CHECK IT OUT

Turkey gave the world the man who would become Santa Claus: St. Nicholas, a fourth-century bishop.

TURKMENISTAN

Capital: Ashgabat
Population: 4,884,887
Area: 188,456 sq. mi. (488,100 sq km)
Language: Turkmen, Russian, Uzbek
Money: Manat
Government: Republic under authoritarian presidential rule

CHECK IT OUT

Turkmenistan's stunning flag incorporates five traditional carpet designs. Each design is associated with a particular tribe.

TUVALU

Capital: Funafuti
Population: 12,373
Area: 10 sq. mi. (26 sq km)
Language: Tuvaluan, English, Samoan
Money: Australian dollar
Government: Constitutional monarchy with parliamentary democracy

CHECK IT OUT

Tuvalu is made up of nine coral atolls in the South Pacific. Eight are inhabited. The word *tuvalu* means "group of eight."

UGANDA

Capital: Kampala
Population: 32,369,558
Area: 91,136 sq. mi. (236,040 sq km)
Language: English, Ganda, Luganda
Money: Shilling
Government: Republic

CHECK IT OUT

Ugandans speak in more than 42 different dialects. In fact, no single language is understood by all Ugandans.

UKRAINE

Capital: Kyiv (Kiev)
Population: 45,700,395
Area: 233,090 sq. mi. (603,700 sq km)
Language: Ukrainian, Russian, Romanian, Polish, Hungarian
Money: Hryvnia
Government: Republic

CHECK IT OUT

Ukraine is the largest country completely landlocked within Europe.

UNITED ARAB EMIRATES

Capital: Abu Dhabi
Population: 4,798,491
Area: 32,278 sq. mi. (83,600 sq km)
Language: Arabic, Persian, English, Hindi, Urdu
Money: Dirham
Government: Federation of emirates

CHECK IT OUT

The United Arab Emirates consists of seven independent Arab states in southwestern Asia. City dwellers live in modern buildings. Country people live in huts, and most wear long robes. Nomadic tribes roam the desert regions with camels, goats, and sheep.

UNITED KINGDOM

Capital: London
Population: 61,113,205
Area: 94,526 sq. mi. (244,820 sq km)
Language: English, Welsh, Scottish form of Gaelic
Money: Pound
Government: Constitutional monarchy

CHECK IT OUT

Today the United Kingdom (UK) consists of England, Scotland, Wales, and Northern Ireland. At one time the British Empire extended to five other continents.

UNITED STATES

Capital: Washington, DC
Population: 307,212,123
Area: 3,794,083 sq. mi. (9,826,630 sq km)
Language: English, Spanish, Hawaiian, other minority languages
Money: Dollar
Government: Federal republic with strong democratic tradition

CHECK IT OUT

What is now the United States was the first European colony to become independent from its motherland (England).

URUGUAY

Capital: Montevideo
Population: 3,494,382
Area: 68,039 sq. mi. (176,220 sq km)
Language: Spanish, Portunol, Brazilero
Money: Peso
Government: Constitutional republic

CHECK IT OUT

Uruguay's name comes from a Guarani word meaning "river of painted birds."

UZBEKISTAN

Capital: Tashkent
Population: 27,606,007
Area: 172,742 sq. mi. (447,400 sq km)
Language: Uzbek, Russian, Tajik
Money: Som
Government: Republic with authoritarian presidential rule

CHECK IT OUT

The cities of Uzbekistan—Samarkand, Bukhara, and Khiva—were well-traveled centers on the Silk Road, an ancient trade route linking Asia to Europe.

VANUATU

Capital: Port-Vila
Population: 218,519
Area: 4,710 sq. mi. (12,200 sq km)
Language: Bislama, English, French, 100 local languages
Money: Vatu
Government: Parliamentary republic

🔎 CHECK IT OUT

Vanuatu is not just one island but more than 80 volcanic islands in a South Pacific archipelago.

VENEZUELA

Capital: Caracas
Population: 26,814,843
Area: 352,144 sq. mi. (912,050 sq km)
Language: Spanish, indigenous dialects
Money: Bolivar Fuerte
Government: Federal republic

🔎 CHECK IT OUT

Venezuela is home to the largest rodents in the world—the capybaras. They measure up to 4.3 feet (1.3 m) long and weigh up to 140 pounds (about 64 kg).

VIETNAM

Capital: Hanoi
Population: 86,967,524
Area: 127,244 sq. mi. (329,560 sq km)
Language: Vietnamese, English, French, Chinese, Khmer
Money: Dong
Government: Communist state

🔎 CHECK IT OUT

Vietnam is shaped like a long, skinny 5. It measures 1,031 miles (1,650 km) from north to south, but at its narrowest point is only 31 miles (50 km) across.

YEMEN

Capital: Sanaa
Population: 23,822,783
Area: 203,850 sq. mi. (527,970 sq km)
Language: Arabic
Money: Rial
Government: Republic

🔎 CHECK IT OUT

According to legend, coffee was discovered by a goat herder who noticed his goats got livelier after eating berries from a certain plant. The plant was brought to Yemen, where it was developed into a drink.

ZAMBIA

Capital: Lusaka
Population: 11,862,740
Area: 290,586 sq. mi. (752,614 sq km)
Language: English, numerous vernaculars
Money: Kwacha
Government: Republic

🔎 CHECK IT OUT

One of the world's highest waterfalls, the Victoria Falls is created by the Zambezi River tumbling over cliffs between Zambia and Zimbabwe. The waterfall is twice as high as Niagara Falls.

ZIMBABWE

Capital: Harare
Population: 11,392,629
Area: 150,804 sq. mi. (390,580 sq km)
Language: English, Shona, Sindebele, minor tribal dialects
Money: Dollar
Government: Parliamentary democracy

🔎 CHECK IT OUT

Zimbabwe means "stone house." Ruins of the stone palaces of African kings can be seen in many parts of the country.

States of the
United States

A country's flag is an important symbol reflecting the nation's spirit and personality. Over the years, as the United States has grown and changed, so has the national flag. In 1777 the first commissioned flag had 13 red and white stripes and 13 white stars representing the original 13 colonies. Over time, as states were added, so were stars. In 1960 the 50th star was added after Hawaii became the 50th state. Today the American flag has 13 stripes and 50 stars on a blue background—showing the world where we came from and where we are now.

One Nation, Fifty Faces

Each state in America has its own capital, state bird, flower, motto, and diverse ethnic makeup. Each state also has a great deal of pride. It doesn't matter whether the state is the biggest in land area (Alaska) or the smallest (Rhode Island). It doesn't matter whether the state has the most people (California) or the least (Wyoming). Each state has a unique story to tell. And the design, colors, and patterns of its flag are some ways to tell that story.

Take a peek through the flags in this section. You will see a variety of plants, animals, stars, moons, and people, reflecting each state's history and personality. You will also learn facts and statistics about each state that may surprise you.

CIRCLE OF LIFE

New Mexico's flag tells a story of its people. The colors—golden yellow and bright red—are the colors of Spain, first brought to New Mexico in the 1500s. The symbol—a circle with four rays emanating in each of four directions—is an ancient Native American sun symbol. The circle has no beginning or end and embodies life and love. The rays symbolize:

★ the four seasons—spring, summer, autumn, winter
★ the four directions—north, south, east, west
★ the four times of day—morning, daytime, afternoon, night
★ the four stages of life—childhood, young adulthood, middle years, old age

★ TAKE a LOOK

There are 21 state flags that feature a star or stars, 26 flags on a field of blue, 8 with birds on them, 2 with bears, and 1 with a moose! Can you find them all? (Answers are on page 350.)

In addition to the 50 states, the United States includes 1 federal district, 2 commonwealths, 3 main territories, and several minor territories. Only one of these places is located within the continental United States. See page 145 for all the information.

CHECK IT OUT!

Alaska

Juneau

Olympia
Washington

Salem

Oregon

Idaho

Boise

Montana

Helena

North Dakota

Bismarck

South Dakota

Pierre

Wyoming

Sacramento Carson City

Nevada

California

Salt Lake City

Utah

Cheyenne

Denver

Colorado

Nebraska

Lincoln

Kansas

Top

Arizona

Phoenix

Santa Fe

New Mexico

Oklaho

Oklahoma

Texas

Austin

Honolulu

Hawaii

U.S. States and Their Capital Cities

sota

Paul

Wisconsin

Madison

Michigan

Lansing

New Hampshire

Maine

Vermont

Augusta

Montpelier

Concord

Massachusetts

Boston

Albany

Providence

New York

Hartford

Rhode Island

Connecticut

Pennsylvania

Trenton

New Jersey

Harrisburg

Dover

Delaware

Ohio

Columbus

Annapolis

Maryland

va

Moines

Illinois

Indiana

Springfield

Indianapolis

West
Virginia

Charleston

Richmond

Washington, DC

fferson City

Frankfort

Virginia

Missouri

Kentucky

Raleigh

Nashville

North Carolina

Arkansas

Tennessee

Columbia

ittle Rock

Atlanta

South
Carolina

Mississippi

Alabama

Georgia

Jackson

Montgomery

Louisiana

Baton
Rouge

Tallahassee

Florida

State Quarters by Release Date (and Statehood Dates)

■ Release Date   ■ Statehood Date

Delaware
January 4, 1999
December 7, 1787

Pennsylvania
March 8, 1999
December 12, 1787

New Jersey
May 17, 1999
December 18, 1787

Georgia
July 19, 1999
January 2, 1788

Connecticut
October 12, 1999
January 9, 1788

Massachusetts
January 3, 2000
February 6, 1788

Maryland
March 13, 2000
April 28, 1788

South Carolina
May 22, 2000
May 23, 1788

New Hampshire
August 7, 2000
June 21, 1788

Virginia
October 16, 2000
June 25, 1788

New York
January 2, 2001
July 26, 1788

North Carolina
March 12, 2001
November 21, 1789

Rhode Island
May 21, 2001
May 29, 1790

Vermont
August 6, 2001
March 4, 1791

Kentucky
October 15, 2001
June 1, 1792

Tennessee
January 2, 2002
June 1, 1796

Ohio
March 11, 2002
March 1, 1803

Louisiana
May 20, 2002
April 30, 1812

Indiana
August 2, 2002
December 11, 1816

Mississippi
October 15, 2002
December 10, 1817

Illinois
January 2, 2003
December 3, 1818

Alabama
March 17, 2003
December 14, 1819

Maine
June 2, 2003
March 15, 1820

Missouri
August 4, 2003
August 10, 1821

Arkansas
October 20, 2003
June 15, 1836

States of the United States

■ Release Date   ■ Statehood Date

Michigan
January 26, 2004
January 26, 1837

Florida
March 29, 2004
March 3, 1845

Texas
June 1, 2004
December 29, 1845

Iowa
August 30, 2004
December 28, 1846

Wisconsin
October 25, 2004
May 29, 1848

California
January 31, 2005
September 9, 1850

Minnesota
April 4, 2005
May 11, 1858

Oregon
June 6, 2005
February 14, 1859

Kansas
August 29, 2005
January 29, 1861

West Virginia
October 14, 2005
June 20, 1863

Nevada
January 31, 2006
October 31, 1864

Nebraska
April 3, 2006
March 1, 1867

Colorado
June 14, 2006
August 1, 1876

North Dakota
August 28, 2006
November 2, 1889

South Dakota
November 6, 2006
November 2, 1889

Montana
January 29, 2007
November 8, 1889

Washington
April 2, 2007
November 11, 1889

Idaho
June 4, 2007
July 3, 1890

Wyoming
September 3, 2007
July 10, 1890

Utah
November 5, 2007
January 4, 1896

Oklahoma
January 28, 2008
November 16, 1907

New Mexico
April 7, 2008
January 6, 1912

Arizona
June 2, 2008
February 14, 1912

Alaska
August 25, 2008
January 3, 1959

Hawaii
November 3, 2008
August 21, 1959

ALABAMA

Capital: Montgomery
Postal Code: AL
Nickname: Heart of Dixie
Flower: Camellia
Bird: Yellowhammer
Area: 52,419 sq. mi. (135,765 sq km)
Population: 4,708,708

CHECK IT OUT

Huntsville, Alabama, is the site where the first rocket that took people to the moon was built.

ALASKA

Capital: Juneau
Postal Code: AK
Nickname: Last Frontier
Flower: Forget-me-not
Bird: Willow ptarmigan
Area: 663,267 sq. mi. (1,726,556 sq km)
Population: 698,473

CHECK IT OUT

Woolly mammoth remains have been found in Alaska's frozen ground.

ARIZONA

Capital: Phoenix
Postal Code: AZ
Nickname: Grand Canyon State
Flower: Saguaro cactus blossom
Bird: Cactus wren
Area: 113,998 sq. mi. (295,253 sq km)
Population: 6,595,778

CHECK IT OUT

There are more species of hummingbirds in Arizona than in any other state.

ARKANSAS

Capital: Little Rock
Postal Code: AR
Nickname: Land of Opportunity
Flower: Apple blossom
Bird: Mockingbird
Area: 53,179 sq. mi. (137,733 sq km)
Population: 2,889,450

CHECK IT OUT

Stuttgart, Arkansas, is home to the annual World's Championship Duck Calling Contest.

CALIFORNIA

Capital: Sacramento
Postal Code: CA
Nickname: Golden State
Flower: Golden poppy
Bird: California quail
Area: 163,696 sq. mi. (423,971 sq km)
Population: 36,961,664

CHECK IT OUT

The highest and lowest points in the continental United States are in California—Mount Whitney (14,494 ft./4,418 m) and Badwater in Death Valley (282 ft./86 m below sea level).

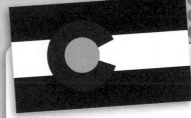

COLORADO

Capital: Denver
Postal Code: CO
Nickname: Centennial State
Flower: Rocky Mountain columbine
Bird: Lark bunting
Area: 104,094 sq. mi. (269,602 sq km)
Population: 5,024,748

CHECK IT OUT

The streets in Victor, Colorado, were actually paved in a low grade of gold back in 1890 to make use of the low-quality ore that couldn't be refined.

CONNECTICUT

Capital: Hartford
Postal Code: CT
Nickname: Constitution State
Flower: Mountain laurel
Bird: American robin
Area: 5,543 sq. mi. (14,356 sq km)
Population: 3,518,288

☝CHECK IT OUT

America's first newspaper, the *Hartford Courant*, was printed in 1764 in Connecticut.

DECEMBER 7, 1787

DELAWARE

Capital: Dover
Postal Code: DE
Nickname: First State
Flower: Peach blossom
Bird: Blue hen chicken
Area: 2,489 sq. mi. (6,446 sq km)
Population: 885,122

☝CHECK IT OUT

Delaware was the first state to ratify the U.S. Constitution.

FLORIDA

Capital: Tallahassee
Postal Code: FL
Nickname: Sunshine State
Flower: Orange blossom
Bird: Mockingbird
Area: 65,755 sq. mi. (170,305 sq km)
Population: 18,537,969

☝CHECK IT OUT

Florida's name comes from the Spanish word for "flowery." Ponce de Leon named it after the beautiful flowers he saw all around when he arrived there in 1513.

Florida wildflowers

GEORGIA

Capital: Atlanta
Postal Code: GA
Nickname: Empire State of the South
Flower: Cherokee rose
Bird: Brown thrasher
Area: 59,425 sq. mi. (153,910 sq km)
Population: 9,829,211

CHECK IT OUT

Georgia's top crops include peaches. The "World's Largest Peach Cobbler," which uses 75 gallons (285 L) of peaches and 150 pounds (68 kg) each of sugar and flour, is the star of the annual Georgia Peach Festival.

HAWAII

Capital: Honolulu
Postal Code: HI
Nickname: Aloha State
Flower: Yellow hibiscus
Bird: Nene, or Hawaiian goose
Area: 10,931 sq. mi. (28,311 sq km)
Population: 1,295,178

CHECK IT OUT

Hawaii is made up of 132 islands. The 8 main ones are Niihau, Kauai, Oahu, Maui, Molokai, Lanai, Kahoolawe, and the Big Island of Hawaii.

IDAHO

Capital: Boise
Postal Code: ID
Nickname: Gem State
Flower: Syringa
Bird: Mountain bluebird
Area: 83,570 sq. mi. (216,445 sq km)
Population: 1,545,801

CHECK IT OUT

The largest freshwater fish ever caught in America was a white sturgeon hauled out of Idaho's Snake River in 1898. It weighed 1,500 pounds (680 kg), about as much as a grown Holstein cow.

ILLINOIS

ILLINOIS

Capital: Springfield
Postal Code: IL
Nickname: Land of Lincoln
Flower: Native violet
Bird: Cardinal
Area: 57,914 sq. mi. (149,997 sq km)
Population: 12,910,409

CHECK IT OUT

The tallest building in the United States is the Willis (formerly Sears) Tower in Chicago, measuring 1,725 feet (526 m) from the ground to the tip of the antenna.

IOWA

INDIANA

Capital: Indianapolis
Postal Code: IN
Nickname: Hoosier State
Flower: Peony
Bird: Cardinal (sometimes called northern cardinal)
Area: 36,418 sq. mi. (94,322 sq km)
Population: 6,423,113

CHECK IT OUT

Santa Claus, Indiana, receives over half a million letters at Christmastime.

IOWA

Capital: Des Moines
Postal Code: IA
Nickname: Hawkeye State
Flower: Wild prairie rose
Bird: Eastern goldfinch (also called American goldfinch)
Area: 56,272 sq. mi. (145,744 sq km)
Population: 3,007,856

CHECK IT OUT

Iowa is the only state name in America that begins with two vowels.

KANSAS

KANSAS

Capital: Topeka
Postal Code: KS
Nickname: Sunflower State
Flower: Native sunflower
Bird: Western meadowlark
Area: 82,277 sq. mi. (213,096 sq km)
Population: 2,818,747

CHECK IT OUT

In 1905, the element helium was discovered at the University of Kansas.

KENTUCKY

Capital: Frankfort
Postal Code: KY
Nickname: Bluegrass State
Flower: Goldenrod
Bird: Northern cardinal
Area: 40,409 sq. mi. (104,659 sq km)
Population: 4,314,113

CHECK IT OUT

The Kentucky Derby, held the first Saturday in May, is the oldest annual horse race in the United States.

LOUISIANA

Capital: Baton Rouge
Postal Code: LA
Nickname: Pelican State
Flower: Magnolia
Bird: Eastern brown pelican
Area: 51,840 sq. mi. (134,265 sq km)
Population: 4,492,076

CHECK IT OUT

Louisiana is the only state divided into parishes instead of counties.

States of the United States

MAINE

Capital: Augusta
Postal Code: ME
Nickname: Pine Tree State
Flower: White pine cone and tassel
Bird: Black-capped chickadee
Area: 35,385 sq. mi. (91,647 sq km)
Population: 1,318,301

CHECK IT OUT

Eastport, Maine, is the first town in America to see the sunrise because it is the town farthest east.

MARYLAND

Capital: Annapolis
Postal Code: MD
Nickname: Old Line State
Flower: Black-eyed Susan
Bird: Baltimore oriole
Area: 12,407 sq. mi. (32,134 sq km)
Population: 5,699,478

CHECK IT OUT

Maryland is famous for having the first dental school in the United States.

MASSACHUSETTS

Capital: Boston
Postal Code: MA
Nickname: Bay State
Flower: Mayflower
Bird: Black-capped chickadee
Area: 10,555 sq. mi. (27,337 sq km)
Population: 6,593,587

CHECK IT OUT

Volleyball was invented in 1895 in Holyoke, Massachusetts, by gym teacher William Morgan. The game was originally called mintonette. Basketball was invented in nearby Springfield.

MICHIGAN

Capital: Lansing
Postal Code: MI
Nickname: Wolverine State
Flower: Apple blossom
Bird: American robin
Area: 96,716 sq. mi. (250,493 sq km)
Population: 9,969,727

CHECK IT OUT

With over 11,000 inland lakes and over 36,000 miles (57,936 km) of rivers and streams, Michigan has the longest freshwater shoreline in the world.

MINNESOTA

Capital: St. Paul
Postal Code: MN
Nickname: Gopher State
Flower: Pink and white lady's slipper
Bird: Common loon
Area: 86,939 sq. mi. (225,171 sq km)
Population: 5,266,214

CHECK IT OUT

The Mall of America in Bloomington, Minnesota, is 9.5 million square feet (8,825,780 sq m)—about the size of 78 football fields!

MISSISSIPPI

Capital: Jackson
Postal Code: MS
Nickname: Magnolia State
Flower: Magnolia
Bird: Mockingbird
Area: 48,430 sq. mi. (125,433 sq km)
Population: 2,951,996

CHECK IT OUT

Edward Adolf Barq Sr. invented root beer in Biloxi, Mississippi, in 1898.

MISSOURI

Capital: Jefferson City
Postal Code: MO
Nickname: Show Me State
Flower: Hawthorn
Bird: Eastern bluebird
Area: 69,704 sq. mi. (180,533 sq km)
Population: 5,987,580

CHECK IT OUT

The St. Louis World's Fair in 1904 was so hot that Richard Blechyden decided to serve his tea over ice—and invented iced tea.

MONTANA

Capital: Helena
Postal Code: MT
Nickname: Treasure State
Flower: Bitterroot
Bird: Western meadowlark
Area: 147,042 sq. mi. (380,837 sq km)
Population: 974,989

CHECK IT OUT

The average square mile (1.6 sq km) of land in Montana contains 1.4 pronghorn antelope, 1.4 elk, and 3.3 deer. Montana has the largest number of mammal species in the United States.

NEBRASKA

Capital: Lincoln
Postal Code: NE
Nickname: Cornhusker State
Flower: Goldenrod
Bird: Western meadowlark
Area: 77,354 sq. mi. (200,346 sq km)
Population: 1,796,619

CHECK IT OUT

About 95 percent of Nebraska's area is taken up by farms and ranches—a higher percentage than any other state. The state's top crop is corn.

NEVADA

Capital: Carson City
Postal Code: NV
Nickname: Silver State
Flower: Sagebrush
Bird: Mountain bluebird
Area: 110,561 sq. mi. (286,352 sq km)
Population: 2,643,085

CHECK IT OUT

The Silver State produces more gold than any other state and is the third highest producer in the world after China and South Africa.

NEW HAMPSHIRE

Capital: Concord
Postal Code: NH
Nickname: Granite State
Flower: Purple lilac
Bird: Purple finch
Area: 9,350 sq. mi. (24,216 sq km)
Population: 1,324,575

CHECK IT OUT

The winds on top of New Hampshire's Mount Washington have been recorded at speeds over 231 miles (372 km) an hour—the fastest winds on Earth!

NEW JERSEY

Capital: Trenton
Postal Code: NJ
Nickname: Garden State
Flower: Purple violet
Bird: Eastern goldfinch
Area: 8,721 sq. mi. (22,587 sq km)
Population: 8,707,739

CHECK IT OUT

The street names in the game Monopoly come from real street names in Atlantic City, New Jersey.

NEW MEXICO

Capital: Santa Fe
Postal Code: NM
Nickname: Land of Enchantment
Flower: Yucca flower
Bird: Roadrunner (also called greater roadrunner)
Area: 121,589 sq. mi. (314,914 sq km)
Population: 2,009,671

CHECK IT OUT

There are more than 110 caves in Carlsbad Caverns. One cave is 22 stories high and is home to tens of thousands of bats.

NEW YORK

Capital: Albany
Postal Code: NY
Nickname: Empire State
Flower: Rose
Bird: Eastern bluebird
Area: 54,556 sq. mi. (141,299 sq km)
Population: 19,541,453

CHECK IT OUT

More than 100 million people have visited the top of the Empire State Building in New York City. The building is 1,453 feet, 8 9/16 inches (443.2 m) from the street to the top of the lightning rod.

New York City, with the Empire State Building far right

NORTH CAROLINA

Capital: Raleigh
Postal Code: NC
Nickname: Tar Heel State
Flower: Dogwood
Bird: Cardinal
Area: 53,819 sq. mi. (139,391 sq km)
Population: 9,380,884

CHECK IT OUT

On March 7, 1914, in Fayetteville, North Carolina, George Herman "Babe" Ruth hit his first professional home run.

States of the United States

NORTH DAKOTA

Capital: Bismarck
Postal Code: ND
Nickname: Flickertail State
Flower: Wild prairie rose
Bird: Western meadowlark
Area: 70,700 sq. mi. (183,112 sq km)
Population: 646,844

CHECK IT OUT

Jamestown, North Dakota, is home to the World's Largest Buffalo monument. It stands 26 feet (7.9 m) high and 46 feet (14 m) long, and weighs 60 tons (54,441 kg).

OHIO

Capital: Columbus
Postal Code: OH
Nickname: Buckeye State
Flower: Scarlet carnation
Bird: Cardinal
Area: 44,825 sq. mi. (116,096 sq km)
Population: 11,542,645

CHECK IT OUT

The first traffic light in America began working on August 5, 1914, in Cleveland, Ohio.

OKLAHOMA

Capital: Oklahoma City
Postal Code: OK
Nickname: Sooner State
Flower: Mistletoe
Bird: Scissor-tailed flycatcher
Area: 69,898 sq. mi. (181,035 sq km)
Population: 3,687,050

CHECK IT OUT

Not every state has a state amphibian, but Oklahoma does—the American bullfrog.

1859

OREGON

Capital: Salem
Postal Code: OR
Nickname: Beaver State
Flower: Oregon grape
Bird: Western meadowlark
Area: 98,381 sq. mi. (254,806 sq km)
Population: 3,825,657

CHECK IT OUT

Two pioneers founded Portland, Oregon. One was from Boston, Massachusetts, and the other was from Portland, Maine. They couldn't decide what to name the city, so they flipped a coin. Guess who won!

PENNSYLVANIA

Capital: Harrisburg
Postal Code: PA
Nickname: Keystone State
Flower: Mountain laurel
Bird: Ruffed grouse
Area: 46,055 sq. mi. (119,282 sq km)
Population: 12,604,767

CHECK IT OUT

In 1953, Dr. Jonas Salk created the polio vaccine at the University of Pittsburgh.

RHODE ISLAND

Capital: Providence
Postal Code: RI
Nickname: Ocean State
Flower: Violet
Bird: Rhode Island Red chicken
Area: 1,545 sq. mi. (4,002 sq km)
Population: 1,053,209

CHECK IT OUT

"I'm a Yankee Doodle Dandy" and "You're a Grand Old Flag" were written by George M. Cohan, who was born in Providence, Rhode Island, in 1878.

States of the United States

SOUTH CAROLINA

Capital: Columbia
Postal Code: SC
Nickname: Palmetto State
Flower: Yellow jessamine
Bird: Great Carolina wren
Area: 32,020 sq. mi. (82,931 sq km)
Population: 4,561,242

CHECK IT OUT

The first battle of the Civil War was fought at Fort Sumter, South Carolina.

SOUTH DAKOTA

Capital: Pierre
Postal Code: SD
Nickname: Mount Rushmore State
Flower: Pasqueflower
Bird: Ring-necked pheasant
Area: 77,116 sq. mi. (199,730 sq km)
Population: 812,383

CHECK IT OUT

The faces of George Washington, Thomas Jefferson, Theodore Roosevelt, and Abraham Lincoln are sculpted into Mount Rushmore, the world's greatest mountain carving. The carvings are taller than a four-story building.

TENNESSEE

Capital: Nashville
Postal Code: TN
Nickname: Volunteer State
Flower: Iris
Bird: Mockingbird
Area: 42,143 sq. mi. (109,150 sq km)
Population: 6,296,254

CHECK IT OUT

More than nine million people visit Smoky Mountain National Park in Tennessee every year, making it America's most visited national park. Over 30 species of salamanders and 1,500 black bears live there year-round.

TEXAS

Capital: Austin
Postal Code: TX
Nickname: Lone Star State
Flower: Bluebonnet
Bird: Mockingbird
Area: 268,581 sq. mi. (695,622 sq km)
Population: 24,782,302

CHECK IT OUT

The name *Texas* is actually derived from a misunderstanding of *tejas*, a Caddo Indian word meaning "friend."

UTAH

Capital: Salt Lake City
Postal Code: UT
Nickname: Beehive State
Flower: Sego lily
Bird: California gull
Area: 84,899 sq. mi. (219,887 sq km)
Population: 2,784,572

CHECK IT OUT

Utah's Great Salt Lake is several times saltier than seawater. It's so salty that you'd float on the surface of the water like a cork if you swam there!

VERMONT

Capital: Montpelier
Postal Code: VT
Nickname: Green Mountain State
Flower: Red clover
Bird: Hermit thrush
Area: 9,614 sq. mi. (24,900 sq km)
Population: 621,760

CHECK IT OUT

Vermont is the only New England state that doesn't border the Atlantic Ocean.

VIRGINIA

Capital: Richmond
Postal Code: VA
Nickname: Old Dominion
Flower: American dogwood
Bird: Cardinal
Area: 42,774 sq. mi. (110,784 sq km)
Population: 7,882,590

CHECK IT OUT

More U.S. presidents come from Virginia than from any other state—George Washington, Thomas Jefferson, James Madison, James Monroe, William Henry Harrison, John Tyler, Zachary Taylor, and Woodrow Wilson.

WASHINGTON

Capital: Olympia
Postal Code: WA
Nickname: Evergreen State
Flower: Coast rhododendron
Bird: Willow goldfinch (also called American goldfinch)
Area: 71,300 sq. mi. (184,666 sq km)
Population: 6,664,195

CHECK IT OUT

Washington is a hotbed of volcanic activity. Mount Rainier erupted in 1969 and Mount St. Helens erupted in 1980.

WEST VIRGINIA

Capital: Charleston
Postal Code: WV
Nickname: Mountain State
Flower: Big rhododendron
Bird: Cardinal
Area: 24,230 sq. mi. (62,755 sq km)
Population: 1,819,777

CHECK IT OUT

Before the Civil War, West Virginia was part of Virginia. It became a separate state and remained part of the Union when Virginia decided to secede at the dawn of the war.

WISCONSIN

1848

WISCONSIN

Capital: Madison
Postal Code: WI
Nickname: Badger State
Flower: Wood violet
Bird: American robin
Area: 65,498 sq. mi. (169,639 sq km)
Population: 5,654,774

CHECK IT OUT

Wisconsin produces 40 percent of all the cheese and 20 percent of all the butter melted, slathered, spread, and devoured in the United States. No wonder folks from Wisconsin are sometimes called "cheeseheads."

WYOMING

Capital: Cheyenne
Postal Code: WY
Nickname: Equality State
Flower: Indian paintbrush
Bird: Western meadowlark
Area: 97,814 sq. mi. (253,337 sq km)
Population: 544,270

CHECK IT OUT

Wyoming's Yellowstone National Park has more than 500 geysers, including Old Faithful, that regularly shoot hot water into the air.

Washington, DC
Our Nation's Capital

Every state has a capital, the city where all the state's official government business takes place. Our country's capital, Washington, DC, is the center for all national, or federal, business. But our nation's capital isn't located in a state. It's part of a federal district, the District of Columbia. Congress wanted the capital to be in a district, not a state, so as not to favor any one state above the others.

The city is named after our first president, George Washington, who chose its location in 1791. It became the capital in 1800. Before that the center of the federal government was Philadelphia, Pennsylvania.

The United States Capitol

WASHINGTON, DC

Flower: American Beauty rose
Area: 68 sq. mi. (177 sq km)
Population: 599,657
Government: Federal district under the authority of Congress; mayor and city council, elected to four-year terms, run the local government

CHECK IT OUT

The White House, at 1600 Pennsylvania Ave., is the official presidential residence. George Washington is the only U.S. president who never lived there.

PUERTO RICO

Besides the 50 states and the District of Columbia, the United States also includes a number of commonwealths and territories. A commonwealth has its own constitution and has more rights and independence than a territory, but neither one has all the rights of a state.

The largest commonwealth is Puerto Rico, which is made up of one large island and three smaller ones in the Caribbean Sea. Puerto Rico was given to the United States by Spain in 1898 and became a commonwealth in 1952.

PUERTO RICO

Capital: San Juan
Area: 3,515 sq. mi. (8,870 sq km)
Population: 3,967,288
Language: Spanish, English
Money: U.S. dollar
Goverment: U.S. territory with commonwealth status

CHECK IT OUT

Puerto Ricans are American citizens, but they cannot vote in U.S. presidential elections.

Other U.S. Commonwealths and Territories

The Northern Mariana Islands in the North Pacific Ocean are the only other U.S. commonwealth. U.S. territories are:

- American Samoa
- Guam
- The U.S. Virgin Islands

The United States Minor Outlying Islands:

- Midway Islands
- Johnston Atoll
- Navassa Island
- Baker, Howland, and Jarvis Islands
- Wake Island
- Kingman Reef
- Palmyra Atoll

Games

Want to Play?

Nintendo Wii, Sony PlayStation 3, smartphone game apps: What would we do without our favorite game console or online game? What *did* we do without them? Thousands of years before technology made electronic games available 24/7, people were playing board games for fun and relaxation.

Get Onboard

The oldest board games date back as far as 3500 BCE. The most famous modern board game, Monopoly, was invented in 1934 by Charles B. Darrow. Monopoly's theme—getting rich fast by buying and selling property—was wildly popular with Americans suffering from the financial problems of the Great Depression. The game has sold 250 million copies to date.

Gaming on the Go

Now you can play Monopoly on a board or as an app on your smartphone. Early video arcade games such as Pac-Man, Pong, Space Invaders, and Asteroids paved the way for today's connected world, where you can play strategy, sports, and action games by yourself or with real or virtual partners almost anywhere.

What Wii All Want

In 2006, the Nintendo company released the Wii, a game console featuring a wandlike controller. Kids loved it. Two years later, the company added Wii Fit, a new way to exercise at home, featuring a balance board, challenging physical activities, and a virtual personal trainer. It was a hit with adults as well as kids. Wii Fit shows that games aren't just for kids anymore. The U.S. Army even has a Wii fitness program!

TAKE a LOOK

Tetris, one of the most popular electronic games of all time, has been adapted for every game console, computer, and phone there is. What were the most popular computer and video games in 2009? Turn the page to see if your favorites made the list.

CHECK IT OUT!

According to a recent survey by the Entertainment Software Association, almost seven out of ten American households play video or computer games. What's your family's favorite game?

Top 10 PC Games in 2009

World of Warcraft

The Sims

The Sims 2

RuneScape

Halo: Combat Evolved

Call of Duty 4: Modern Warfare

Left 4 Dead

Call of Duty

Diablo II

Fallout 3

Top Video Game Console Usage in 2009

Console	Usage Minutes (%)
Xbox 360	23.1
PlayStation 2	20.4
Wii	19.0
PlayStation 3	10.2
Xbox	6.0
GameCube	2.3
Other	19.0

Top 10 Best-Reviewed Video Games of 2009

Uncharted 2: Among Thieves (PS3)

Call of Duty: Modern Warfare 2 (PS3)

Street Fighter IV (PS3)

Call of Duty: Modern Warfare 2 (Xbox 360)

Grand Theft Auto: Chinatown Wars (Nintendo DS)

Braid (PS3)

Street Fighter IV (Xbox 360)

God of War Collection (PS3)

Batman: Arkham Asylum (Xbox 360)

Forza Motorsport 3 (Xbox 360)

Games

Top 10 Xbox 360 Games of 2009

Assassin's Creed II

Forza 3

Batman: Arkham Asylum

Call of Duty: Modern Warfare 2

Shadow Complex

Guitar Hero: Metallica

The Beatles: Rock Band

UFC 2009: Undisputed

FIFA Soccer 10

Afro Samurai

Top 10 Wii Games of 2009

New Super Mario Bros Wii

Wii Fit

Wii Sports Resort

Mario Kart Wii with Wii Wheel

Mario and Sonic at the Olympic Winter Games

Wii Play with Remote

The Beatles: Rock Band

Toy Story Mania

We Ski

Lego Rock Band

Top 10 iPhone Game Apps

Scrabble

Bejeweled 2

Solitaire

Sudoku

Flick Fishing

PAC-MAN Lite

Touch Hockey: FS5

Checkers

MONOPOLY Here & Now: The World Edition

Crash Bandicoot Nitro Kart 3D

Geography
World & U.S.

A Curious World

If you hung out on your street for your whole life, you'd never know anything except your own neighborhood. Can you imagine what kind of world it would be if people never left home?

Lucky for us, people have always been driven to explore. Some searched for better hunting grounds or warmer climates. Some wanted riches, spices, new kingdoms, or more land. Some were just curious to see what was around the next corner. And in leaving home, these explorers found new and never-before-seen worlds.

All Over the Map

Of course, explorers couldn't take everyone along on their journeys. But such people as Marco Polo, Christopher Columbus, Meriwether Lewis, William Clark, and others captured their voyages in the form of journals and diaries. (In fact, the word *geographia* means "to describe or write about the earth.") Explorers also created maps showing where they had been and how they got there.

A Flat-out Mistake

Early explorers and scientists had a lot to work through when it came to mapping the world. First of all, up until the 1500s many people believed that Earth was flat. That meant a sailing ship could sail off into the horizon and drop over the edge. An expedition led by Magellan successfully circumnavigated the world and proved that Earth was a globe.

LINE UP, PLEASE!

Navigators and mapmakers needed new tools to plot out voyages and measure distances on the globe. A system of imaginary lines was created.

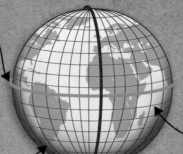

The equator circles the middle of the globe like a giant belt. It divides the world in half horizontally.

Parallels run east and west, parallel to the equator. They are used to measure latitude, or distance north or south of the equator.

Meridians run north and south, looping around the poles. The prime meridian divides the world in half vertically. Meridians are used to measure longitude, or distance east or west of the prime meridian.

We measure longitude and latitude by degrees. The equator is at 0 degrees latitude. The prime meridian is at 0 degrees longitude.

TAKE a LOOK

Each point on a map is described by two sets of degrees depending on distance north or south of the equator and east or west of the prime meridian. For instance, Kansas City, Missouri, has a latitude of 39° N and a longitude of 94° W. On a map, find the latitude of your city and state. Then reverse the direction. (If it's north, change it to south, for example.) Next, find the longitude of your location. Subtract it from 180 and reverse its direction, too. The new location will be the place directly opposite your home on the other side of the globe.

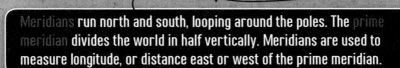

CHECK IT OUT!

The prime meridian passes through the city of Greenwich, England. That's why it's also known as the Greenwich meridian.

Greenwich, England

How to Read a Map

Directions

When you're reading a map, how do you figure out which way is which? On most—but not all—maps:

⬆️ **Up means north**   ⬇️ **Down means south**   ⬅️ **Left means west**   ➡️ **Right means east**

Some maps are turned or angled so that north is not straight up. Always look for a symbol called a compass rose to show you exactly where north is on the map you're reading.

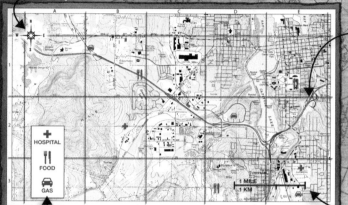

HOSPITAL
FOOD
GAS

1 MILE
1 KM

Location

Maps that show large areas such as countries and continents include lines of longitude and latitude. Maps of cities and streets are divided into blocks called grids. Grid maps have numbers on one side and letters on another. They also have an index that gives a number—letter combination for every place on the map.

Distance

You can look at a map and think it's a hop, skip, and a jump from Maine to Maryland, but it's really a few million hops. The map scale shows you how many miles (or km) a certain length of map represents.

Shapes and Symbols

Every picture, object, shape, and line on a map stands for something. A tiny red airplane stands for an airport. A thick line is one kind of road and a dotted line is another. A map's legend, or key, shows these symbols and explains what they stand for.

A Map Is a Map Is a Map . . .

All maps are not created equal. There are different maps for different purposes:

- A bathymetric map shows the depths and contours of the bottom of a body of water.
- A geological map shows earthquake faults, volcanoes, minerals, rock types, underground water, and landslide areas.
- A physical map shows mountains, lakes, and rivers.
- A planimetric map shows horizontal (not vertical, such as elevations) features.
- A political map shows boundaries of cities, states, countries, and provinces.
- A relief map uses different colors to show different elevations.
- A road map shows roads, highways, cities, and towns.
- A topographic map shows elevations.
- A weather map shows temperatures, fronts, rain, snow, sleet, storms, fog, and other weather conditions.

Geographical Terms

Term	Definition
Altitude	the distance above sea level
Archipelago	a group or chain of islands clustered together in an ocean or sea
Atlas	a book of maps
Atoll	an ocean island made out of an underwater ring of coral
Bay	a body of water protected and partly surrounded by land
Cartographer	a mapmaker
Compass rose	a four-pointed design on a map that shows north, south, east, and west
Continent	one of Earth's seven largest land masses
Degree	a unit of measurement used to calculate longitude and latitude
Delta	a flat, triangular piece of land that fans out at the mouth of a river
Elevation	the height of a point on the earth's surface above sea level
Equator	an imaginary circle around the earth halfway between the North Pole and the South Pole
Globe	a 3-D spherical map of the earth
GPS	short for Global Positioning System; finds longitude and latitude by bouncing information off satellites in space
Grid	a crisscross pattern of lines forming squares on a map
Hemisphere	one half of the world
Island	land that is surrounded by water on all sides
Isthmus	a narrow strip of land (with water on both sides) that connects two larger land areas
Latitude	distance north or south of the equator
Legend	a key to the symbols on a map
Longitude	distance east or west of the prime meridian
Map	a flat picture of a place drawn to scale
Meridian	an imaginary line running north and south and looping around the poles used to measure longitude
North Pole	the most northerly point on Earth
Ocean	the body of salt water surrounding the great land masses and divided by the land masses into several distinct portions
Parallel	an imaginary line parallel to the equator, used to measure latitude
Peninsula	a body of land surrounded by water on three sides
Scale	a tool on a map that helps calculate real distance
Sea level	the surface of the ocean
South Pole	the most southerly point on Earth
Strait	a narrow body of water that connects two larger bodies
Topography	the physical features of a place, such as mountains

Continental Drift

Maps are all well and good if things don't change. "Go east one mile and turn south and find Mt. Crumpet" works only if Mt. Crumpet doesn't decide to walk a few miles north. Sound ridiculous? Actually, the earth didn't always look like it does today. About 250 million years ago, all the continents were scrunched together in one lump called Pangaea.

Gradually the land drifted and changed into the seven continents we know today in a process called continental drift. And the land is still moving.

Pangaea

Journey to the Center of the Earth

Earth isn't just one big blue ball with the same stuff all the way through. It's made up of layers.

The part we walk around on is the crust, or lithosphere. It's only about 60 miles (100 km) deep.

Beneath the lithosphere is the mantle. It's a layer about 1,800 miles (2,897 km) deep.

Beneath that is the core, which is made of two parts:

The outer core (1,375 miles, or 2,200 km, thick) is almost as big as the Moon and made up of soupy molten iron.

The inner core is about 781 miles (1,250 km) thick and about as hot as the surface of the Sun.

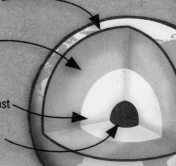

Earth's Layers

The Continents Today

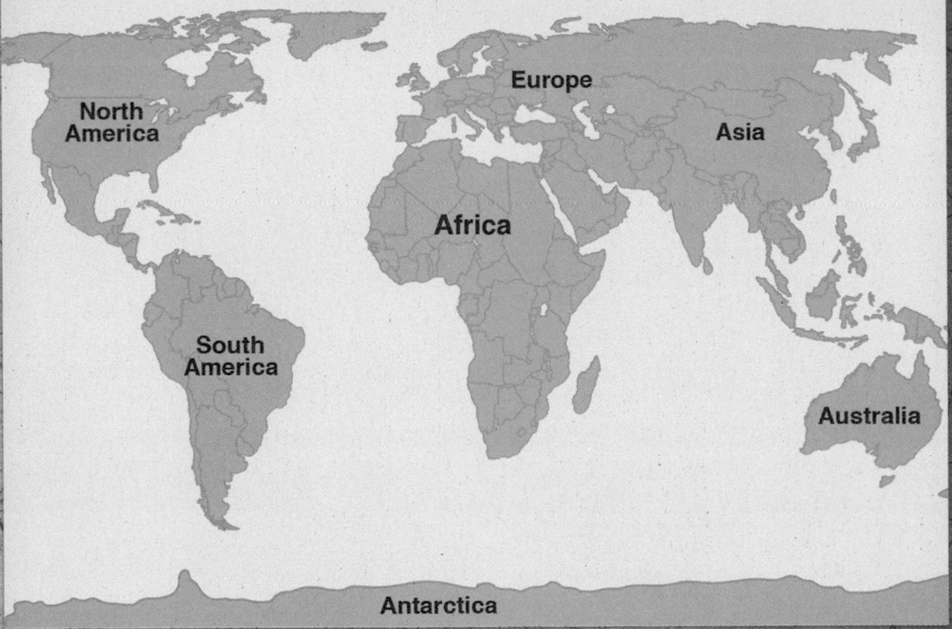

Europe

North
America

Asia

Africa

South
America

Australia

Antarctica

30% LAND

70% WATER

CHECK IT OUT !

The total surface area of the world is 196,937,583 square miles (510,066,000 sq km). However, about 70 percent of that is water. Turn the page to read about the continents in detail. Turn to pages 170–171 to read about the world's major oceans.

Arctic Ocean

LAND

NEW SIBERIAN
ISLANDS

East Siberian
Sea

Barents Sea

SEVERNAYA
ZEMLYA

Laptev
Sea

NOVAYA
ZEMLYA

Kara Sea

KHREBET CHERS

Tiksi

S I B E R I A

RUSSIA

Yakutsk

Nizhniy
Novgorod

Perm'

Noril'sk

Arctic Circle

VERKHOYANSK KHREBET

Vilyuy

Kazan'

Yekaterinburg

Irtysh

Angara

Chita

Samara

Ufa

Chelyabinsk

Omsk

Krasnoyarsk

Novosibirsk

Irkutsk

Lake
Baikal

VABONOVYY KHREBET

DA HINGGAN LING

Shenya

Atryaū
(Atryau)

Astana

Qaraghandy
(Karaganda)

Ürümqi

Ulaanbaatar

MONGOLIA

Baotou

Beijing

Tbilisi

GEO.

ARM.

Yerevan

AZERBALIAN

Caspian
Sea

Aral
Sea

KAZAKHSTAN

QIZILQUM

Lake
Balkhash

Almaty

TIEN SHAN MTS.

GOBI DESERT

Tianjin

Taiyuan

Qin

Baku

Tabrīz

QIZILQUM

UZBEKISTAN

TURKMENISTAN

Ashgabat

KARAKUM

Tashkent

Bishkek

KYRGYZSTAN

TIEN

Kashi

TAKLA MAKAN
DESERT

Jinan

ZAGROS MTS.

Tehran

Eṣfahān

Mashhad

Dushanbe

TAJIKISTAN

KUNLUN MOUNTAINS

Lanzhou

Zhengzhou

Nanjing

CHINA

Xi'an

IRAN

Shīrāz

AFGHANISTAN

Kabul

Line of Control

Indian
claim

Xizang

Wuhan

Kandahār

Bandar
'Abbās

Islamabad

Faisalabad

Line of Control
(In Kashmir)

QING ZANG GAOYUAN

Chengdu

Chongqing

Changsha

Persian
Gulf

Doha

QATAR

Abu
Dhabi

U.A.E.

Muscat

Quetta

Lahore

Ludhiāna

MT. Everest
(highest point in the world,
8850 m)

Lhasa

HENGDUAN SHAN

Gulyang

SAUDI
ARABIA

OMAN

PAKISTAN

Karāchi

**New
Delhi**

Jaipur

Lucknow

Kānpur

NEPAL

Kathmandu

Patna

BHUTAN

Thimphu

Brahmaputra

Kunming

Xi Jiang

Guangzhou

Hon

Macau

Ahmadābād

Indore

INDIA

Nāgpur

Kolkata

BANGLADESH

Dhaka

Nanning

Mumbai

Surat

Pune

DECCAN

Hyderābād

Vishākhapatnam

Chittagong

Mandalay

Hanoi

Haiphong

Hainan
Dao

Macau

Arabian
Sea

WESTERN GHATS

EASTERN GHATS

Bengaluru

Chennai

Bay of
Bengal

BURMA

Nay Pyi
Taw

LAOS

Vientiane

Da Nang

Sou
Ch
Se

LAKSHADWEEP
(INDIA)

Cochin

Jaffna

Laccadive
Sea

ANDAMAN
ISLANDS
(INDIA)

Andaman
Sea

Rangoon

THAILAND

Bangkok

VIETNAM

SPRATLY
ISLANDS

MALDIVES

Male

Colombo

SRI LANKA

NICOBAR
ISLANDS
(INDIA)

Gulf of
Thailand

CAMBODIA

**Phnom
Penh**

Ho Chi Minh
City

Bandar
Begaw

BRUNEI

Medan

MALAYSIA

**Kuala
Lumpur**

SINGAPORE
Singapore

Pontianak

MALAYSI

Scale 1:48,000,000

Azimuthal Equal-Area Projection

Sumatra

Palembang

INDO

Jakarta

Semarang

0   800 Kilometers

0   800 Miles

Bandung

Java

Boundary representation is
not necessarily authoritative.

Christmas Island
(AUSTL.)

ASIA can be described best in one word: BIG. It's the biggest continent in size, covering about 30 percent of Earth's land area. It's biggest in population, with about 60 percent of all the people in the world living there. And in terms of contributions to the world, it's enormous. Asians founded the first cities; set up the first legal system; invented writing paper, printing, the magnetic compass, and gunpowder; and much more. All of the world's major religions began in Asia.

Asia rules in world-class geographical features, too. It has:
- The highest mountain range, the Himalayas, as well as the most mountains of any continent.
- The highest point on Earth, Mt. Everest, and the lowest, the Dead Sea.

Asia at a Glance

Area
17,226,200 sq. mi. (44,614,000 sq km)

Population
4,075,742,000

Number of countries
50

Largest country
China
3,705,407 sq. mi. (9,596,960 sq km)

Most populated city
Shanghai, China
11,283,714 people

Longest river
Yangtze, China
3,915 mi. (6,300 km)

Largest lake
Lake Baikal, Russia
12,200 sq. mi. (31,500 sq km)

Highest point
Mt. Everest, Nepal/China
29,035 ft. (8,850 m) above sea level

Lowest point
Dead Sea, Israel/Jordan
1,380 ft. (421 m) below sea level

CHECK IT OUT!

Asia has some of the world's largest international business centers, such as Tokyo, Japan; Singapore; and Hong Kong. Yet about half of all Asians are farmers.

AFRICA

North Atlantic Ocean

GERMANY • Brussels ★ LUX. POLAND
BEL. Prague ★ ★ Kyiv
Paris CZ. REP. SLOV. UKRAINE
FRANCE SWITZ. Vienna ★ ★ Budapest MOL.
AUS. HUNG. ROM.
SLO. CRO. Belgrade ★ Bucharest
PORTUGAL BOS.& SER. Sofia Black Sea
AND. HER. MONT. KOS. BULG. Ankara
Madrid ★ Corsica ★ Rome MAC. TURKE
AZORES Lisbon ★ ITALY Athens CYPRUS LE
(PORTUGAL) SPAIN Sardinia GREECE Beiru
Algiers Sicily Jerusalem ★ Amman
MADEIRA ISLANDS Oran ★ Tunis MALTA Alexandria ISRAEL JORDAN
(PORTUGAL) Rabat ★ Constantine TUNISIA Mediterranean Sea Cairo
Casablanca Fès Al Jīzah
MOROCCO Tripoli ★ Banghāzī Aswān
Marrakech EGYPT
CANARY ISLANDS Admin.
(SPAIN) Laayoune ALGERIA LIBYA Al Jawf Boundary
(El Aaiún)
Western Port
Sahara Sudan
Nouadhibou S A H A R A
MAURITANIA NIGER Omdurman
CAPE VERDE Nouakchott Tombouctou Agadez Khartoum
Praia MALI CHAD SUDAN
Dakar BURKINA Zinder N'Djamena Add
SENEGAL Bamako FASO Niamey Kano Abal
Banjul Ouagadougou
THE GAMBIA Bissau BENIN NIGERIA Moundou
GUINEA-BISSAU GUINEA Abuja CENTRAL AFRICAN Juba
Conakry GHANA TOGO Ogbomoso REPUBLIC
Freetown CÔTE Ibadan
SIERRA LEONE D'IVOIRE Lomé Lagos Bangui CONGO
Monrovia Yamoussoukro Accra Porto- CAMEROON Congo UGANDA
LIBERIA Abidjan Novo Douala Kisangani Kampala
Malabo Yaoundé
EQUATORIAL GUINEA REP. OF RWANDA Kigali
Gulf of Guinea Libreville THE Bukavu
SAO TOME GABON CONGO BASIN DEM. REP. Bujumbura
AND PRINCIPE São Tomé OF THE CONGO BURUNDI
Annobón Brazzaville TANZAN
(EQUA. GUI.) Pointe-Noire Kinshasa
ANGOLA Mbuji-Mayi
(Cabinda) Luanda
Lubumbashi
Kitwe MALAWI
ANGOLA ZAMBIA Lilongwe
Namibe Lubango Lusaka Blant
Harare MOZA
ZIMBABWE Beira
Windhoek BOTSWANA
Walvis Bay KALAHARI
DESERT
NAMIBIA Gaborone
Johannesburg Pretoria
Mbabane Maputo
SOUTH SWAZILAND
AFRICA Maseru
LESOTHO Durban
Cape Town Port Elizabeth
India

Scale 1:51,400,000
Azimuthal Equal-Area Projection
0 800 Kilometers
0 800 Miles
Boundary representation is not necessarily authoritative.

AFRICA is second to Asia in area and population, but it tops all continents in other categories:

- Biggest desert: The Sahara, covering about 3.5 million square miles (9 million sq km), or about one-third of the continent
- Longest freshwater lake: Lake Tanganyika, 420 miles (680 km)
- Most independent countries: 53

Africa is a land of treasures, from the lions, giraffes, rhinos, and other spectacular wildlife that inhabit its rain forests and grasslands to its rich supplies of gold and diamonds. However, most Africans remain poor because of drought, famine, disease, and other ongoing serious problems.

Africa at a Glance

Area
11,684,000 sq. mi. (30,262,000 sq km)

Population
1,027,783,000

Largest country
Sudan
967,500 sq. mi. (2,505,813 sq km)

Most populated city
Cairo, Egypt
About 8 million people

Longest river
Nile
4,132 mi. (6,650 km)

Largest lake
Lake Victoria, Tanzania/Uganda/Kenya
26,828 sq. mi. (69,484 sq km)

Highest point
Mount Kilimanjaro, Tanzania
19,340 ft. (5,895 m) above sea level

Lowest point
Lake Assal, Djibouti
509 ft. (155 m) below sea level

CHECK IT OUT!

From fossils found in Africa, scientists say that the earliest human beings lived here about 2 million years ago.

Cherskiy

RUSSIA

Pevek

Anadyr'

East Siberian Sea

Arctic Ocean

Alert

Ellesmere Island

Greenla (DENMA

Qaanaaq (Thule)

Chukchi Sea

Providéniya

Barrow

QUEEN ELIZABETH ISLANDS

Baffin Bay

Bering Strait

Nome

Prudhoe Bay

Beaufort Sea

Banks Island

Resolute

Pond Inlet

Baffin Island

Bering Sea

UNITED STATES

Mt. McKinley (highest point in North America, 6194 m)

Fairbanks

ALASKA

Bethel

Inuvik

Victoria Island

Cambridge Bay

Gjoa Haven

Iqaluit

Anchorage

Dawson

Valdez

Gulf of Alaska

ALEUTIAN TRENCH

Whitehorse

Great Bear Lake

Rankin Inlet

Juneau

Fort Nelson

Great Slave Lake

CANADA

Arviat

Hudson Bay

ROCKY

River

Churchill

Chisasibi

Prince George

Fort McMurray

Lake Athabasca

North

Edmonton

Saskatoon

Lake Winnipeg

Moosonee

Ch (Sa

Vancouver

Calgary

Regina

Thunder Bay

Me

Pacific

Victoria

Seattle

Winnipeg

Lake Superior

Sudbury

Ottaw

Portland

MOUNTAINS

Fargo

Lake Huron

Toronto

Hamilton

London

Detroit

Boise

Minneapolis

Lake Michigan

Milwaukee

Cleveland

Pittsburgh

Ocean

SIERRA NEVADA

CASCADE

Great Salt Lake

Chicago

Columbus

Cincinnati

Sacramento

Salt Lake City

Omaha

UNITED

Indianapolis

Saint Louis

Louisville

San Francisco

San Jose

Death Valley (lowest point in North America, -86 m)

Denver

Kansas City

Nashville

Fresno

Las Vegas

STATES

Memphis

Los Angeles

Albuquerque

Oklahoma City

Atlant

Tijuana

San Diego

Phoenix

Dallas

Birmingham

Mexicali

Tucson

El Paso

Austin

Jacksonv

Ciudad Juárez

San Antonio

Houston

New Orleans

Or

Hermosillo

Chihuahua

Gulf of Mexico

Guadeloupe

Torreón

Monterrey

Matamoros

La Paz

Culiacán

MEXICO

San Luis Potosí

Tampico

Can

Mérida

Guadalajara

Aguascalientes

León

Querétaro

Bahía de Campeche

ISLAS REVILLAGIGEDO (MEXICO)

Morelia

Toluca

Mexico

Puebla

Veracruz

Acapulco

Oaxaca

BEL

Belmo

HO

Guatemala

Teg

GUATEMALA

San Salvador

EL SALVADOR

Scale: 1:36,000,000

Lambert Conformal Conic Projection, standard parallels 25°N and 77°N

0   300   600 Kilometers

0   300   600 Miles

NORTH AMERICA, the third-largest continent in area and the fourth-largest in population, is all about variety. The continent has an enormous mix of climates and habitats, from the frozen Arctic to warm, humid Central American rain forests, which support an amazing number of plants and animals. North American human inhabitants live in a variety of environments, too, from rural farms to such bustling, densely populated urban centers as Mexico City. Many—but not all—North Americans enjoy a high standard of living compared to inhabitants of the rest of the world.

Of all the continents, North America has:
- The world's largest island: Greenland,* 836,330 square miles (2,166,086, sq km)
- The world's largest freshwater lake: Lake Superior
- The longest coastline: 190,000 miles (300,000 km), or more than 60,000 times the distance across the Atlantic Ocean

*Except for Australia, which is classified as a continent as well as an island

North America at a Glance

Area
9,352,000 sq. mi. (24,220,000 sq km)

Population
538,417,000

Number of countries
23

Largest country
Canada
3,855,101 sq. mi. (9,984,670 sq km)

Most populated city
Mexico City, Mexico
8,720,916

Longest river
Mississippi-Missouri, United States
3,710 mi. (5,971 km) long

Largest lake
Lake Superior, United States/Canada
31,700 sq. mi. (82,100 sq km)

Highest point
Mt. McKinley, Alaska
20,320 ft. (6,194 m) above sea level

Lowest point
Death Valley, California
282 ft. (86 m) below sea level

CHECK IT OUT !

Nearly half of all Canadians and about a third of Americans come from English, Irish, Scottish, or Welsh ancestors. However, North America's first settlers were from Asia. Scientists say that these Native Americans, now sometimes called Indians, walked across the Bering Strait, which was dry land between 15,000 and 35,000 years ago. Before they came, there were no people on the continent.

eguciglapa
NICARAGUA
Managua
San José
COSTA RICA
Panama
PANAMA

Providencia
(COLOMBIA)
Isla de
San Andrés
(COLOMBIA)

Aruba
(NETH.)
Antilles
(NETH.)

ST. VINCENT AND
THE GRENADINES
GRENADA

BARBADOS

Port-of-Spain
TRINIDAD AND
TOBAGO

Barranquilla
Cartagena
Maracaibo
Barquisimeto
Valencia
Caracas
Barcelona

COCOS RIDGE

Cúcuta
San
Cristobal
Bucaramanga
Medellín

VENEZUELA

Ciudad
Guayana

Río Orinoco

Georgetown

Paramaribo

GUYANA
SURINAME
French
Guiana
(FRANCE)

Cayenne

Isla de Malpelo
(COLOMBIA)

Pereira
Ibagué
Cali

Bogotá

COLOMBIA

Boa
Vista

GUIANA
HIGHLANDS

Quito
ECUADOR
Guayaquil
Cuenca

Macapá

Equator

Belém

A M A Z O N

Río Negro

Amazon

Iquitos

Manaus
Santarém

Piura
Chiclayo
Trujillo

Pucallpa

B A S I N

Río Madeira

PERU

Huánuco
Huancayo
Lima
Ica
Cusco

Rio
Branco

Pôrto
Velho

B R A Z I L

BRAZIL

South
Pacific
Ocean

Arequipa

ANDES

PERU-CHILE TRENCH

Trinidad

MATO GROSSO
PLATEAU

Cuiabá

Goiânia

Brasilia

HIGHL

NAZCA RIDGE

Arica
Iquique

La Paz
BOLIVIA
Cochabamba
Sucre
Potosí

Santa
Cruz

ATACAMA DESERT

ALTIPLANO

Campo
Grande

Uberlândia

Antofagasta

Tropic of Capricorn

Salta

PARAGUAY

Asunción

Ciudad
del Este

Río Paraná

Londrina
São Paulo

Campinas
Santos

Curitiba
Joinvile

San Miguel
de Tucumán

Resistencia

Florianópolis

Ambrosio
(CHILE)

CHILE

Cerro Aconcagua
(highest point in
South America, 6962 m)

Valparaíso
Santiago

Córdoba

Mendoza

Santa
Fe
Rosario

Porto Alegre

Salto

URUGUAY

PAMPAS

Buenos Aires
La Plata

Montevideo

S
At
o

Concepcion

ARGENTINA

Bahía Blanca

Temuco

ANDES

San Carlos de
Bariloche

Puerto Montt

PATAGONIA

Comodoro
Rivadavia

Laguna del Carbón
(lowest point in South America and
the Western Hemisphere, -105 m)

SOUTH

Scale 1:35,000,000
Azimuthal Equal-Area Projection

0   500 Kilometers
0   500 Miles

Río
Gallegos

Stanley
Falkland Islands
(Islas Malvinas)
(administered by U.K.,
claimed by ARGENTINA)

Punta Arenas

Strait of
Magellan

Boundary representation is
not necessarily authoritative.

Ushuaia

Cape
Horn

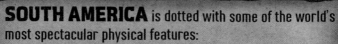

SOUTH AMERICA is dotted with some of the world's most spectacular physical features:

- The longest mountain range, the Andes, stretching 4,500 miles (7,200 km) from Chile in the south, to Venezuela and Panama in the north.
- The largest rain forest, the Amazon, covering about 2 million square miles (5.2 million sq km), or two-fifths of the continent.
- The highest waterfall, Angel Falls in Venezuela, plunging 3,212 feet (979 m).

South America is the fourth-largest continent, but only Australia and Antarctica have fewer people. About 80 percent of the people live in urban areas such as São Paulo, Brazil. South America's economy is growing fast, led by Brazil, Argentina, Colombia, and Chile.

South America at a Glance

Area
6,887,000 sq. mi. (17,836,000 sq km)

Population
396,258,000

Number of countries
12

Largest country
Brazil
3,287,613 sq. mi. (8,514,877 sq km)

Most populated city
São Paulo, Brazil
10,434,252 people

Longest river
Amazon, Brazil
4,000 mi. (6,437 km)

Largest lake
Lake Maracaibo, Venezuela
5,217 sq. mi. (13,512 sq km)

Highest point
Aconcagua, Argentina
22,835 ft. (6,960 m) above sea level

Lowest point
Valdes Peninsula, Argentina
131 ft. (40 m) below sea level

rtaleza

Natal

João
Pessoa

Recife

Maceió

Aracajú

dor

20

RIO
GRANDE
RISE

CHECK IT OUT!

The Amazon rain forest is home to an estimated one in ten plant and animal species on Earth.

163

Jan Mayen
(NORWAY)

Nordkapp

Hammerfest

Greenland
Sea

Denmark
Strait

Norwegian Sea

Tromsø

Kiruna

Arctic Circle

Luleå

Oulu

NORWAY

Reykjavik
ICELAND

Umeå

FINLAN

Trondheim

SWEDEN

Gulf
of
Bothnia

Tampere

Faroe Islands
(DENMARK)

Bergen

Gävle

Turku

Helsinki

Tórshavn

SHETLAND
ISLANDS

Oslo

Stockholm

ÅLAND
ISLANDS

Tal

EST

ORKNEY
ISLANDS

Stavanger

Gotland

Riga

Skagerrak

HEBRIDES

Göteborg

Baltic Sea

LITHUA

Aberdeen

North
Sea

Öland

Vilr

Glasgow
Edinburgh

UNITED

DENMARK
Copenhagen

Malmö

Kaliningrad

RUSSIA

Belfast

Malmö

Bornholm

Gdańsk

Isle
of
Man
(U.K.)

Leeds

Hamburg

Poznań

Warsaw

Dublin

Liverpool

Manchester

Bremen

Berlin

POLAND

IRELAND

Irish
Sea

KINGDOM

Birmingham

Amsterdam

Essen

Leipzig

Łódź
Wrocław

Cardiff

NETH.

Cologne

Kraków

Celtic
Sea

London

Rotterdam

Brussels

Bonn

GERMANY

Prague

CZECH REPUBLIC

English
Channel

Lille

BEL.

Frankfurt

Brno

SLOVAKIA

Guernsey (U.K.)
Jersey (U.K.)

Paris

LUX.

Luxembourg

Stuttgart

Bratislava

Strasbourg

Munich

Vienna

Budapes

Nantes

LIECH.

AUSTRIA

HUNGARY

Zürich
Bern

Vaduz

SWITZ.

Bay of
Biscay

FRANCE

Geneva

SLOVENIA

Ljubljana

Zagreb

A Coruña

MASSIF
CENTRAL

Lyon

Milan

Venice

Turin

CROATIA

BOSNIA AND
HERZEGOVINA

Belgr

Bordeaux

Genoa

SAN
MARINO

Bilbao

Toulouse

MONACO

Florence

Sarajevo

MONT

Porto

PYRENEES

Andorra
la Vella

Marseille

Ligurian
Sea

Corsica

ITALY

Adriatic
Sea

Podgorica

Zaragoza

ANDORRA

VATICAN
CITY

Rome

Tirana

PORTUGAL

Madrid

Barcelona

AL

Lisbon

Valencia

Balearic
Sea

Sardinia

Naples

SPAIN

Tyrrhenian
Sea

BALEARIC
ISLANDS

Cagliari

Sevilla

Ionian
Sea

Gibraltar
(U.K.)

Málaga

Palermo

Ceuta
(SPAIN)

Alborán
Sea

Mediterranean Sea

Sicily

Strait of Gibraltar

Melilla
(SPAIN)

Oran

Algiers

Tunis

Scale 1:

Valletta

Lambert Conform

Rabat

MALTA

standard paralle

Casablanca

MOROCCO

ALGERIA

TUNISIA

0

EUROPE is a small continent divided into many individual countries, with at least 50 different languages and up to 100 different dialects spoken. With the third-largest population and the second-smallest area of any continent, Europe is densely populated. Still, there's plenty of natural beauty in its rivers, lakes, canals, and towering mountain ranges such as the Urals and the Alps. Straddling the border between Europe and Asia is the largest inland body of water in the world, the saltwater Caspian Sea, which covers 149,200 square miles (386,400 sq km). European contributions in art, music, philosophy, and culture formed the basis for Western civilization.

Europe at a Glance

Area
4,033,000 sq. mi. (10,445,000 sq km)

Population
706,966,000

Number of countries
49

Largest country (entirely in Europe)
Ukraine
233,090 sq. mi. (603,628 sq km)

Most populated city
Moscow, Russia
10.5 million people

Longest river
Volga, Russia
2,194 mi. (3,531 km) long

Largest lake
Lake Ladoga, Russia
6,835 sq. mi. (17,702 sq km)

Highest point
Mt. Elbrus, Russia
18,510 ft. (5,642 m) above sea level

Lowest point
Shore of the Caspian Sea
92 ft. (28 m) below sea level

CHECK IT OUT!

Europe has some of the world's longest railroad tunnels, including the Channel Tunnel, or Chunnel, which runs 31.1 miles (50 km) under the English Channel and connects the United Kingdom and France.

Arkhangel'sk

Lake Onega

USSIA

Moscow

Smolensk

Chernihiv

Kyiv

RAINE

Vinnytsya

Mykolayiv

Chisinau

Odesa

OVA

Constanța

Varna

Black Sea

IA

Istanbul

Bursa

TURKEY

Izmir

Rhodes

Crete

oundary representation is
t necessarily authoritative.

South Atlantic
Ocean

area of
enlargement

Queen Maud Land

Enderby
Land

Halley

Weddell Sea

Mac. Robertso
Land

Palmer
Land

Ronne
Ice Shelf

80

Bellingshausen
Sea

Ellsworth

Vinson Massif
(highest point in Antarctica, 4897 m)
Land

South Pole
2800 m.

Peter I Island

Bentley Subglacial Trench
(lowest point in Antarctica, -2540 m)

Marie Byrd
Land

Ross
Ice Shelf

Amundsen
Sea

80

Ross Sea

average minimum
extent of sea ice

Victoria Land

Wilke

Scott
Island

70

Antarctic Circle

BALLENY
ISLANDS

South
Pacific
Ocean

ANTARCTICA is the southernmost continent and the coldest place on Earth. It's almost entirely covered with ice that in some places is ten times as high as Chicago's Willis Tower, the tallest building in the United States. Gusts of wind up to 120 miles per hour (190 kph) make it feel even colder.

Antarctica is so cold, windy, and dry that humans never settled there. There are no countries, cities, or towns. However, researchers and scientists from different countries come to study earthquakes, the environment, weather, and more at scientific stations established by 19 countries. Some of these nations have claimed parts of Antarctica as their national territory, although other countries do not recognize the claims.

Few land animals can survive the continent's harsh conditions. The biggest one is a wingless insect called a midge, which is only one-half inch long. However, a great variety of whales, seals, penguins, and fish live in and near the surrounding ocean.

Antarctica at a Glance

Area
About 5,400,000 sq. mi. (14,000,000 sq km)

Population
No native people, but researchers come for various periods

Number of countries claiming territory
7

Number of research stations
60

Longest river
Onyx River 19 mi. (31 km) long

Highest point
Vinson Massif
16,050 ft. (4,892 m) above sea level

Lowest point
Bentley Subglacial Trench
8,383 ft. (2,555 m) below sea level

CHECK IT OUT !

The ice sheets covering Antarctica form the largest body of fresh water or ice in the world—7.25 million cubic miles (30 million cubic km), or about 70 percent of the world's fresh water.

Oceania
(Including Australia)

Samarinda
Balikpapan
Banjarmasin
Palu
Ternate
Molucca Sea
Celebes
Buru
Ceram
Kendari
Ambon
Sorong
Biak
Jayapura
Wewak
Bismarck Sea
New Ireland
Makassar

Java Sea
Surabaya
Jawa
Bali
Sumbawa
Flores
Denpasar
Lombok
Sumba
Kupang

INDONESIA
Banda Sea
Dili
TIMOR-LESTE
Timor
Timor Sea

PAPUA NEW GUINEA
Madang
Mount Hagen
New Guinea
Lae
New Britain
Bougainville
Solomon Sea
Port Moresby
Awara

Ashmore and Cartier Island (AUSTRALIA)
Darwin
Arafura Sea
Torres Strait
Gulf of Carpentaria

Cor Isl.
Coral

Indian Ocean

KING LEOPOLD RANGE
MACDONNELL RANGE

Cairns
Townsville

GREAT

20
Port Hedland
HAMMERSLEY RANGE
GREAT SANDY DESERT
Mount Isa
Mackay
Rockhampton
Gladstone

DIVIDING

GIBSON DESERT
Alice Springs

AUSTRALIA

SIMPSON DESERT
Toowoomba
Brisbane
Gold Coast

Geraldton
GREAT VICTORIA DESERT
Lake Eyre (lowest point in Australia, -15 m)
Broken Hill

RANGE

DARLING RANGE
Kalgoorlie
FLINDERS RANGE
Whyalla

Perth
Rockingham
Bunbury
Esperance
Adelaide
Newcastle
Sydney
Wollongong

Canberra

Mount Kosciuszko (highest point in Australia, 2229 m)
Melbourne
Geelong

Great Australian Bight

Bass Strait

Tasm Sea

40

Pacific Islands

Johnston Atoll (U.S.)
North Pacific Ocean
CLARION FRACTURE

Enewetak
MARSHALL ISLANDS
Kwajalein
Majuro
Kingman Reef (U.S.)
CLIPPERTON FRACTURE ZONE

Pohnpei
Palikir
Palmyra Atoll (U.S.)
Kiritimati (Christmas Island) (KIRIBATI)

Tarawa
KIRIBATI (GILBERT ISLANDS)
Howland Island (U.S.)
Equator

Banaba
Baker Island (U.S.)
Jarvis Island (U.S.)

Yaren District
NAURU
RAWAKI (PHOENIX ISLANDS)
KIRIBATI
LINE ISLANDS
ÎLES MARQUISES

Bougainville
SOLOMON ISLANDS
Honiara
Guadalcanal
SANTA CRUZ ISLANDS
TUVALU
Funafuti
Tokelau (N.Z.)
Swains Island

Rotuma
Cook Islands (N.Z.)
SOCIETY ISLANDS
ARCHIPEL DES TUAMOTU

Wallis and Futuna (FRANCE)
Mata-Utu
SAMOA
Apia
Pago Pago
American Samoa (U.S.)
Papeete
Tahiti

Coral Sea
New Caledonia (FRANCE)
Vanua Levu
VANUATU
Port-Vila
FIJI
Suva
Viti Levu
TONGA
Alofi
Niue (N.Z.)
Avarua
French Polynesia (FRANCE)
Mururoa
Adamstow

Noumea
Ceva-i-Ra
Nuku'Alofa
ÎLES TUBUAI

Minerva Reefs
Tropic of Capricorn

NEW CALEDONIA
LORD HOWE BASIN

KERMADEC ISLANDS (N.Z.)
Kingston
Norfolk Island (AUSTRALIA)

ISLANDS)

AUSTRALIA is an island. No, it's a continent. Wait, it's a country. Actually, it's all three. Australia is technically an island because it's surrounded on all sides by water, but geographers classify it as a continent because of its size. It's also the only continent that is also a country.

Australia is part of a large geographical area called Oceania, which includes new Zealand, Tasmania, Papua New Guinea and thousands of other smaller islands. Most of Australia is low and flat, with deserts covering about one-third of the continent. The world's largest coral reef, the Great Barrier Reef, is in the Coral Sea off the coast of Queensland in northeast Australia. Huge cattle and sheep ranches make Australia a leading producer of beef, mutton, and wool. Still, 90 percent of Australians live in cities and towns.

Minerva

ston

KER
ISL
lk Island (
STRALIA)

North
Island
Auckland
Hamilton Tauranga

Palmerston Hastings
North

ND
Wellington

Christchurch

South Island

Dunedin

rt Island

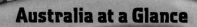

Australia at a Glance

Area
2,967,909 sq. mi. (7,686,850 sq km)
Population
21,262,241
Number of countries
1
Most populated city
Sydney
4,119,190 people
Longest river
Murray-Darling
2,094 mi. (3,376 km) long
Largest lake
Lake Eyre
3,708 sq. mi. (9,300 sq km)
Highest point
Mt. Kosciuszko
7,310 ft. (2,228 m) above sea level
Lowest point
Lake Eyre
52 ft. (16 m) below sea level

CHECK
IT OUT
!

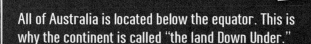

All of Australia is located below the equator. This is why the continent is called "the land Down Under."

The Continents and Major Oceans

HOW MANY oceans are there? Actually, there's only one. Although the seven continents split the ocean into five major parts, the ocean is one huge connected body of water. This *world ocean* has an average depth of 13,000 feet (4,000 m), with parts plunging almost three times that deep. On the ocean floor is a landscape of valleys and ridges that is constantly changing, as magma from underwater volcanoes seeps out and forms new land.

The ocean provides food, energy, medicines, minerals, and most of the precipitation that falls to the earth. It regulates the world's climate by storing and releasing heat from the Sun. Without the ocean, there could be no life on our planet.

North
America

Atlantic
Ocean

Pacific
Ocean

South
America

Area
About 66 million sq. mi.
(171 million sq km)
Greatest depth
35,840 ft. (10,924 m), in the
Challenger Deep
Surface temperature
Highest: 82°F (28° C), near the
equator in August
Lowest: 30°F (−1° C), in the
polar region in winter

Area
About 34 million sq. mi.
(88 million sq km)
Greatest depth
28,232 ft. (8,605 m) in the
Puerto Rico Trench
Surface temperature
Highest: About 86°F (30° C),
near the equator in summer
Lowest: 28°F (−2° C), at and
near the boundary with the
Southern Ocean in winter

Area
About 3,680,000 sq. mi. (9,530,000 sq km)
Greatest depth
18,399 ft. (5,608 m), in Molloy Hole, northwest of Svalbard
Surface temperature
Highest: 29°F (-1.5°C), in July
Lowest: 28°F (-2°C), in January

Arctic Ocean

Asia

Europe

Area
About 26.6 million sq. mi.
(69 million sq km)
Greatest depth
23,812 ft. (7,258 m), in the Java Trench
Surface temperature
Highest: 90°F (32° C), in the Persian
Gulf and Red Sea during July
Lowest: Below 30°F (-1° C), near the
Southern Ocean during July

Africa

Indian Ocean

Australia

Southern Ocean

Antarctica

Area
About 8.5 million sq. mi. (22 million sq km)
Greatest depth
23,737 ft. (7,235 m), at the southern end of
the South Sandwich Trench
Surface temperature
Highest: 30 to 43°F (-1 to 6°C), near 60°
south latitude in February
Lowest: 28 to 30°F (-2 to-1°C), near
Antarctica in August

171

World's 5 Deepest Oceans and Seas

(Ranked by average depth)

Pacific Ocean
14,040 ft. (4,279 m)

Indian Ocean
12,800 ft. (3,900 m)

Atlantic Ocean
11,810 ft. (3,600 m)

Caribbean Sea
8,448 ft. (2,575 m)

Sea of Japan
5,468 ft. (1,666 m)

World's 5 Largest Lakes

Caspian Sea
Azerbaijan/Iran/Kazakhstan/
Russia/Turkmenistan
146,101 sq. mi.
(378,401 sq km)

Lake Superior
Canada/United States
31,699 sq. mi.
(378,401 sq km)

Lake Victoria
Kenya/Tanzania/Uganda
26,828 sq. mi.
(69,485 sq km)

Lake Huron
Canada/United States
23,004 sq. mi.
(59,580 sq km)

Lake Michigan
United States
22,278 sq. mi.
(57,700 sq km)

World's 5 Highest Waterfalls

Angel
Venezuela
Tributary of Caroni River
3,212 ft. (979 m)

Tugela
South Africa
Tugela River
3,110 ft. (948 m)

Tres Hermanas
Peru
Cutivireni River
3,000 ft. (914 m)

Olo'upena
United States
2,953 ft. (900 m)

Yumbilla
Peru
2,938 ft. (896 m)

World's 5 Longest River Systems

Nile
Tanzania/Uganda/Sudan/Egypt
4,145 mi.
(6,670 km)

Amazon
Peru/Brazil
4,007 mi.
(6,448 km)

Yangtze-Kiang
China
3,915 mi.
(6,300 km)

Mississippi-Missouri-Red
United States
3,710 mi.
(5,971 km)

Yenisey-Angara-Selenga
Mongolia/Russia
2,500 mi.
(4,000 km)

World's 5 Highest Mountains

(Height of principal peak; lower
peaks of same mountain excluded)

Mt. Everest
Nepal/Tibet
29,035 ft. (8,850 m)

K2
Kashmir/China
28,250 ft. (8,611 m)

Kanchenjunga
Nepal/Sikkim
28,208 ft. (8,598 m)

Lhotse
Tibet
27,923 ft. (8,511 m)

Makalu
Nepal/Tibet
27,824 ft. (8,480 m)

Redwood Forest
Location: California

Grand Canyon
Location: Arizona

Yellowstone
Location: Wyoming

Bryce Canyon
Location: Utah

Crater Lake
Location: Oregon

10 Largest States in Total Area

1. Alaska	663,267 sq. mi. (1,717,854 sq km)
2. Texas	268,581 sq. mi. (695,622 sq km)
3. California	163,696 sq. mi. (423,971 sq km)
4. Montana	147,042 sq. mi. (380,837 sq km)
5. New Mexico	121,589 sq. mi. (314,914 sq km)
6. Arizona	113,998 sq. mi. (295,253 sq km)
7. Nevada	110,561 sq. mi. (286,352 sq km)
8. Colorado	104,094 sq. mi. (269,602 sq km)
9. Oregon	98,381 sq. mi. (254,806 sq km)
10. Wyoming	97,814 sq. mi. (253,337 sq km)

10 Smallest States in Total Area

1. Rhode Island	1,545 sq. mi. (4,002 sq km)
2. Delaware	2,489 sq. mi. (6,446 sq km)
3. Connecticut	5,543 sq. mi. (14,356 sq km)
4. New Jersey	8,721 sq. mi. (22,587 sq km)
5. New Hampshire	9,350 sq. mi. (24,216 sq km)
6. Vermont	9,614 sq. mi. (24,900 sq km)
7. Massachusetts	10,555 sq. mi. (27,337 sq km)
8. Hawaii	10,931 sq. mi. (28,311 sq km)
9. Maryland	12,407 sq. mi. (32,134 sq km)
10. West Virginia	24,230 sq. mi. (62,755 sq km)

5 Highest U.S. Mountains

Mt. McKinley
Alaska
20,320 ft. (6,194 m)

Mt. St. Elias
Alaska–Yukon
18,008 ft. (5,489 m)

Mt. Foraker
Alaska
17,400 ft. (5,304 m)

Mt. Bona
Alaska
16,550 ft. (5,044 m)

Mt. Blackburn
Alaska
16,390 ft. (4,996 m)

10 Longest U.S. Rivers

Mississippi
2,348 mi. (3,779 km)

Missouri
2,315 mi. (3,726 km)

Yukon
1,979 mi. (3,186 km)

Rio Grande
1,900 mi. (3,058 km)

Arkansas
1,459 mi. (2,348 km)

Red
1,290 mi. (2,076 km)

Columbia
1,243 mi. (2,000 km)

Snake
1,038 mi. (1,670 km)

Ohio
981 mi. (1,579 km)

St. Lawrence
800 mi. (1,287 km)

10 Largest U.S. National Historical Parks

(By total acreage and hectares)

Chaco Culture
New Mexico
33,960 acres (13,743 h)

Cumberland Gap
Kentucky/Tennessee/Virginia
22,365 acres (9,050 h)

Jean Lafitte
Louisiana
20,001 acres (8,094 h)

Chesapeake & Ohio Canal
Maryland/West Virginia/
Washington, DC
19,615 acres (7,938 h)

Klondike Gold Rush
Alaska/Washington
12,996 acres (5,259 h)

Colonial
Virginia
8,676 acres (3,511 h)

Pecos
New Mexico
6,669 acres (2,699 h)

Nez Perce
Idaho/Montana/
Oregon/Washington
4,570 acres (1,849 h)

Harpers Ferry
West Virginia/Maryland/Virginia
3,647 acres (1,476 h)

Cedar Creek & Belle Grove
Virginia
3,712 acres (1,502 h)

The Great Lakes—Facts and Figures

Lake Superior
Area	31,700 sq. mi. (82,103 sq km)
Borders	Minnesota, Wisconsin, Michigan (United States); Ontario (Canada)
Major Ports	Duluth, Superior, Sault Ste. Marie (United States); Sault Ste. Marie, Thunder Bay (Canada)

Lake Huron
Area	23,000 sq. mi. (59,570 sq km)
Borders	Michigan (United States); Ontario (Canada)
Major Ports	Port Huron (United States); Sarnia (Canada)

Lake Michigan
Area	22,300 sq. mi. (57,570 sq km)
Borders	Illinois, Indiana, Michigan, Wisconsin (United States)
Major Ports	Milwaukee, Racine, Kenosha, Chicago, Gary, Muskegon (United States)

Lake Erie
Area	9,940 sq. mi. (25,745 sq km)
Borders	Michigan, New York, Ohio, Pennsylvania (United States); Ontario (Canada)
Major Ports	Toledo, Sandusky, Lorain, Cleveland, Erie, Buffalo (United States)

Lake Ontario
Area	7,340 sq. mi. (19,011 sq km)
Borders	New York (United States); Ontario (Canada)
Major Ports	Rochester, Oswego (United States); Toronto, Hamilton (Canada)

The Great Lakes from Space

An easy way to remember the names of the Great Lakes is the mnemonic *HOMES*:

HURON **O**NTARIO **M**ICHIGAN **E**RIE **S**UPERIOR

CHECK IT OUT!

National Parks by State

Alaska
Denali
Gates of the Arctic
Glacier Bay
Katmai
Kenai Fjords
Kobuk Valley
Lake Clark
Wrangell–St. Elias

Arizona
Grand Canyon
Petrified Forest
Saguaro

Arkansas
Hot Springs

California
Channel Islands
Death Valley
Joshua Tree
Kings Canyon
Lassen Volcanic
Redwood
Sequoia
Yosemite

Colorado
Black Canyon of the Gunnison
Great Sand Dunes
Mesa Verde
Rocky Mountain

Florida
Biscayne
Dry Tortugas
Everglades

Hawaii
Haleakala
Hawaii Volcanoes

Idaho
Yellowstone

Kentucky
Mammoth Cave

Maine
Acadia

Michigan
Isle Royale

Minnesota
Voyageurs

Montana
Glacier
Yellowstone

Nevada
Death Valley
Great Basin

New Mexico
Carlsbad Caverns

North Carolina
Great Smoky Mountains

North Dakota
Theodore Roosevelt

Ohio
Cuyahoga Valley

Oregon
Crater Lake

South Carolina
Congaree

South Dakota
Badlands
Wind Cave

Tennessee
Great Smoky Mountains

Texas
Big Bend
Guadalupe Mountains

Utah
Arches
Bryce Canyon
Capitol Reef
Canyonlands
Zion

Virginia
Shenandoah

Washington
Mount Rainier
North Cascades
Olympic

Wyoming
Grand Teton
Yellowstone

10 Most Visited U.S. National Parks

Park (Location)	Visitors in 2009
Great Smoky Mountains (Tennessee/North Carolina)	9,491,437
Grand Canyon (Arizona)	4,348,068
Yosemite (California)	3,737,472
Yellowstone (Wyoming)	3,295,187
Olympic (Washington)	3,276,459
Rocky Mountain (Colorado)	2,822,325
Zion (Utah)	2,735,402
Cuyahoga Valley (Ohio)	2,589,288
Grand Teton (Wyoming)	2,580,081
Acadia (Maine)	2,227,698

Geography—World & U.S.

U.S. National Memorials

Memorial	State	Description
Arkansas Post	Arkansas	First permanent French settlement in the lower Mississippi River valley
Arlington House (Robert E. Lee Memorial)	Virginia	Lee's home overlooking the Potomac
Chamizal	Texas	Commemorates 1963 settlement of 99-year border dispute with Mexico
Coronado	Arizona	Commemorates first European exploration of the Southwest
De Soto	Florida	Commemorates 16th-century Spanish explorations
Father Marquette	Michigan	Commemorates Father Jacques Marquette, a French Jesuit missionary who helped establish Michigan's first European settlement at Sault Ste. Marie in 1668
Federal Hall	New York	First seat of U.S. government under the Constitution
Flight 93	Pennsylvania	Commemorates the passengers and crew of Flight 93, who lost their lives to bring down a plane headed to attack the nation's capital on September 11, 2001
Fort Caroline	Florida	On St. Johns River; overlooks site of a French Huguenot colony
Fort Clatsop	Oregon	Lewis and Clark encampment, 1805–1806
Franklin Delano Roosevelt	DC	Statues of President Roosevelt and First Lady Eleanor Roosevelt, as well as waterfalls and gardens; dedicated May 2, 1997
General Grant	New York	Grant's Tomb
Hamilton Grange	New York	Home of Alexander Hamilton
Jefferson National Expansion Monument	Missouri	Commemorates westward expansion
Johnstown Flood	Pennsylvania	Commemorates tragic flood of 1889
Korean War Veterans	DC	Dedicated in 1995; honors those who served in the Korean War
Lincoln Boyhood	Indiana	Site of Lincoln cabin, boyhood home, and grave of Lincoln's mother
Lincoln Memorial	DC	Marble statue of the 16th U.S. president
Lyndon B. Johnson Grove on the Potomac	DC	Honors the 36th president; overlooks the Potomac River vista of the capital
Mount Rushmore	South Dakota	World-famous sculpture of four presidents
Oklahoma City	Oklahoma	Commemorates the April 19, 1995, bombing of the Alfred P. Murrah Federal Building
Perry's Victory and International Peace Memorial	Ohio	The world's largest Doric column, constructed 1912–1915, promotes pursuit of international peace through arbitration and disarmament
Roger Williams	Rhode Island	Memorial to founder of Rhode Island
Thaddeus Kosciuszko	Pennsylvania	Memorial to Polish hero of the American Revolution
Theodore Roosevelt Island	DC	Statue of the 26th president in wooded island sanctuary
Thomas Jefferson Memorial	DC	Statue of the 3rd president in a circular, colonnaded structure
USS Arizona	Hawaii	Memorializes American losses at Pearl Harbor
Vietnam Veterans	DC	Black granite wall inscribed with names of those missing or killed in action in the Vietnam War
Washington Monument	DC	Obelisk honoring the 1st U.S. president
World War II	DC	Oval plaza with central pool commemorating those who fought and died in World War II
Wright Brothers	North Carolina	Site of first powered flight

Stones River, Tennessee
Scene of battle that began Union
offensive to trisect Confederacy

Fort Donelson, Tennessee
Site of first major Union victory

Antietam, Maryland
Battle here ended first Confederate
invasion of North, Sept. 17, 1862

Big Hole, Montana
Site of major battle between Nez Perce
and U.S. Army

Petersburg, Virginia
Scene of 10-month Union
campaigns, 1864–1865

Fort Necessity, Pennsylvania
Some of the first battles of
French and Indian War

Wilson's Creek, Missouri
Scene of Civil War battle
for control of Missouri

Tupelo, Mississippi
Site of crucial Civil War battle
over Sherman's supply line

Cowpens, South Carolina
American Revolution battlefield

Monocacy, Maryland
Civil War battle in defense of
Washington, DC, fought here July 9, 1

Moores Creek, North Carolina
1776 battle between Patriots and
Loyalists commemorated here

Stats on the Statue of Liberty

The Statue of Liberty was designed by French sculptor Frederic Auguste Bartholdi and arrived
in 214 packing cases from Rouen, France, in June 1885. The completed statue was dedicated on
October 28, 1886, by President Grover Cleveland. It was designated a National Monument in 1924
and is one of America's most famous symbols of freedom.

Part of Statue	Measurement
Height from heel to torch	151 ft. 1 in. (45.3 m)
Height from base of pedestal to torch	305 ft. 1 in. (91.5 m)
Length of hand	16 ft. 5 in. (5 m)
Length of index finger	8 ft. 0 in. (2.4 m)
Circumference at second finger joint	3 ft. 6 in. (1 m)
Size of fingernail	13 x 10 in. (33 x 25 cm)
Height of head from chin to cranium	17 ft. 3 in. (5 m)
Thickness of head from ear to ear	10 ft. 0 in. (3 m)
Distance across eye	2 ft. 6 in. (0.76 m)
Length of nose	4 ft. 6 in. (1.4 m)
Length of right arm	42 ft. 0 in. (12.8 m)
Thickness of right arm at thickest point	12 ft. 0 in. (3.7 m)
Thickness of waist	35 ft. 0 in. (10.7 m)
Width of mouth	3 ft. 0 in. (1 m)
Length of tablet	23 ft. 7 in. (7.2 m)
Width of tablet	13 ft. 7 in. (4.1 m)
Thickness of tablet	2 ft. 0 in. (0.6 m)

Select National Sites of Washington, DC

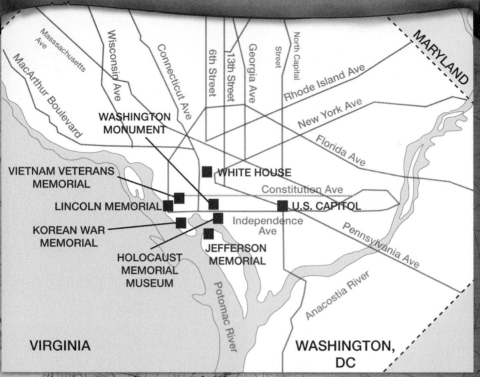

U.S. Capitol
The Capitol is open to the public for guided tours 8:45 AM–3:30 PM, Monday through Saturday. Tickets are available at tour kiosks at the east and west fronts of the Capitol. Phone: (202) 226-8000

Holocaust Memorial Museum
The museum is open daily, 10:00 AM–5:30 PM, except Yom Kippur and December 25. 100 Raoul Wallenburg Pl., SW (formerly 15th St., SW) near Independence Ave. Phone: (202) 488-0400

Jefferson Memorial
The memorial, which is located on the south edge of the Tidal Basin, is open 24 hours a day. An elevator and curb ramps for the disabled are in service. Phone: (202) 426-6841

Korean War Memorial
The $18 million military memorial, which was funded by private donations, is open 24 hours a day. Phone: (202) 426-6841

Lincoln Memorial
The memorial, which is located in West Potomac Park, is open 24 hours a day. An elevator and curb ramps for the disabled are in service. Phone: (202) 426-6841

Vietnam Veterans Memorial
The memorial is open 24 hours a day. Phone: (202) 426-6841

Washington Monument
The memorial is open 9:00 AM–5:00 PM daily, except July 4 and December 25. Tickets are required for entry and can be either reserved ahead of time or picked up same day. Phone: (202) 426-6841

The White House
Free reserved tickets for guided tours can be obtained up to six months in advance. Contact your senators or representatives for tickets. Phone: (202) 224-3121

To Your Health

Unless you happen to be sick and unable to do what you want to do, you probably take your health for granted. But keeping healthy is the most important thing you can do for yourself. The first step is to eat a healthy diet with lots of vegetables, lean proteins, whole grains, and fruits. But you also need to do other things: keep moving and keep clean.

Shake a Leg

Running, jumping rope, playing tag, skating, skiing, playing basketball, baseball, swimming, or riding a bike is serious fun. Activity is good for you, too. Every day you should play outside for at least an hour. The more you move, the more you protect yourself from being overweight and running the risk of getting diseases like asthma, diabetes, high blood pressure, cancer, and heart disease. Get up and get out!

ZZZZZZZZZZZ

You snooze, you lose. Actually, that's not true. You need your sleep.

Every night you need to shut down and reboot your system by sleeping for at least eight hours. When you sleep, your brain reshuffles information, spreads a few chemicals around, repairs damage done during the day, and maybe even solves problems! Sleeping is also the time when your body grows. So go to bed—and grow up!

Keep It Clean!

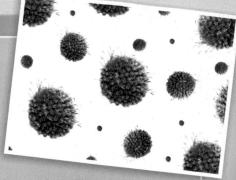

Ever had a cold? Who hasn't? Colds and flu are spread by tiny pathogens called viruses, which like to get into your body through your eyes, nose, and mouth. They're riding around on doorknobs, pencils, desks, and faucets, just waiting for a chance to jump aboard when you reach out and touch something. The next thing you know, you're rubbing your eye, scratching your nose, or touching your lips, and *BOOM!*—the virus has an invitation. So it's really important to keep your hands germ-free at all times. Wash!

TAKE a LOOK

After poking around in this section—and getting up close and personal with your body systems—take a good look at your personal health habits. How do you measure up? What are some things you can do to be as healthy as possible? What are your favorite "power" foods? What's your favorite way to exercise?

CHECK IT OUT!

When you wash your hands, be sure to use warm water and lots of soap—and take your time. Health experts say you should wash your hands for 20 seconds every time you come inside. Not sure how long 20 seconds is? Try singing "Happy Birthday" when you wash your hands. (Sing it softly or to yourself if others start to object!)

The Six Systems of the Human Body

Skeletal System

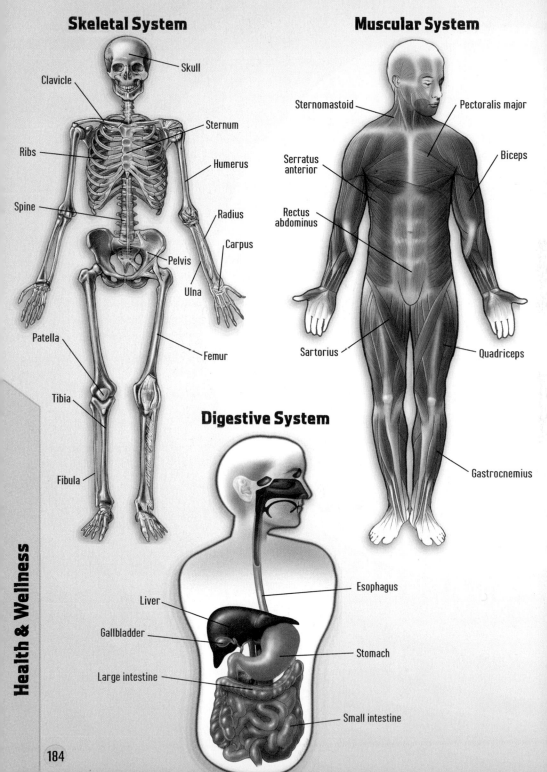

Skull
Clavicle
Sternum
Ribs
Humerus
Spine
Radius
Carpus
Pelvis
Ulna
Patella
Femur
Tibia
Fibula

Muscular System

Sternomastoid
Pectoralis major
Serratus anterior
Biceps
Rectus abdominus
Sartorius
Quadriceps
Gastrocnemius

Digestive System

Esophagus
Liver
Gallbladder
Stomach
Large intestine
Small intestine

Health & Wellness

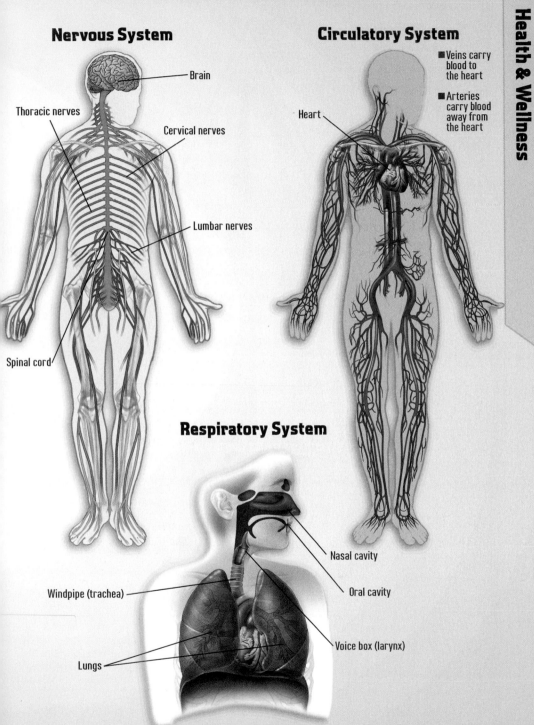

Nervous System

- Brain
- Thoracic nerves
- Cervical nerves
- Lumbar nerves
- Spinal cord

Circulatory System

- Heart

■ Veins carry blood to the heart

■ Arteries carry blood away from the heart

Respiratory System

- Nasal cavity
- Oral cavity
- Windpipe (trachea)
- Voice box (larynx)
- Lungs

The New Food Pyramid

In 2005, the U.S. Department of Agriculture (USDA) created a new food pyramid. The colored parts of the pyramid stand for different food groups. The width of each part shows what portion of your daily diet should be from that food group.

The amounts shown below are based on what a 12-year-old boy of average height and weight who is moderately active should eat every day. To figure out your own personal food pyramid plan, go to **www.mypyramid.gov**.

The most popular fruit in the world is one you may think is a vegetable—the tomato. Scientifically speaking, a tomato is considered a fruit because it comes from a flowering plant that contains seeds. Sixty million tons of tomatoes are produced every year.

CHECK IT OUT!

Grains	Vegetables	Fruits	Milk	Meat & Beans
Seven ounces of bread, cereal, crackers, rice, or pasta every day. At least half should be whole grains.	Three cups every day, fresh or frozen. Dark green, orange, light green—mix it up!	Two cups of nature's sweet treats a day. Go easy on the fruit juice.	Three cups a day. Choose nonfat or lowfat milk products.	Six ounces of lean protein a day: meat, fish, or poultry, or nuts, seeds, beans, and peas.

Oils Oils aren't a food group, but you need some for good health. Nuts and fish are good sources. Be sure to limit sugars and solid fats such as butter. Read the labels—you might be surprised!

Health & Wellness

Kids' Top 5 Favorite Activities

According to a survey by the Outdoor Foundation, these were the favorite activities of kids between ages 6 and 17 in 2009:

1. Bicycling   2. Running/ Jogging   3. Camping   4. Hiking   5. Skateboarding

The survey shows that more kids participated in certain outdoor activities, such as hiking and biking, than they did the year before. But overall, outdoor participation among kids ages 6 to 12 decreased more than 7 percent in 2008. Whatever your favorite activity is, go for it!

Your Amazing Body, by the Numbers

Your heart pumps blood along 60,000 miles (97,000 km) of veins and arteries. It beats 100,000 times a day—that's 40 million times a year and more than 3 billion times in an average lifetime.

Your brain weighs only about 3 pounds (1.4 kg), but it has about 100 billion nerve cells. Nerves help you think, move, dream, feel happy or sad, and regulate unconscious activities such as digesting food and breathing.

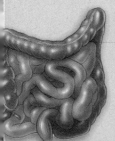

Your digestive system consists of about 30 feet (9 m) of tubes that carry food along a journey from top to bottom, squeezing out nutrients to keep you healthy and processing waste materials.

Your skin is your body's largest organ, weighing about 8 pounds (3.6 kg) and measuring about 22 square feet (2 sq m). Be good to your skin by keeping it clean and well protected from the Sun.

Inventors & Inventions

Flip a Switch and Say Thanks

From texting to snowboarding to brushing your teeth and even turning on a light, you've got an inventor to thank for almost everything you do. Sometimes you have more than one. For instance, without Benjamin Franklin, we'd still be in the dark. Franklin's famous experiment with lightning showed the world that this force was a form of electricity—a power that could be harnessed and used. Thomas Edison invented the electric lightbulb and lit up our world.

Phoning It In

Nowadays we take for granted how easy it is to chat or text on a cell phone. But someone had to invent the technology first. In this case it was Martin Cooper, in 1973. Actually, a hundred years before that you couldn't even talk on a regular telephone. Thank Alexander Graham Bell for changing all that.

Moving Along

Some inventions made it easier for us to get from one place to another:

- Richard Trevithick of England invented the locomotive in 1803.

- Gottlieb Daimler of Germany came up with the first gas-engine motorcycle in 1885. In Germany that same year, Karl Benz came up with the first automobile with an internal combustion engine.

- American Benjamin Holt made the first tractor in 1904.

- The Wright brothers, Wilbur and Orville, gave us the first airplane in 1903. (Thankfully, France's Louis-Sébastien Lenormand had already given the world the parachute in 1783!)

SWEET SURPRISES

Percy Lebaron Spencer had a chocolate bar in his pocket as he worked on a new technology for radar called magnetrons in 1945. The magnetrons melted the chocolate and got him thinking. Many experiments and two years later, he invented the first microwave oven! (It was as big as a full-size refrigerator.)

This kind of accidental discovery happens all the time in the process of inventing. It's called serendipity. Other accidental inventions were penicillin, vulcanized rubber, Velcro—and the Popsicle. The frozen fruit treat was accidentally invented in 1905 by 11-year-old Frank Epperson. Frank left his glass of fruit punch out on the porch with a stir stick in it. The weather turned cold; the punch froze with the stick in it; and the Epsicle ice pop was created. Epperson's children named it Popsicle for their dad many years later.

TAKE a LOOK

Take a look at your day. Make a list of all the inventions that impact you. Then have a peek through this section to see who's responsible for making it all possible. Can you come up with any new ideas for inventions to make your life better? Tastier? Comfier?

CHECK IT OUT!

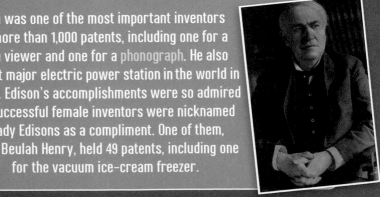

Thomas Edison was one of the most important inventors ever. He had more than 1,000 patents, including one for a motion picture viewer and one for a phonograph. He also set up the first major electric power station in the world in New York City. Edison's accomplishments were so admired that several successful female inventors were nicknamed Lady Edisons as a compliment. One of them, Beulah Henry, held 49 patents, including one for the vacuum ice-cream freezer.

3500 BCE
Wheeled vehicle
Mesopotamia

1590
Microscope
Zacharias Jansen

1783
Hot-air balloon
Joseph-Michel and
Jacques-Étienne Montgolfier

Date
Invention
Inventor / origin o

1608
Telescope
Hans Lippershey

900
Gunpowder
China

1785
Power loom
Edmund Cartwright

185
Elevator
Elisha

105 CE
Paper
China

1765
Steam engine
James Watt

1803
Steam locomotive
Richard Trevithick

1709
Piano
Bartolomeo
Cristofori

1839
Vulcanized rubber
Charles Goodyear

1821
Electric motor
Michael Faraday

640
Windmill
Persia

1835
Revolver
Samuel Colt

1447
Movable type
Johannes Gutenberg

1592
Thermometer
Galileo Galilei

1752
Lightning rod
Benjamin Franklin

1656
Pendulum clock
Christian Huygens

1783
Parachute
Louis-Sébastien
Lenormand

1793
Cotton gin
Eli Whitney

1829
Braille
Louis Braille

1846
Sewing machine
Elias Howe

1784
Bifocal lens
Benjamin Franklin

1816
Photography
Joseph Nicéphore Niépce

1837
Telegraph
Samuel Morse

1865
Antiseptic
Joseph Lister

186
Dynar
Alfred

CHECK IT OUT!

Robert Fulton launched the first commercially successful
steamship in the United States, the *Clermont*, in 1807. But Fulton did
not invent the steamship. Frenchman Claude de Jouffroy d'Abbans
is credited with building the first boat to run successfully on steam,
in 1783. In 1802, a Scottish inventor named William Symington built
a steam-powered tugboat that ran on the Forth and Clyde Canal. In
fact, inventors had been working with ways to use a steam engine
for marine power since the early 1700s.

Important Inventions and Their Inventors

These are just a few of the inventions that have shaped our world and changed our lives. The inventors listed are either those who received patents for the invention or the ones widely credited with introducing the version of the invention we use today. But in many cases, other inventors contributed to the invention by doing experiments or making earlier versions. Do some additional research for the whole story behind these inventions and others.

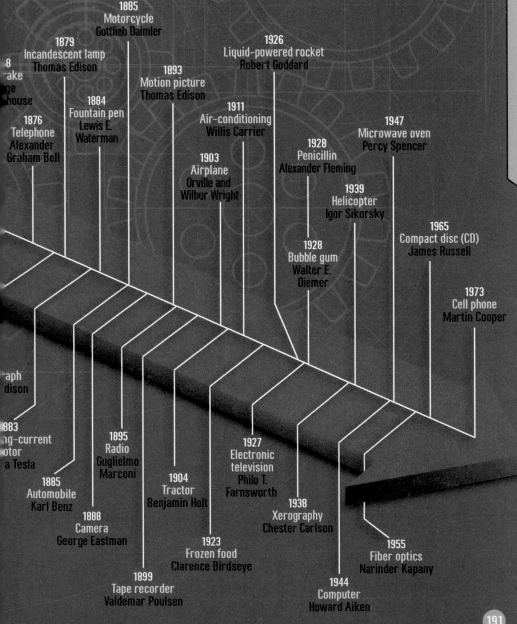

8
ake
ge
house

1876
Telephone
Alexander
Graham Bell

1879
Incandescent lamp
Thomas Edison

1884
Fountain pen
Lewis E.
Waterman

1885
Motorcycle
Gottlieb Daimler

1893
Motion picture
Thomas Edison

1903
Airplane
Orville and
Wilbur Wright

1911
Air-conditioning
Willis Carrier

1926
Liquid-powered rocket
Robert Goddard

1928
Penicillin
Alexander Fleming

1928
Bubble gum
Walter E.
Diemer

1939
Helicopter
Igor Sikorsky

1947
Microwave oven
Percy Spencer

1965
Compact disc (CD)
James Russell

1973
Cell phone
Martin Cooper

·aph
dison

·883
·ng-current
·otor
·a Tesla

1885
Automobile
Karl Benz

1888
Camera
George Eastman

1895
Radio
Guglielmo
Marconi

1904
Tractor
Benjamin Holt

1899
Tape recorder
Valdemar Poulsen

1923
Frozen food
Clarence Birdseye

1927
Electronic
television
Philo T.
Farnsworth

1938
Xerography
Chester Carlson

1944
Computer
Howard Aiken

1955
Fiber optics
Narinder Kapany

Languages

Hell

Hola

おはよう
ございま

你好

Bonso

Let's Talk

There are thousands of languages spoken around the world. A language is a system of communicating by using signals, sounds, or letters that all mean something. Language lets people express written and spoken thoughts in a way that can be understood by others. Though other animals may communicate with one another and with people, strictly speaking, language is thought to be mostly a human skill.

Speak English?

William Shakespeare was a poet and playwright in the late 16th and early 17th centuries. His words still communicate thoughts and ideas, but the English language has changed a lot since his time—and it's still changing. Grammar rules come and go, new words are adopted, and common phrases and sayings evolve. A language that is developing and changing is considered a living language. A language is considered dead when it is no longer spoken as a native language.

Take a look at the following sentences by Shakespeare. Can you match them up to the modern translations? (Answers are on page 350.)

Shakespeare

They that thrive well take counsel of their friends.

Stand and unfold thyself.

Mere prattle, without practice.

Headstrong liberty is lash'd with woe.

Modern

It's all just talk.

Too much freedom can be trouble.

Tell me who you are.

It's good to get advice from your friends.

TALK AMERICA

Most Americans speak English at home, but it's certainly not the only language spoken in the United States. The history of our country begins with people coming here from all over the world. As a result, our country is a rich blend of many languages. Spanish, Chinese, French, and German are just a few of the languages being spoken in our schools and homes.

TAKE a LOOK

Hi may mean "hello" to English speakers, but to the Japanese *hai* also means "yes." Take a look at pages 195 and 196 to see if you can tell your *dōmo* from your *gogo*.

안녕하세요

שָׁלוֹם

Ciao

Aloha

CHECK IT OUT !

unfriend, v.
To remove someone as a friend on a social network such as Facebook

Have you unfriended anyone lately—or been unfriended yourself? Don't worry—it happens all the time. In fact, unfriending has become so common that in 2009 Oxford University Press listed *unfriend* as a new English word in the *Oxford English Dictionary*, along with *blogosphere* and others.

193

Common Words and Phrases in Select Languages

MANDARIN CHINESE

Hello	Ni hao (nee how)
Good-bye	Zài jiàn (zay GEE-en)
Yes	Shide (SURE-due)
No	Bu shi (BOO sure)
Please	Qing (ching)
Thank you	Xièxiè (shieh-shieh)
You're welcome	Búkèqi (boo-keh-chee)
Excuse me	Duìbúqi (doo-ee-boo-chee)

SPANISH

Hello	Hola (OH-lah)
Good-bye	Adiós (ah-dee-OHSS)
Good morning	Buenas días (BWAY-nahs DEE-ahs)
Good afternoon	Buenas tardes (BWAY-nahs TAHR-dehs)
Good evening	Buenas noches (BWAY-nahs NOH-chehs)
Yes	Sí (SEE)
No	No (NOH)
Please	Por favor (por fa-VOHR)
Thank you	Gracias (GRAH-see-ahs)
You're welcome	De nada (DE nada)
What's going on?	¿Qué pasa? (kay PAH-sah)
How are you?	¿Cómo está usted? (COH-mo es-TAH oo-STEHD)

GERMAN

Hello	Guten Tag (GOO-tin TAHK)
Good-bye	Auf Wiedersehen (ahf VEE-dehr-zeh-hehn)
Good morning	Guten Morgen (GOO-tin MOR-gun)
Yes	Ja (yah)
No	Nein (nain)
Please	Bitte (BIT-uh)
Thank you	Danke (DAHN-keh)
You're welcome	Bitte schön (BIT-uh shane)

Privet!

góðan dag

salut

ITALIAN

Hi, 'bye (informal)	
Good-bye	Arrivederci (ah-ree-vay-
Good morning, good afternoon, or a general hello	Buon giorno (bwoh
Yes	Sì (SEE)
No	No (NOH)
Please	Per favore (purr fa-VO-ray)
Thank you	Grazie (GRAH-tsee-ay)
You're welcome	Prego (PRAY-go)
How are you?	Come sta? (KOH-may STAH)
Fine, very well	Molto bene (MOHL-toh BAY-nay)
Excuse me	Scusi (SKOO-zee)

EGYPTIAN ARABIC

Good morning	Sabah el khair (sa-BAH el KHAIR)
Good-bye	Ma salama (MA sa-LA-ma)
Yes	Aiwa (aye-wa)
No	La (la)
Please	Min fadlak (min FAD-lak)
Thank you	Shukran (SHU-kran)
No problem	Ma fee mushkila (ma FEE mush-KI-la)
How are you?	Izzayak? (iz-ZAY-ak)
What is your name?	Ismak ay? (IS-mak AY)

JAPANESE

Hi	Konnichiwa (koh-nee-chee-wah)
Good-bye	Ja mata (jahh mah-tah)
Yes	Hai (hah-ee)
No	Iie (EE-eh)
Good morning	Ohayō gozaimasu (oh-hah-yohh goh-zah-ee-mahs)
Excuse me	Sumimasen (soo-mee-mah-sehn)
Pleased to meet you	Yoroshiku (yoh-roh-shee-koo)
One	Ichi (ee-chee)
Thank you	Dōmo arigatō (dohh-moh ah-ri-gah-toh)

hoi

195

FRENCH

Hello	Bonjour (bohn-zhoor)
Good-bye	Au revoir (oh reh-vwah)
Yes	Oui (wee)
No	Non (no)
Excuse me	Pardonnez-moi (par-dough-nay mwah)
Please	S'il vous plaît (see voo play)
Thank you	Merci (mare-SEE)
How are you?	Comment allez-vous? (co-mahn-tah-lay voo)

KOREAN

Hello	Anyŏng haseyo (ahn-n'yohng hah-say-yoh)
Good-bye	Anyŏng-hi kyeseyo (ahn-n'yohng-he kuh-say-yoh)
Please	Jwe-song-ha-ji-mahn (chey-song-hah-gee-mon)
Thank you	Kamsahamnida (kahm-sah-hahm-need-dah)
Excuse me	Miam hamnida (Me-ahn hahm-nee-dah)
One	Hana (hah-nah)
Ten	Yeol (yuhl)

xin chào

Hi

NIGERIAN
(four of the major Nigerian language groups)

English	Fulani	Hausa	Ibo	Yoruba
I'm fine	Jam tan (JAM-taan)	Kalau (KA-lay-U)	Adimnma (ah-DEE-mm-NMAA)	A dupe (ah-DEW-pa
one	gogo (GO-quo)	daya (DA-ya)	otu (o-TOO)	eni (EE-nee)
two	didi (DEE-dee)	biyu (BEE-you)	abua (ah-BOO-ah)	eji (EE-gee)
three	tati (TA-tea)	uku (OO-coo)	ato (ah-TOE)	eta (EE-ta)
nine	jeenayi (gee-NA-yee)	tara (TAA-ra)	iteghete (IT-egg-HE-tee)	esan (EE-san)
ten	sappo (SAP-poe)	goma (GO-ma)	iri (EE-ree)	ewa (EE-wa)

Languages

196

Which Languages Are Spoken Most?

The following languages have the most speakers in the world. The languages combine individual varieties and dialects that may have different names. The numbers include only first-language (mother-tongue) speakers.

Language	Estimated Number of Speakers (in millions)
Chinese	1,213
Spanish	329
English	328
Arabic	221
Hindi	182
Bengali	181
Portuguese	178
Russian	144
Japanese	122
German	90
Javanese	85
Abaza	83
Lahnda	78
Telugu	70
Vietnamese	69
French	68
Marathi	68
Korean	66
Tamil	66
Italian	62
Urdu	61

dzień dobry

talofa

hej

alô

CHECK IT OUT!

Portugal isn't the only place where people speak Portuguese. About 150 million people speak it in Brazil, where it is the official language.

Math

Got Your Number

Humans have been using numbers to help understand the world around them for a very long time—about 20,000 years, according to some scientists. That's the estimated age of a bone tool with three carved columns of numbers found in the Congo area of Africa in 1960. Called the Ishango bone, the relic is thought by some mathematicians to be a kind of ancient calculator—proof that even way back then, people knew how to multiply.

Give Us a Hand

Over many thousands of years, numerical systems kept developing. One ancient Egyptian system used straight lines to represent small numbers and a special mark for the number ten. In the seventh century, scholars in India invented a system in which all numbers were made from only ten symbols—0, 1, 2, 3, 4, 5, 6, 7, 8, and 9. This was the basis for the decimal system we use today.

Why ten? It's the number of fingers on our two hands. In fact, another word for both numbers and fingers is *digits*.

It All Adds Up

Today we use numbers all day long, in countless activities.

- "I am 12 years old."
- "Will we be there in 20 minutes?"
- "Hey! Who ate three-quarters of my pizza?"

Even tiny numbers can be important. A split second can be the difference between an Olympic gold medal and a so-so finish. The circumference of an NCAA regulation basketball can't be greater than 30 inches (76.2 cm).

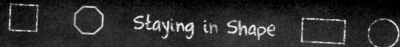

Staying in Shape

But math goes way beyond numbers. The octagon-shaped stop sign, the circular wheel on your bike, the rectangle of your desk—they're examples of a part of math called geometry. Buildings, cars, trains, planes, and even toys involve structure, which depends on math, too. And then there's logic—drawing conclusions that make sense about time, distance, money, and so many other things. We use math theories to predict and describe everything from which TV shows people will watch to where the tennis player will hit the ball to how people will spend their money. You name the process—it starts with math.

TAKE a LOOK

Browse through this chapter and then write down all the ways math enters into your daily life. Include whole numbers, fractions, decimals, minutes, hours, geometric shapes, notes on a musical scale, percentages, estimates, and so on. If you have any time left over, start counting to one million. It should take you about 12 days. If you still have time on your hands, count to one billion. Allowing one second per count, it will take about 32 years.

The googol is the number 1 followed by 100 zeros (see below). Mathematicians say that the googolplex, the number 1 followed by a googol of zeros, is the largest named number in the world.

10,000,000,000,000,000,000,000,000,000
,000,000,000,000,000,000,000,000,
000,000,000,000,000,000,000,000,000,
000,000,000,000,000,000,000

CHECK IT OUT!

MULTIPLICATION TABLE

	1	2	3	4	5	6	7	8	9	10	11	12
1	1	2	3	4	5	6	7	8	9	10	11	12
2	2	4	6	8	10	12	14	16	18	20	22	24
3	3	6	9	12	15	18	21	24	27	30	33	36
4	4	8	12	16	20	24	28	32	36	40	44	48
5	5	10	15	20	25	30	35	40	45	50	55	60
6	6	12	18	24	30	36	42	48	54	60	66	72
7	7	14	21	28	35	42	49	56	63	70	77	84
8	8	16	24	32	40	48	56	64	72	80	88	96
9	9	18	27	36	45	54	63	72	81	90	99	108
10	10	20	30	40	50	60	70	80	90	100	110	120
11	11	22	33	44	55	66	77	88	99	110	121	132
12	12	24	36	48	60	72	84	96	108	120		144

Squares and Square Roots

Multiplying a number by itself is also called squaring it (or raising it to its second power). For example, 3 squared (3^2) is 9. By the same token, the square root of 9 is 3. The symbol for square root is called a radical sign ($\sqrt{}$).

Examples of Squaring

2 squared: $2^2 = 2 \times 2 = 4$

3 squared: $3^2 = 3 \times 3 = 9$

4 squared: $4^2 = 4 \times 4 = 16$

Examples of Square Roots

Square root of 16: $\sqrt{16} = 4$

Square root of 9: $\sqrt{9} = 3$

Square root of 4: $\sqrt{4} = 2$

SQUARE ROOTS TO 40

$\sqrt{1} = 1$	$\sqrt{36} = 6$	$\sqrt{121} = 11$	$\sqrt{256} = 16$	$\sqrt{441} = 21$	$\sqrt{676} = 26$	$\sqrt{961} = 31$	$\sqrt{1,296} = 36$
$\sqrt{4} = 2$	$\sqrt{49} = 7$	$\sqrt{144} = 12$	$\sqrt{289} = 17$	$\sqrt{484} = 22$	$\sqrt{729} = 27$	$\sqrt{1,024} = 32$	$\sqrt{1,369} = 37$
$\sqrt{9} = 3$	$\sqrt{64} = 8$	$\sqrt{169} = 13$	$\sqrt{324} = 18$	$\sqrt{529} = 23$	$\sqrt{784} = 28$	$\sqrt{1,089} = 33$	$\sqrt{1,444} = 38$
$\sqrt{16} = 4$	$\sqrt{81} = 9$	$\sqrt{196} = 14$	$\sqrt{361} = 19$	$\sqrt{576} = 24$	$\sqrt{841} = 29$	$\sqrt{1,156} = 34$	$\sqrt{1,521} = 39$
$\sqrt{25} = 5$	$\sqrt{100} = 10$	$\sqrt{225} = 15$	$\sqrt{400} = 20$	$\sqrt{625} = 25$	$\sqrt{900} = 30$	$\sqrt{1,225} = 35$	$\sqrt{1,600} = 40$

Some Mathematical Formulas

To find the CIRCUMFERENCE of a:
- Circle—Multiply the diameter by π

To find the AREA of a:
- Circle—Multiply the square of the radius by π
- Rectangle—Multiply the base by the height
- Sphere (surface)—Multiply the square of the radius by π and multiply by 4
- Square—Square the length of one side
- Trapezoid—Add the two parallel sides, multiply by the height, and divide by 2
- Triangle—Multiply the base by the height and divide by 2

π (pi) = 3.1416
(See page 204.)

To find the VOLUME of a:
- Cone—Multiply the square of the radius of the base by π, multiply by the height, and divide by 3
- Cube—Cube (raise to the third power) the length of one edge
- Cylinder—Multiply the square of the radius of the base by π and multiply by the height
- Pyramid—Multiply the area of the base by the height and divide by 3
- Rectangular prism—Multiply the length by the width by the height
- Sphere—Multiply the cube of the radius by π, multiply by 4, and divide by 3

LARGE NUMBERS AND HOW MANY ZEROS THEY CONTAIN

million	6	1,000,000
billion	9	1,000,000,000
trillion	12	1,000,000,000,000
quadrillion	15	1,000,000,000,000,000
quintillion	18	1,000,000,000,000,000,000

sextillion	21	1,000,000,000,000,000,000,000
septillion	24	1,000,000,000,000,000,000,000,000
octillion	27	1,000,000,000,000,000,000,000,000,000
nonillion	30	1,000,000,000,000,000,000,000,000,000,000
decillion	33	1,000,000,000,000,000,000,000,000,000,000,000

NUMBERS GLOSSARY

COUNTING NUMBERS
Counting numbers, or natural numbers, begin with the number 1 and continue into infinity.

WHOLE NUMBERS
Whole numbers are the same as counting numbers, except that the set of whole numbers begins with 0.

INTEGERS
Integers include 0, all counting numbers (called positive whole numbers), and all whole numbers less than 0 (called negative whole numbers).

RATIONAL NUMBERS
Rational numbers include any number that can be written in the form of a fraction (or a ratio), as long as the denominator (the bottom number of the fraction) is not equal to 0. All counting numbers and whole numbers are also rational numbers because all counting numbers and whole numbers can be written as fractions with a denominator equal to 1.

PRIME NUMBERS
Prime numbers are counting numbers that can be divided by only two numbers: 1 and themselves.

Prime numbers between 1 and 1,000
2, 3, 5, 7, 11, 13, 17, 19, 23, 29, 31, 37, 41, 43, 47, 53, 59, 61, 67, 71, 73, 79, 83, 89, 97, 101, 103, 107, 109, 113, 127, 131, 137, 139, 149, 151, 157, 163, 167, 173, 179, 181, 191, 193, 197, 199, 211, 223, 227, 229, 233, 239, 241, 251, 257, 263, 269, 271, 277, 281, 283, 293, 307, 311, 313, 317, 331, 337, 347, 349, 353, 359, 367, 373, 379, 383, 389, 397, 401, 409, 419, 421, 431, 433, 439, 443, 449, 457, 461, 463, 467, 479, 487, 491, 499, 503, 509, 521, 523, 541, 547, 557, 563, 569, 571, 577, 587, 593, 599, 601, 607, 613, 617, 619, 631, 641, 643, 647, 653, 659, 661, 673, 677, 683, 691, 701, 709, 719, 727, 733, 739, 743, 751, 757, 761, 769, 773, 787, 797, 809, 811, 821, 823, 827, 829, 839, 853, 857, 859, 863, 877, 881, 883, 887, 907, 911, 919, 929, 937, 941, 947, 953, 967, 971, 977, 983, 991, 997

COMPOSITE NUMBERS
Composite numbers are all counting numbers that are not prime numbers. In other words, composite numbers are numbers that have more than two factors. The number 1, because it has only one factor (itself), is not a composite number.

Composite numbers between 1 and 100
4, 6, 8, 9, 10, 12, 14, 15, 16, 18, 20, 21, 22, 24, 25, 26, 27, 28, 30, 32, 33, 34, 35, 36, 38, 39, 40, 42, 44, 45, 46, 48, 49, 50, 51, 52, 54, 55, 56, 57, 58, 60, 62, 63, 64, 65, 66, 68, 69, 70, 72, 74, 75, 76, 77, 78, 80, 81, 82, 84, 85, 86, 87, 88, 90, 91, 92, 93, 94, 95, 96, 98, 99, 100

Roman Numerals

I	1	XI	11	CD	400
II	2	XIX	19	D	500
III	3	XX	20	CM	900
IV	4	XXX	30	M	1,000
V	5	XL	40	$\overline{V}$	5,000
VI	6	L	50	$\overline{X}$	10,000
VII	7	LX	60	$\overline{L}$	50,000
VIII	8	XC	90	$\overline{C}$	100,000
IX	9	C	100	$\overline{D}$	500,000
X	10	CC	200	$\overline{M}$	1,000,000

Fractions, Decimals, and Percents

To find the equivalent of a fraction in decimal form, divide the numerator (top number) by the denominator (bottom number). To change from a decimal to a percent, multiply by 100. To change from a percent to a decimal, divide by 100.

Fraction	Decimal	Percent
1/16 (= 2/32)	0.0625	6.25
1/8 (= 2/16)	0.125	12.5
3/16 (= 6/32)	0.1875	18.75
1/4 (= 2/8; = 4/16)	0.25	25.0
5/16 (= 10/32)	0.3125	31.25
1/3 (= 2/6; = 4/12)	0.333	33.3
3/8 (= 6/16)	0.375	37.5
7/16 (= 14/32)	0.4375	43.75
1/2 (= 2/4; = 4/8; = 8/16)	0.5	50.0
9/16 (= 18/32)	0.5625	56.25
5/8 (= 10/16)	0.625	62.5
2/3 (= 4/6; = 8/12)	0.666	66.6
11/16 (= 22/32)	0.6875	68.75
3/4 (= 6/8; = 12/16)	0.75	75.0
13/16 (= 26/32)	0.8125	81.25
7/8 (= 14/16)	0.875	87.5
15/16 (= 30/32)	0.9375	93.75
1 (= 2/2; = 4/4; = 8/8; = 16/16)	1.0	100.0

Geometry Glossary

Term	Definition	
Acute angle	Any angle that measures less than 90°	
Angle	Two rays that have the same endpoint form an angle	
Area	The amount of surface inside a closed figure	
Chord	A line segment whose endpoints are on a circle	
Circumference	The distance around a circle	
Congruent figures	Geometric figures that are the same size and shape	
Degree (angle)	A unit for measuring angles	45°
Diameter	A chord that passes through the center of a circle	
Endpoint	The end of a line segment	
Line of symmetry	A line that divides a figure into two identical parts if the figure is folded along the line	
Obtuse angle	Any angle that measures greater than 90°	
Perimeter	The distance around the outside of a plane figure	
Pi (π)	The ratio of the circumference of a circle to its diameter; when rounded to the nearest hundredth, pi equals 3.14	
Polygon	A simple closed figure whose sides are straight lines	
Protractor	An instrument used to measure angles	
Quadrilateral	A polygon with four sides	
Radius	A straight line that connects the center of a circle to any point on the circumference of the circle	
Ray	A straight line with one endpoint	
Rectangle	A four-sided figure with four right angles	
Right angle	An angle that measures 90°	
Square	A rectangle with congruent sides and 90° angles in all four corners	
Surface area	The total outside area of an object	
Symmetrical	A figure that, when folded along a line of symmetry, has two halves that superimpose exactly on each other	
Triangle	A three-sided figure	
Vertex	The common endpoint of two or more rays that form angles	
Vertices	The plural of vertex	

All About Polygons

Polygons are two-dimensional, or flat, shapes formed from three or more line segments.

Examples

Triangles

Triangles are polygons that have three sides and three vertices; the common endpoints of two or more rays form angles.

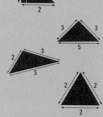

- **Right triangles** are formed when two of three line segments meet in a 90° angle. In a right triangle, the longest side has a special name: the hypotenuse.

- **Isosceles triangles** have two sides of equal length.

- **Scalene triangles** have no sides of equal length.

- **Equilateral triangles** have three sides of equal length.

Quadrilaterals

Quadrilaterals are polygons that have four sides and four vertices.

- **Trapezoids** are quadrilaterals that have one pair of parallel sides.

- **Parallelograms** are quadrilaterals that have parallel line segments in both pairs of opposite sides.

- **Rectangles** are parallelograms formed by line segments that meet at right angles. A rectangle always has four right angles.

- **Squares** are rectangles that have sides of equal length and four right angles.

- **Rhombuses** are parallelograms that have sides of equal length but don't meet at right angles.

Circles

A circle is a set of points within a plane. Each point on the circle is at an equal distance from a common point inside the circle called the center.

The distance from the center of the circle to any point on the circle is called the radius (r = radius).

A line segment drawn through the center of the circle to points on either side of the circle is called the diameter (d = diameter). The circle is bisected, or cut in two equal parts, along the diameter line. Diameter is equal to two times the radius (2r = diameter).

The distance around the circle is called the circumference (πd or π2r = circumference).

Military

In Our Defense

Armed forces have been part of human history since the time of ancient Assyria, Egypt, China, Greece, and Rome—and probably before. A nation's military protects, defends, and maintains security for its political interests, land, and citizens. In the United States, the military accomplishes those goals through five branches: the Army, Navy, Air Force, Marines, and Coast Guard.

Large Armies—or None at All

The United States and other world powers have armed forces numbering in the millions, but some countries rely on small groups or civilian militias. Others have no military at all. For example, Costa Rica formally abolished the military in its constitution. The island nations of Nauru and Palau have no armies of their own, but are protected by the militaries of Australia and the United States.

Growth of a Military

The first U.S. military was the Continental Army, formed in 1775 to fight for independence from England. In 1898, the United States became a world power when it fought in the Spanish-American War. Since then it has fought many times alongside other leading nations to protect against threats to world peace.

FINAL RESTING PLACE

Brigadier General Montgomery C. Meigs established Arlington National Cemetery in 1864. Today it is the final resting ground for more than 300,000 war veterans, casualties of wars (including the wars in Iraq and Afghanistan), presidents, explorers, and notable Americans. The most visited site is the Tomb of the Unknowns, which honors unidentified members of the military lost in battle.

TAKE a LOOK

Every man and woman who serves in the U.S. military deserves the respect and thanks of its citizens. For particularly brave actions, some members of the military are honored with medals such as the Purple Heart. What is the highest military medal? See the full list on page 209.

CHECK IT OUT!

The Army and Air Force National Guard is a reserve force of about 500,000 members who perform peacetime duties and can be called into active service in a crisis or emergency.

Best-Armed Nations*

The world's strongest militaries are built with manpower, financial resources, training, and equipment.

Country	Armed Forces	Annual Defense Budget	Air Force Planes	Navy Ships
United States	1,385,122	$607 billion	22,700	1,600
China	2,255,000	$84.9 billion	2,400	760
Russia	1,245,000	$58.6 billion	6,500	760
India	1,325,000	$30.0 billion	1,250	145
United Kingdom	195,000	$65.3 billion	2,670	140
France	225,000	$65.7 billion	1,900	135
Germany	250,000	$46.8 billion	1,100	130
Brazil	287,000	$23.3 billion	1,650	90
Japan	239,000	$46.3 billion	2,700	150
Turkey	958,000	$14.5 billion	1,530	180

*All figures are approximate

Bring in the 'Bots

In today's military, high-tech devices help keep humans out of harm's way.

Explosive Ordinance Disposal (EOD) is a military unit that consists of robots designed to handle chemical, biological, radiological, nuclear, and explosive threats.

Precision Urban Hopper is a GPS-guided robot that can hop more than 25 feet (7.6 m) in the air, allowing it to jump over fences and barricades. It's designed especially to be used in cities.

MQ-1 Predator is a plane that can be piloted remotely for surveillance and attack.

Branches of the U.S. Military

Army
The oldest and largest branch of the United States military serves to defend and protect the nation at home and abroad. The most elite units, Army Rangers and Special Forces, train in advanced combat methods.

Navy
Members are especially skilled to handle any operations on and under the sea and in the air. Navy Divers and SEALs undergo specialized training for the most complex warfare operations.

Marines
The smallest branch of the nation's military is known for being the first on the ground in combat. Marines live by a strict code of honor, courage, and commitment.

Air Force
The technologically advanced members of the Air Force specialize in air and space operations to protect American interests.

Coast Guard
During peacetime, this branch protects national waterways, providing law enforcement, environmental cleanup, as well as search and rescue operations. During wartime, Coast Guard members serve with the Navy.

Beyond the Call of Duty

Military medals, or decorations, are awarded for bravery in and out of combat, loss of life or injury in combat, and other reasons. Most medals can be awarded to a member of any branch of the armed forces. The top 12 awards are listed in order, beginning with the highest.

Military Medals
1. Medal of Honor
2. Army Distinguished Service Cross, Navy Cross, Air Force Cross
3. Distinguished Service Medal
4. Silver Star
5. Defense Superior Service Medal
6. Legion of Merit
7. Distinguished Flying Cross
8. Soldier's Medal, Navy and Marine Corps Medal, Airman's Medal, Coast Guard Medal
9. Gold Lifesaving Medal
10. Bronze Star
11. Purple Heart
12. Defense Meritorious Service Medal

CHECK IT OUT!

Liquid Body Armor is made of Kevlar soaked with Shear Thickening Fluid (STF), silica particles mixed with polyethylene glycol. The material's liquid form makes it lightweight and flexible, but it hardens in milliseconds if struck by a bullet or shrapnel.

Movies & TV

Now Available on DVD and Blu-ray from Twentieth Century Fox Home Entertainment

True Blue

Last year, *blue* meant "green" at the box office—*blue* as in *Avatar*, and *green* as in money. Director James Cameron's epic story about a race of towering blue humanoids on the planet Pandora and their fight to save their unspoiled environment raked in out-of-this-world piles of cash. As of March 2010, *Avatar* had earned $1.85 billion at the box office, beating Cameron's previous smash hit, *Titanic*, to become the most financially successful film in history.

In Your Face

If blue was the top color at the movies, three was the magic number. Three-dimensional, or 3-D, films such as *Avatar*, *Monsters vs. Aliens*, and *Up* pulled eager audiences out of their seats and into the action. If you like the in-your-face technique, there's lots more coming. Disney Studios announced that all of its animated movies will be released in 3-D in the future.

New Technology, Old Shows

More networks broadcast in high definition (HD) last year, but favorite shows remained the same: *American Idol*, *Dancing with the Stars*, and crime shows like *NCIS* nailed down the top ratings. *American Idol* got a new judge, Ellen DeGeneres, who replaced Paula Abdul.

One, Two, Three-D

The glasses look different today, but 3-D movies are not new. In the early 1950s, Hollywood producers were looking for something new to lure people away from their new television sets and back into movie theaters. They released several films in 3-D, including *House of Wax*, a creepy horror film starring Vincent Price as a mad sculptor who turns his victims into wax statues. It was immensely popular and has become a classic. You can see it today on DVD.

TAKE a LOOK

Which stars and shows did kids like best in 2009? Learn who won the Nickelodeon Kids' Choice and Teen Choice Awards. If you didn't vote this year, discover how you can make your voice heard next time around. See pages 213–215.

CHECK IT OUT !

Three of the top-grossing movies in 2009 were adapted from books: *Harry Potter and the Half-Blood Prince*, *The Twilight Saga: New Moon*, and *The Blind Side*.

Ellen DeGeneres

Movies

10 Top-Grossing Movies of 2009*

Movie	Box-Office Receipts
1. *Transformers: Revenge of the Fallen*	$402,100,000
2. *Harry Potter and the Half-Blood Prince*	$302,000,000
3. *Up*	$293,000,000
4. *The Twilight Saga: New Moon*	$284,600,000
5. *Avatar*	$283,800,000
6. *The Hangover*	$277,400,000
7. *Star Trek*	$256,700,000
8. *The Blind Side*	$209,100,000
9. *Monsters vs. Aliens*	$198,400,000
10. *Ice Age: Dawn of the Dinosaurs*	$196,600,000

*Figures are as of January, 2010

Sandra Bullock

2010 Oscar Winners

Best Picture: *The Hurt Locker*

Best Director: Katherine Bigelow, *The Hurt Locker*

Best Actor: Jeff Bridges, *Crazy Heart*

Best Supporting Actor: Christoph Waltz, *Inglourious Basterds*

Best Actress: Sandra Bullock, *The Blind Side*

Best Supporting Actress: Mo'Nique, *Precious*

Best Animated Film: *Up*

Best Foreign Film: *The Secret in Their Eyes*, Argentina

Best Original Screenplay: *The Hurt Locker*, Mark Boal

Best Adapted Screenplay: *Precious*, Geoffrey Fletcher

2010 Golden Globe Winners
Best Picture, Drama: *Avatar*
Best Actor, Drama: Jeff Bridges, *Crazy Heart*
Best Actress, Drama: Sandra Bullock, *The Blind Side*
Best Picture, Comedy or Musical: *The Hangover*
Best Actor, Comedy or Musical: Robert Downey Jr., *Sherlock Holmes*
Best Actress, Comedy or Musical: Meryl Streep, *Julie & Julia*
Best Director: James Cameron, *Avatar*
Best Supporting Actor: Christoph Waltz, *Inglourious Basterds*
Best Supporting Actress: Mo'Nique, *Precious*
Best Animated Film: *Up*
Best Foreign Film: *The White Ribbon*, Germany
Best Screenplay: *Up in the Air*, Jason Reitman and Sheldon Turner

2009 Nickelodeon Kids' Choice Awards Movie Winners
Favorite Movie: *Alvin and the Chipmunks: The Squeakquel*
Favorite Movie Actor: Taylor Lautner
Favorite Movie Actress: Miley Cyrus
Favorite Animated Movie: *Up*
Favorite Voice from an Animated Movie: Jim Carrey

Taylor Lautner

2009 Teen Choice Awards Movie Winners
Fresh Face, Female: Ashley Greene
Fresh Face, Male: Taylor Lautner
Villain: Cam Gigandet
Actress, Music/Dance: Miley Cyrus
Actor, Music/Dance: Zac Efron
Actress, Comedy: Anne Hathaway
Actor, Comedy: Zac Efron
Actress, Action Adventure: Jordana Brewster
Actor, Action Adventure: Hugh Jackman
Actress, Drama: Kristen Stewart
Actor, Drama: Robert Pattinson
Horror/Thriller: *Friday the 13th*
Comedy: *Night at the Museum: Battle of the Smithsonian*
Music/Dance: *High School Musical 3: Senior Year*
Action Adventure: *X-Men Origins: Wolverine*
Drama: *Twilight*
Bromantic Comedy: *Marley & Me*
Romance: *Twilight*

ne Hathaway

213

Television

Most-Watched TV Shows of 2009

American Idol
Dancing with the Stars
NBC Sunday Night Football
NCIS: Los Angeles
NCIS
NFL Regular Season
The Good Wife

Ryan Seacrest

2009 Emmy Award Winners

Outstanding Series, Drama: *Mad Men*
Outstanding Series, Comedy: *30 Rock*
Outstanding Reality Program, Competition: *The Amazing Race*
Outstanding Actor, Drama: Bryan Cranston, *Breaking Bad*
Outstanding Actress, Drama: Glenn Close, *Damages*
Outstanding Actor, Comedy: Alec Baldwin, *30 Rock*
Outstanding Actress, Comedy: Toni Collette, *United States of Tara*
Outstanding Supporting Actor, Drama: Michael Emerson, *Lost*
Outstanding Supporting Actress, Drama: Cherry Jones, *24*
Outstanding Supporting Actor, Comedy: Jon Cryer, *Two and a Half Men*
Outstanding Supporting Actress, Comedy: Kristin Chenoweth, *Pushing Daisies*

2009 Nickelodeon Kids' Choice Awards TV Winners

Favorite TV Show: *iCarly*
Favorite Reality Show: *American Idol*
Favorite TV Actor: Dylan Sprouse
Favorite TV Actress: Selena Gomez
Favorite Cartoon: *SpongeBob SquarePants*

Dylan and Cole Sprouse

2009 Teen Choice Awards
TV Winners

Breakout Female: Demi Lovato
Breakout Male: Frankie Jonas
Breakout Show: *J.O.N.A.S.*
Villain: Ed Westwick
Personality: Ryan Seacrest
Actress, Comedy: Miley Cyrus
Actor, Comedy: Jonas Brothers
Actress, Action Adventure: Hayden Panettiere
Actor, Action Adventure: Tom Welling
Actress, Drama: Leighton Meester
Actor, Drama: Chace Crawford
Female, Reality/Variety: Lauren Conrad
Male, Reality/Variety: Adam Lambert
Comedy: *Hannah Montana*
Action Adventure: *Heroes*
Drama: *Gossip Girl*
Reality: *The Hills*
Reality Competition: *American Idol*
Animated Show: *SpongeBob SquarePants*

Demi Lovato

CHECK IT OUT !

More than 115 million votes were cast for the 2010 Nickelodeon Kids' Choice Awards. If yours wasn't one of them, don't miss your chance next year. Learn how to cast a vote for your favorites at www.nick.com.

Music & Dance

A Swift Rise to Stardom

Taylor Alison Swift was born in Wyomissing, Pennsylvania, on December 13, 1989. She started writing songs and singing at festivals and fairs when she was 10. At age 14, she became the youngest staff songwriter hired by a music publishing branch of Sony. At 16, she made her first album and was well on her way to stardom. Her second album, *Fearless*, was released when she was 19. It sold 3.2 million copies in 2009, becoming the bestselling album of the year. What's the secret to Taylor's phenomenal success?

For one thing, her music has crossover appeal. Fans of both country and pop music love it equally. Also, her songs are both personal and universal. She sings about situations teens and young people can relate to, like having a crush on someone who doesn't care about you. She says, "If you listen to my album, it's like reading my diary." It's a formula that seems to work for the queen of country/pop.

No One Passes These Peas!

The Black Eyed Peas had the top two most digitally downloaded songs of 2009. Topping the charts is nothing new for the hip-hop/pop group whose members include Fergie, will.i.am, Taboo, and Apl.de.ap. Since the Black Eyed Peas formed in 1995, they've sold 56 million albums and singles.

Catching Bieber Fever

Sixteen-year-old Canadian pop superstar Justin Bieber's name isn't Gaga, but fans go wild for him just the same. So many "Biebettes" flocked to buy his album *My World 2.0* that it zoomed to the top of the charts as soon as it came out. Last year, a car he was riding in was dented by girls who jumped on it, trying to get closer. Justin's career got its start when he was 12, and his mom posted videos of him singing on YouTube for family and friends.

TAKE a LOOK

In the 1970s, Donny Osmond was a teenage pop star and host of a TV show with his sister, Marie. Last year, Donny scored on TV again, this time as the celebrity winner of *Dancing with the Stars*.

92150123 - "Adam Larkey" © ABC/Gettyimages

As of spring 2010, Justin Bieber's YouTube channel had 162 million views—more than half the population of the United States.

CHECK IT OUT !

Top 10 Albums of 2009

Album	Artist
Fearless	Taylor Swift
I Dreamed a Dream	Susan Boyle
Number Ones	Michael Jackson
The Fame	Lady Gaga
My Christmas	Andrea Bocelli
Hannah Montana: The Movie	Miley Cyrus
The E.N.D.	The Black Eyed Peas
Relapse	Eminem
The Blueprint 3	Jay-Z
Only by the Night	Kings of Leon

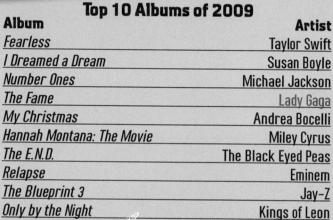

Top 10 Digitally Downloaded Songs of 2009

Song	Artist
"Boom Boom Pow"	The Black Eyed Peas
"I Gotta Feeling"	The Black Eyed Peas
"Poker Face"	Lady Gaga
"Right Round"	Flo Rida
"Just Dance"	Lady Gaga, featuring Colby O'Donis
"Party in the U.S.A."	Miley Cyrus
"Down"	Jay Sean
"Gives You Hell"	The All-American Rejects
"Fireflies"	Owl City
"Whatcha Say"	Jason DeRulo

2010 Grammy Award Winners

Record of the Year: "Use Somebody," Kings of Leon
Album of the Year: *Fearless*, Taylor Swift
Song of the Year: "Single Ladies (Put a Ring on It)," Thaddis Harrell,
Beyoncé Knowles, Terius Nash, Christopher Stewart
Best New Artist: Zac Brown Band
Best Rap Album: *Relapse*, Eminem
Best Rap Song: "Run This Town," Jeff Bhasker, Shawn Carter,
Robyn Fenty, Kanye West, Ernest Wilson
Best R&B Album: *I Am . . . Sasha Fierce*, Beyoncé
Best R&B Song: "Single Ladies (Put a Ring on It)," Thaddis Harrell,
Beyoncé Knowles, Terius Nash, Christopher Stewart
Best Rock Album: *21st Century Breakdown*, Green Day
Best Rock Song: "Use Somebody," Caleb, Jared, Matthew, and
Nathan Followill (Kings of Leon)
Best Alternative Music Album: *Wolfgang Amadeus Phoenix*, Phoenix
Best Pop Vocal Album: *The E.N.D.*, The Black Eyed Peas
Best Country Song: "White Horse," Liz Rose and Taylor Swift

2009 Teen Choice Awards

Rock Track: "Decode," Paramore
Rock Group: Paramore
Rap/Hip-Hop Track: "Boom Boom Pow," The Black Eyed Peas
R&B Track: "Single Ladies (Put a Ring on It)," Beyoncé
Love Song: "Crush," David Archuleta
Breakout Artist: David Archuleta
R&B Artist: Beyoncé
Rap Artist: Kanye West
Female Artist: Taylor Swift
Male Artist: Jason Mraz
Single: "The Climb," Miley Cyrus

2010 Nickelodeon Kids' Choice Awards

Favorite Music Group: The Black Eyed Peas
Favorite Song: "You Belong with Me," Taylor Swift
Favorite Male Singer: Jay-Z
Favorite Female Singer: Taylor Swift

Plants

Silent Partners

Take a breath. Let it out. Do it again—and again—and again. Humans inhale and exhale about 14 times a minute. It may seem as if we're going through this process alone, but we're not. When it comes to the air we breathe, plants and people are a natural partnership.

Give and Take

Through a process called photosynthesis, plants convert energy from the Sun into sugars they store as food. Photosynthesis releases oxygen, which humans breathe in. When we breathe out, we give something back to plants. We release carbon dioxide, a waste gas needed for photosynthesis to work. This cycle goes on and on countless times a day, all over the earth.

Let's Eat

Of the 275,000–300,000 plant species on Earth, not all get their food through photosynthesis. About 4,000 species are parasites, which feed on other plants. Another 400 or so plants are meat eaters. Plants such as the pitcher plant and sundew have hairs that trap insects inside their leaves. Then the plants' digestive juices help them consume their victims. Other carnivorous plants even eat frogs, birds, and mice!

Extreme Plants

The smallest plants are duckweeds, which can measure only 0.01–0.04 inches (0.5–1.2 mm). The rafflesia plant in Southeast Asia has the largest flowers in the world. It has a reddish brown blossom that can measure up to 3 feet (91 cm) wide and weigh up to 15 pounds (7 kg). This plant is commonly known as the stinking corpse lily because it smells like a rotting carcass! But don't turn up your nose. The foul odor has a purpose—it attracts flies, which pollinate the flower.

TAKE a LOOK

Explore the plant variety outside your school or home. How many different kinds of plants can you find? Draw pictures and write descriptions of your plants in a notebook, and try to figure out where they fit into the plant kingdom, shown on the next page. (Don't pick any plants that aren't on your property, and don't eat any, regardless of where you find them. Many plants are poisonous.)

CHECK IT OUT!

Plants don't have to be big to be deadly. The tiny bladderwort is the fastest killer of the carnivorous plants. It can suck in prey in less than one-fiftieth of a second.

Biological Classification of Plants

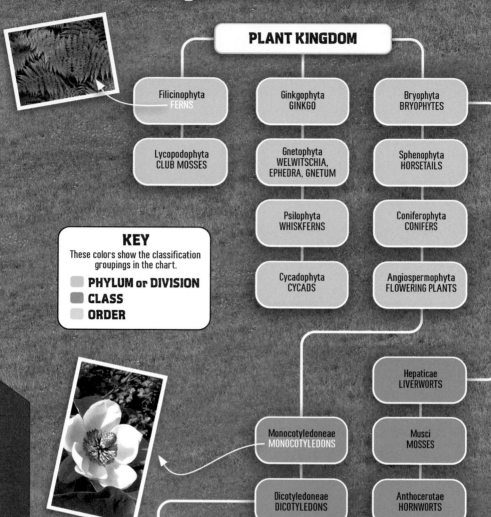

PLANT KINGDOM

Filicinophyta
FERNS

Ginkgophyta
GINKGO

Bryophyta
BRYOPHYTES

Lycopodophyta
CLUB MOSSES

Gnetophyta
WELWITSCHIA,
EPHEDRA, GNETUM

Sphenophyta
HORSETAILS

Psilophyta
WHISKFERNS

Coniferophyta
CONIFERS

Cycadophyta
CYCADS

Angiospermophyta
FLOWERING PLANTS

Hepaticae
LIVERWORTS

Monocotyledoneae
MONOCOTYLEDONS

Musci
MOSSES

Dicotyledoneae
DICOTYLEDONS

Anthocerotae
HORNWORTS

KEY
These colors show the classification
groupings in the chart.

■ **PHYLUM or DIVISION**
■ **CLASS**
■ **ORDER**

Liliaceae	LILY, TULIP	Roasceae	APPLE, ROSE
Orchidaceae	ORCHIDS	Fabaceae	BEAN, PEANUT
Poaceae	WHEAT, BAMBOO	Magnoliaceae	MAGNOLIA, TULIP TREE
Iridaceae	IRIS, GLADIOLUS	Apiaceae	CARROT, PARSLEY
Arecaceae	COCONUT PALM, DATE PALM	Solonaceae	POTATO, TOMATO
Bromeliaceae	BROMELIAD, PINEAPPLE	Lamiaceae	MINT, LAVENDER
Cyperaceae	SEDGES	Asteraceae	SUNFLOWER, DANDELION
Juncaceae	RUSHES	Salicaceae	WILLOW, POPLAR
Musaceae	BANANA	Cucurbitaceae	MELON, CUCUMBER
Amaryllidaceae	DAFFODIL, AMARYLLIS	Malvaceae	HIBISCUS, HOLLYHOCK
Ranunculaceae	BUTTERCUP, DELPHINIUM	Cactaceae	CACTUS
Brassicaceae	CABBAGE, TURNIP		

Plants

Where Do Plants Grow?

Plants grow everywhere in the world, except where there is permanent ice. However, different types of plants grow best in different regions. A region's plant life depends on the climate, the amount of water and sun, the type of soil, and other features. For instance, plants in the tundra grow close to the ground, away from the region's icy winds. Desert plants have thick skins to hold in every drop of water. This map shows five major regions where certain kinds of plants grow best, and the areas where the climate is too harsh for any plant life at all.

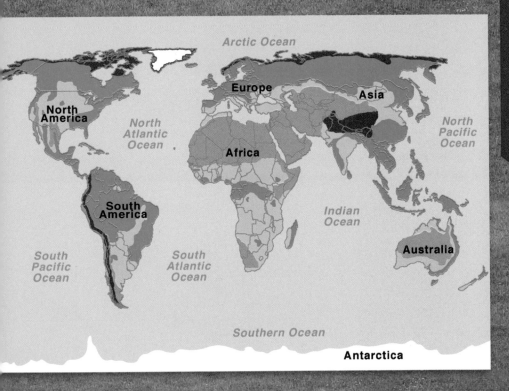

Region	Types of Plants
Aquatic	Cattails, seaweed
Grassland	Short and tall grasses
Forest	Trees, shrubs, ferns, wildflowers
Tundra	Small shrubs, mosses
Desert	Many kinds of cacti
Permanent ice	No plant life

Population

See How We've Grown

We live in a big world, and it's getting bigger all the time. Earth isn't expanding, but increasing number of people are calling it home. There are about 6.8 billion people on the planet today. Since 1959 the population has more than doubled. In your lifetime the population is expected to grow by at least another 50 percent.

Two at the Top

Where do all those people live? China and India top the population charts with more than a billion people apiece. That means about two out of every five people in the world are Chinese or Indian. Researchers predict that India will overtake China in population within the next twenty-five years.

Born in the USA—or Not

Although the United States is far behind India and China in population, it ranks third in the world. Our country's population is more than 300 million people, and we've added about 100 million since 1970. In 1790, the entire population was only about 4 million.

More and more of the U.S. population gain comes from immigrants, continuing an American tradition. The United States was founded by immigrants from Europe. Today our culture, ideas, languages, and lives are still being enriched by people who come from other places. In fact, almost one in five Americans speaks a language other than English at home.

Hispanic Americans: A Major Minority

Hispanics are people from Spanish, or Central or South American, cultures. As of July 1, 2008, there were about 46.9 million Hispanics in the United States, an increase of about 1.5 million from the previous July.

TAKE a LOOK

Everybody's from somewhere! Where are you from? How about the people you know? Ask classmates, friends, and neighbors about the towns, states, or countries where they were born. Then make a chart or graph that shows the diversity of the place you all now call home.

CHECK IT OUT!

Do you speak a language other than English? According to the U.S. Census Bureau, more than 55 million Americans do. Spanish is the top language. Chinese is second, and Tagalog, a major language of the Philippines, is number three.

Population by Continent

Continent	Population
Asia	4,052,332,000
Africa	1,027,783,000
Europe	706,966,000
North America	538,417,000
South America	396,258,000
Oceania, including Australia	34,685,745

CHECK IT OUT !

The continent of Antarctica is not listed above because it has no permanent population. Scientists, researchers, and tourists come and go.

5 Most Populous Countries

Country	Population
China	1,338,612,968
India	1,166,079,217
United States	307,212,123
Indonesia	240,271,522
Brazil	198,739,269

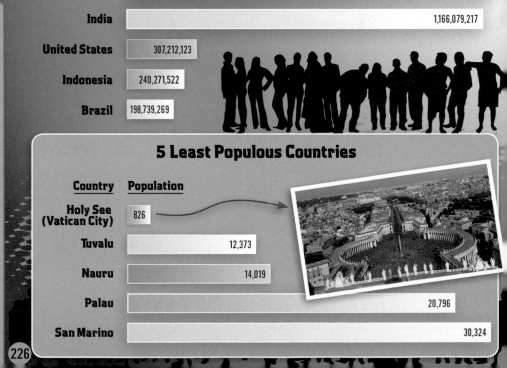

5 Least Populous Countries

Country	Population
Holy See (Vatican City)	826
Tuvalu	12,373
Nauru	14,019
Palau	20,796
San Marino	30,324

Population

5 Most Densely Populated Countries

Country	Persons per sq. mi. (persons per sq km)
Monaco	43,953 (16,905.1)
Singapore	19,325.9 (6,720.8)
Holy See (Vatican City)	4,858.8 (1,877.2)
Maldives	3,416.7 (1,321.1)
Malta	3,321.0 (1,282.2)

5 Most Sparsely Populated Countries

Country	Persons per sq. mi. (persons per sq km)
Mongolia	5.0 (1.9)
Namibia	6.6 (2.6)
Australia	7.1 (2.8)
Suriname	7.6 (2.9)
Iceland	7.7 (3.0)

5 Largest World Cities

City	Population (includes surrounding densely populated areas)
Tokyo, Japan	35,676,000
New York, New York, United States	19,040,000
Mexico City, Mexico	19,028,000
Mumbai, India	18,978,000
Sao Paulo, Brazil	18,845,000

CHECK IT OUT!

You can figure out population density by dividing the population by the land area. Land areas for all countries can be found on pages 90–121. Land areas for each state of the United States, Puerto Rico, and Washington, DC, can be found on pages 128–145.

10 Most Populous States

State	Population
California	36,961,664
Texas	24,782,302
New York	19,541,453
Florida	18,537,969
Illinois	12,910,409
Pennsylvania	12,604,767
Ohio	11,542,645
Michigan	9,969,727
Georgia	9,829,211
North Carolina	9,380,884

10 Least Populous States

State	Population
Wyoming	544,270
Vermont	621,760
North Dakota	646,844
Alaska	698,473
South Dakota	812,383
Delaware	885,122
Montana	974,989
Rhode Island	1,053,209
Hawaii	1,295,178
New Hampshire	1,324,575

U.S. Population Growth 1790–2009

Year	Population (in millions)
1790	3.9
1830	12.9
1870	38.6
1890	62.9
1910	92.2
1930	123.2
1950	151.3
1970	203.2
1990	248.7
2000	281.4
2008	304.1
2009	307.2

Population

10 Largest U.S. Cities

City	Population
New York, NY	8,363,710
Los Angeles, CA	3,833,995
Chicago, IL	2,853,114
Houston, TX	2,242,193
Phoenix, AZ	1,567,924
Philadelphia, PA	1,447,395
San Antonio, TX	1,351,505
Dallas, TX	1,279,910
San Diego, CA	1,279,329
San Jose, CA	948,279

10 Fastest-Growing Major U.S. Cities

City	Percent Increase from 2007 to 2008
New Orleans, LA	8.2
Round Rock, TX	8.2
Cary, NC	6.9
Gilbert, AZ	5.0
McKinney, TX	4.8
Roseville, CA	3.8
Irvine, CA	3.8
Raleigh, NC	3.8
Killeen, TX	3.8
Fort Worth, TX	3.6

U.S. Racial Makeup

Race	Population
White	223,965,009
Black	37,131,771
Another race	17,538,990
Asian	13,164,169
American Indian, Native Alaskan	2,419,895
Native Hawaiian, other Pacific Islander	446,164

Hispanic is an ethnic background, not a race. Hispanic people can be of any race. There are 46,943,613 Hispanics in the United States. California leads the nation in Hispanic population, with 13,457,397.

States with the Highest Population by Race

White
California	28,170,328
Texas	20,046,078
New York	14,310,269

Black
New York	3,362,736
Florida	2,916,174
Texas	2,898,143

Asian
California	4,581,890
New York	1,368,585
Texas	841,016

American Indian, Native Alaskan
California	443,719
Arizona	315,727
Oklahoma	291,390

Native Hawaiian, other Pacific Islander
California	157,727
Hawaii	117,004
Washington	31,822

Population

States with the Highest Percentage of Foreign-Born Residents

State	Percentage
California	26.8
New York	21.7
New Jersey	19.8
Nevada	18.9
Florida	18.5

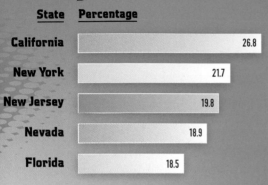

In Los Angeles, California, and Miami, Florida, about half the residents speak a language other than English at home. Los Angeles and Miami also have the highest percentage of foreign-born residents. St. Louis, Missouri, has the lowest percentage.

Racial and Hispanic Makeup of 10 Largest U.S. Cities

New York, NY
White	44.7%
Black	26.6%
Hispanic	27.8%
Asian	9.8%
American Indian, Native Alaskan	0.5%
Native Hawaiian, other Pacific Islander	0.1%

Philadelphia, PA
White	45.0%
Black	43.2%
Hispanic	8.5%
Asian	4.5%
American Indian, Native Alaskan	0.3%
Native Hawaiian, other Pacific Islander	0%

Los Angeles, CA
White	46.9%
Black	11.2%
Hispanic	46.5%
Asian	10.0%
American Indian, Native Alaskan	0.8%
Native Hawaiian, other Pacific Islander	0.2%

San Antonio, TX
White	32.1%
Black	6.8%
Hispanic	58.7%
Asian	1.6%
American Indian, Native Alaskan	0.8%
Native Hawaiian, other Pacific Islander	0.1%

Chicago, IL
White	42.0%
Black	36.8%
Hispanic	26.0%
Asian	4.3%
American Indian, Native Alaskan	0.4%
Native Hawaiian, other Pacific Islander	0.1%

Dallas, TX
White	50.8%
Black	25.9%
Hispanic	35.6%
Asian	2.7%
American Indian, Native Alaskan	0.5%
Native Hawaiian, other Pacific Islander	0%

Houston, TX
White	49.3%
Black	25.3%
Hispanic	37.4%
Asian	5.3%
American Indian, Native Alaskan	0.4%
Native Hawaiian, other Pacific Islander	0.1%

San Diego, CA
White	60.2%
Black	7.9%
Hispanic	25.4%
Asian	13.6%
American Indian, Native Alaskan	0.6%
Native Hawaiian, other Pacific Islander	0.5%

Phoenix, AZ
White	71.1%
Black	5.1%
Hispanic	34.1%
Asian	2.0%
American Indian, Native Alaskan	2.0%
Native Hawaiian, other Pacific Islander	0.1%

San Jose, CA
White	47.5%
Black	3.5%
Hispanic	30.2%
Asian	26.9%
American Indian, Native Alaskan	0.8%
Native Hawaiian, other Pacific Islander	0.4%

Religion

Looking for Answers

A religion is a system of beliefs and holy practices, called rituals, that help guide people in their lives. Today there are about 20 major religions in the world, with thousands of other smaller religious groups. At the heart of most religions is a desire to find answers to important questions such as: How should I live my life? What happens when you die? Why do some people suffer? In most religions, people seek these answers with guidance from one or more supreme beings or forces.

Supreme Beings

A supreme being or force offers people a perspective from beyond the physical world. Christians, Jews, and Muslims believe in one supreme being, or god. Practitioners of Hinduism believe in one divine principle, known as Brahman, and various gods who represent parts of that principle.

Major Religions

Christians make up the largest religious group in the world, numbering more than two billion. About half of all Christians belong to the Roman Catholic Church, whose spiritual leader is the Pope. Muslims are the second-largest group, with more than 1.5 billion members. With close to a billion believers, Hindus are the third-largest group. See pages 234 and 235 for detailed information.

Holy Places

Most religions have specific places on the planet that are considered holy. Christians, Jews, and Muslims may make trips to their holy lands in Egypt, Israel, or Jordan. Hindus sprinkle the ashes of their dead relatives in the Ganges River. The Bighorn Medicine Wheel in Wyoming is sacred to many Native Americans, and members of the Buddhist and Shinto faith believe Mount Fuji in Japan to be a sacred place.

TAKE a LOOK

Take a look at the information in this section and explore how other people approach the mysteries of life. How do you answer the big questions? What kinds of things are important to you on a spiritual level?

CHECK IT OUT!

Most major religions have five features in common: belief in a god or supreme force, a doctrine of salvation, a code of conduct, rituals, and the telling of sacred stories.

Major Religions of the World

Buddhism

Buddhism began about 525 BCE, reportedly in India. This religion is based on the teachings of Gautama Siddhartha, the Buddha, who achieved enlightenment through intense meditation. The Buddha taught that though life is full of pain, you can break the cycle and achieve peace by being mindful, meditating, and doing good deeds. There are Buddhists all over the world, but mostly in Asia. The Buddha's teachings can be read in spiritual texts, or scriptures, called sutras.

Christianity

Christianity is the world's biggest religion, with over 2 billion worshippers in the world. It is based on the teachings of Jesus Christ, who lived between 8 BCE and 29 CE. The Old and New Testaments of the Bible are the key scriptures. Christians believe that Jesus Christ is the son of God, who died on the cross to save humankind and later rose from the dead.

Hinduism

To Hindus, there is one overarching divine principle, with a variety of gods such as Vishnu, Shiva, and Shakti representing different parts of it. Hindus believe that by being mindful and doing good deeds you can break meaningless cycles and improve the purity of your actions, known as your karma. Hinduism was founded about 1500 BCE. The main scriptures are called Vedas.

Islam

Islam was founded in 610 CE by Muhammad. People who practice Islam are called Muslims. They believe in one god, Allah, who gave the spiritual writings of the Qu'ran (also known as the Koran) to Muhammad so he could teach truth and justice to all people. There are two major Muslim groups, the Shiites and the Sunni.

Judaism

Judaism was founded about 2000 BCE. The prophet Abraham is recognized as the founder. Jews believe in one god. They believe God created the universe, and they believe in being faithful to God and in following God's laws as outlined in key scriptures such as the Torah and the Hebrew Bible. There are people practicing Judaism all over the world. Many of them are in Israel and the United States.

5 Largest World Religions

Religion	Members
Christianity	2,264,492,000
Islam	1,523,212,150
Hinduism	935,460,000
Buddhism	463,821,000
Traditional Chinese	454,579,800

CHECK IT OUT !

Most religions celebrate holy days throughout the year, including at least one day dedicated to their founder or a leading deity. Christians celebrate the birth of Christ on December 25, but in other religions exact dates change from year to year. Buddhists mark the birth of Buddha in April or May. In February or March, Muslims celebrate the birthday of Muhammad and Hindus hold a festival dedicated to Shiva.

Science

I Wonder Why

Scientists like to look at things. They also like to ask questions. The way scientists observe, question, come up with a possible answer, and then test that *hypothesis* is called the scientific process.

Let's Get Physical

Physical scientists study invisible forces such as light and sound. One of the most famous physical scientists was Sir Isaac Newton, who came up with theories that explained mysteries such as motion and gravity.

That's Life

Life scientists are also called *biologists*. They study animals, plants, ecology, diseases, and more, observing in a lab or in the wild. Biologist Anton von Leeuwenhoek discovered bacteria, which he called "wee creatures," when he saw them through a microscope. Jane Goodall lived in Africa with chimpanzees for many years. Through her observations we know that chimps can use tools and have individual personalities.

Rock Stars

If you want to know when an earthquake is coming, or how the Grand Canyon was formed, ask an earth scientist. Earth scientists study geography, weather, the ocean, rocks, earthquakes, and volcanoes.

Cool Science Jobs

Want to spend your life building robotic cockroaches? How about designing faster roller coasters or taming tarantulas? Then think about becoming a scientist! All those cool jobs and many more are held by scientists. Advances in technology and a rapidly changing world will keep creating more exciting careers in science.

TAKE a LOOK

CaRRy aRound a notebook and obseRve plants, people, the weatheR, oR anything that catches youR eye. WRite down what you see. DRaw pictuRes. ObseRve changes oveR time and make a hypothesis about what caused the change. Then tRy to pRove it with an expeRiment.

CHECK IT OUT!

In addition to the life, earth, and physical branches of science, there is a fourth branch called the social sciences. Social scientists study people, governments, and cultures in fields such as sociology and psychology.

The 5 Kingdoms of Life

To understand living things, life scientists divide them into groups that share certain features. This process is called classification. A classification system created in 1735 by Carolus Linnaeus divides life-forms into five kingdoms: animals, plants, fungi, protista, and monera. Here are some (not all) of the types of life-forms within each kingdom.

ANIMAL KINGDOM	Vertebrates (such as mammals, birds, and reptiles), sponges, worms, insects and arthropods, crustaceans, and jellyfish
PLANT KINGDOM	Ferns, mosses, ginkgos, horsetails, conifers, flowering plants, liverworts, and bladderworts
FUNGI KINGDOM	Molds, mildews, blights, smuts, rusts, mushrooms, puffballs, stinkhorns, lichens, dung fungi, yeasts, morels, and truffles
PROTISTA KINGDOM	Yellow-green algae, golden algae, protozoa, green algae, brown algae, and red algae
MONERA KINGDOM	Bacteria and blue-green algae

The kingdoms are subdivided into smaller and more specific groups.

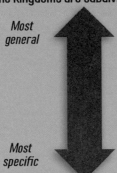

Most general

Most specific

Category	Example: Human Being
Kingdom	Animal
Phylum	Chordate
Subphylum	Vertebrate (animals with backbones)
Superclass	Vertebrate with jaws
Class	Mammal
Subclass	Advanced mammal
Infraclass	Placental mammal
Order	Primate
Family	Hominid
Genus	*Homo*
Species	*Homo sapiens*

The Domain System

In 1990, biologist Carl R. Woese and other scientists proposed a slightly different classification system. They suggested dividing living things into three domains, based on their cell structure. Domain Eukaryota includes multi-celled organisms: animals, plants, fungi, and protista. Domains Archaea and Bacteria are made up of microscopic one-celled organisms. The huge majority of all living things belong to these two domains. Scientists believe that Archaea are among the oldest forms of life on Earth.

Science

Some Major Discoveries in Life Science

Year	Discovery
400 BCE	Aristotle classifies 500 species of animals into 8 classes.
1628 CE	William Harvey discovers how blood circulates in the human body.
1683	Anton van Leeuwenhoek observes bacteria.
1735	Carolus Linnaeus introduces the classification system.
1859	Charles Darwin publishes *On the Origin of Species*, which explains his theories of evolution.
1860	Gregor Mendel discovers the laws of heredity through experiments with peas and fruit flies.
1861	Louis Pasteur, the "father of bacteriology," comes up with a theory that certain diseases are caused by bacteria.
1953	James D. Watson and Francis H. Crick develop the double helix model of DNA, which explains how traits are inherited.
1953	Jonas Salk invents the polio vaccine.
1981	Chinese scientists successfully clone a goldfish.
1996	Dolly the sheep is cloned in Scotland.
2009	Doctors successfully treat blindness, brain disorders, and immune system deficiencies by inserting genes into patients' cells and tissues. Scientists are hopeful that gene therapy may someday be effective against cancer, but the procedure remains controversial because of dangerous side effects.

CHECK OUT!

In 1952, nearly 60,000 cases of polio, with 3,000 deaths, were reported in the United States. Because of the Salk vaccine, the disease was virtually wiped out in this country by 1979. However, polio is circulating in at least six countries today, and it could spread. Until it's eliminated worldwide, it's important that kids continue to get vaccinated.

The Rock Cycle

Rocks don't grow like plants and animals, but they change from one form to another in a never-ending process called the **rock cycle**. Geologists, or scientists who study rocks, divide them into three groups.

Igneous

Igneous rock makes up about 95 percent of the upper part of Earth's crust. There are two kinds:

Granite

Intrusive igneous rock forms when melted rock, or magma, cools beneath Earth's surface. Granite is a common type of intrusive igneous rock. Intrusive igneous rocks are constantly being pushed up to the surface by natural forces.

Extrusive igneous rock forms when the melted rock erupts as lava and cools on Earth's surface. Basalt is a common type of extrusive igneous rock.

Basalt

Sedimentary

Igneous rocks on Earth's surface can be broken down into tiny pieces and moved around by wind, rain, and ocean waves. These little pieces, called sediments, pile up in water and are squeezed into layers with other sediments such as bits and pieces of plants or dead animals. Limestone is a common type of sedimentary rock.

Limestone

Metamorphic

Pressure and heat can flatten and fold igneous or sedimentary rock into a whole new shape, color, and mineral structure. Marble is a metamorphic rock that often comes from limestone.

Marble

CHE IT O !

Plymouth Rock in Plymouth, Massachusetts, is made of granite scientists think was formed more than 600 million years ago. The famous landmark is much smaller today than it was in 1620, when the Pilgrims arrived from England. It has been worn down by erosion and chipped away by souvenir-hunting tourists.

What's the Difference Between Rocks and Minerals?

The difference is simple: Rocks are made of minerals, but minerals are not made of rocks. Minerals are chemical compounds found on, in, and below Earth's crust. There are about 4,000 known minerals on Earth.

Quartz is one of the most common minerals, making up about 12 percent of Earth's crust. Some quartz is so clear you can see straight through it. Other types are pink, green, yellow, or purple. The color varies depending on how the quartz was formed. But quartz does more than look pretty. Under certain conditions, quartz can generate electricity to power clocks, computers, TVs, heaters, and other devices.

A Scratch Test for Minerals

The Mohs Scale, invented by German mineralogist Frederich Mohs, ranks ten minerals on hardness based on their resistance to scratches. Minerals with higher numbers can scratch minerals with lower numbers.

Mineral	Rank
Talc	1
Gypsum	2
Calcite	3
Fluorite	4
Apatite	5
Orthoclase feldspar	6
Quartz	7
Topaz	8
Corundum	9
Diamond	10

Hard to Say

Here's how certain items would rank in hardness on the Mohs scale.

Fingernails	2.5
Gold, silver	2.5–3
Copper penny	3
Iron	4–5
Knife blade	5.5
Glass	6–7
Hardened steel file	7+

Periodic Table of Elements

If rocks are made of minerals, what are minerals made of? Elements! Everything in the world is made of elements, which are found in nature or made by scientists. The first element discovered was phosphorus, in 1669. Since then 110 elements have been added. Some elements are named for scientists. Some are named for places or characters in mythology. Others are named after a certain feature of the element. Scientists put elements in groups called periods on the periodic table.

Period

IA	IIA	IIIB	IVB	VB	VIB	VIIB		V

1 **H** Hydrogen 1.00794								
3 **Li** Lithium 6.941	4 **Be** Beryllium 9.012182							
11 **Na** Sodium 22.989770	12 **Mg** Magnesium 24.3050							
19 **K** Potassium 39.0983	20 **Ca** Calcium 40.078	21 **Sc** Scandium 44.955910	22 **Ti** Titanium 47.867	23 **V** Vanadium 50.9415	24 **Cr** Chromium 51.9961	25 **Mn** Manganese 54.938049	26 **Fe** Iron 55.845	27 **C** Co 58.9
37 **Rb** Rubidium 85.4678	38 **Sr** Strontium 87.62	39 **Y** Yttrium 88.90585	40 **Zr** Zirconium 91.224	41 **Nb** Niobium 92.90638	42 **Mo** Molybdenum 95.94	43 **Tc** Technetium (98)	44 **Ru** Ruthenium 101.07	45 **R** Rho 102.
55 **Cs** Cesium 132.90545	56 **Ba** Barium 137.327		72 **Hf** Hafnium 178.49	73 **Ta** Tantalum 180.9479	74 **W** Tungsten 183.84	75 **Re** Rhenium 186.207	76 **Os** Osmium 190.23	77 Iri 192
87 **Fr** Francium (223)	88 **Ra** Radium (226)		104 **Rf** Rutherfordium (261)	105 **Db** Dubnium (262)	106 **Sg** Seaborgium (266)	107 **Bh** Bohrium (264)	108 **Hs** Hassium (277)	109 **M** Meitn (2

Period: 1, 2, 3, 4, 5, 6, 7

Atomic Number
Symbol
Name
Atomic Weight

58
Ce
Cerium
140.116

Lanthanides

57 **La** Lanthanum 138.9055	58 **Ce** Cerium 140.116	59 **Pr** Praseodymium 140.90765	60 **Nd** Neodymium 144.24	61 **Pm** Promethium (145)	62 **S** Sam 150

Actinides

89 **Ac** Actinium (227)	90 **Th** Thorium 232.0381	91 **Pa** Protactinium 231.03588	92 **U** Uranium 238.02891	93 **Np** Neptunium (237)	94 **P** Plut (2

Science

Solids
Liquids
Gases
Artificially Prepared

VIIIA

| | | | | | | 2 He Helium 4.002602 |

IIIA	IVA	VA	VIA	VIIA	
5 B Boron 10.811	6 C Carbon 12.0107	7 N Nitrogen 14.0067	8 O Oxygen 15.9994	9 F Fluorine 18.9984032	10 Ne Neon 20.1797
13 Al Aluminum 26.981538	14 Si Silicon 28.0855	15 P Phosphorus 30.973761	16 S Sulfur 32.065	17 Cl Chlorine 35.453	18 Ar Argon 39.948

IB   IIB

| 29 Cu Copper 63.546 | 30 Zn Zinc 65.409 | 31 Ga Gallium 69.723 | 32 Ge Germanium 72.64 | 33 As Arsenic 74.92160 | 34 Se Selenium 78.96 | 35 Br Bromine 79.904 | 36 Kr Krypton 83.798 |

| 47 Ag Silver 107.8682 | 48 Cd Cadmium 112.411 | 49 In Indium 114.818 | 50 Sn Tin 118.710 | 51 Sb Antimony 121.760 | 52 Te Tellurium 127.60 | 53 I Iodine 126.90447 | 54 Xe Xenon 131.293 |

| 79 Au Gold 196.96655 | 80 Hg Mercury 200.59 | 81 Tl Thallium 204.3833 | 82 Pb Lead 207.2 | 83 Bi Bismuth 208.98038 | 84 Po Polonium (209) | 85 At Astatine (210) | 86 Rn Radon (222) |

| 111 Uuu Unununium (272) | 112 Uub Ununbium (285) | | 114 Uuq Ununquadium (289) | | 116 Uuh Ununhexium (292) | | |

| 64 Gd Gadolinium 157.25 | 65 Tb Terbium 158.92534 | 66 Dy Dysprosium 162.500 | 67 Ho Holmium 164.93032 | 68 Er Erbium 167.259 | 69 Tm Thulium 168.93421 | 70 Yb Ytterbium 173.04 | 71 Lu Lutetium 174.967 |

| 96 Cm Curium (247) | 97 Bk Berkelium (247) | 98 Cf Californium (251) | 99 Es Einsteinium (252) | 100 Fm Fermium (257) | 101 Md Mendelevium (258) | 102 No Nobelium (259) | 103 Lr Lawrencium (262) |

Signs & Symbols

Getting the Message

Signs and symbols are an important part of communication, especially in a fast-moving world. A sign uses some combination of shapes, colors, pictures, and words to deliver information quickly. Symbols are visual representations of something bigger, such as a country, a brand, an emotion, or an organization. Signs and symbols are a universal language all their own.

Signs of the Times

The best signs are clear and easy to recognize and understand. Some give directions: NO PARKING, DO NOT ENTER. Others tell where to find important places such as hospitals, restrooms, and public telephones. Street signs help us find our way around a city or neighborhood, and danger signs alert us to poison, explosives, or icy roads.

Color Code

The color of a sign can indicate what kind of information it gives. On a highway, blue-and-white signs often point the way to services such as restaurants, lodging, gas stations, and rest areas. Signs that warn against danger are black, white, and red. Traffic signs can be red and white, like STOP, or black on yellow for SCHOOL AHEAD or YIELD.

SYMBOLS

Symbols are like shortcuts: They're quick ways to express a bigger idea. When someone gives you a thumbs-up, you know it means agreement or approval. A heart stands for love. A four-leaf clover stands for luck. In U.S. politics, the elephant symbolizes the Republican Party and the donkey stands for Democrats. Symbols are probably one of the oldest human inventions, and there are thousands of them in use today. How many symbols do you use or see every day?

TAKE a LOOK

Scientists say that the strongest color contrast seen by the human eye is black and yellow. Many important traffic signs have black writing on a yellow background so people can read them easily. Check out the signs on page 246 and then take a look around your city or neighborhood. What color are the signs that catch your eye?

YIELD

CHECK IT OUT!

Can gorillas speak? Koko the Gorilla can't speak any human languages. However, she has learned to communicate with humans through the use of American Sign Language, a series of hand gestures that represent letters, words, and ideas. She expresses her feelings, names things, and asks questions. Using the alphabet on page 247, how many things can you "say" without speaking?

Basic Signs

Fire extinguisher

Women's room

Men's room

First aid

Elevator

Information

Disabled (parking, restrooms, access)

Bus

Recycle

Fallout shelter

No smoking

No admittance

No parking

Danger

Poison

Stop

Yield

Do not enter

No left turn

Falling rock

Stop ahead

Bicycle path

Traffic light ahead

Railroad crossing

Pedestrian crossing

Intersection ahead

Left turn

Right turn

Two-way traffic

Slippery when wet

Signs & Symbols

246

American Sign Language

In the manual alphabet of the hearing impaired, the fingers of the hand are moved to positions that represent the letters of the alphabet. Whole words and ideas are also expressed in sign language.

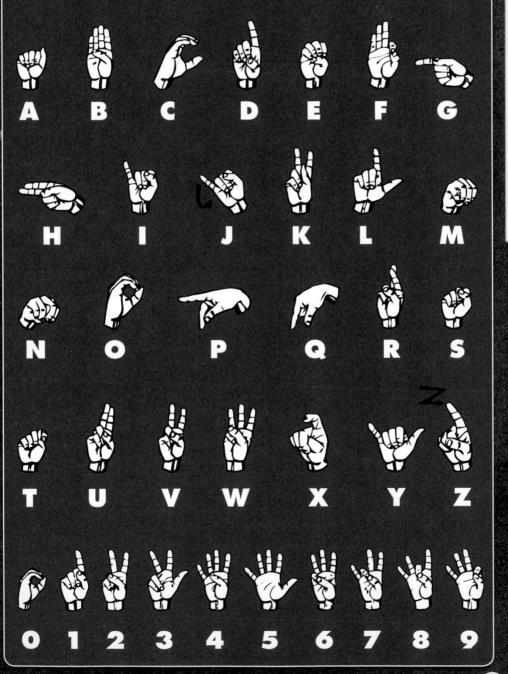

Space

Welcome to the Neighborhood

Go outside and look up. What do you see? Whether it's the clear blue sky, the Moon, the Sun, stars, planets, or just deep, inky blackness, you're looking at space. Within the vastness of space, Earth's solar system is one tiny neighborhood in a very big community.

The Star of the Show

The word *solar* means "of the sun," and the Sun is the star of our little corner of the universe. It's the closest star to Earth, which is why we can see it clearly and be warmed by its light. (Compared to other stars, our Sun is only average in size.) Eight major planets and five dwarf planets revolve around our Sun.

All the major planets except Mercury and Venus have one or more moons orbiting around them, for a total of at least 167 moons, and there may be many more. Also spinning around the Sun are trillions of comets, tens of thousands of asteroids, and countless spheres of space dust and ice.

Spin City

Our entire solar system spins around the center of the Milky Way galaxy. It takes about 230 million years to make one orbit! The Milky Way includes roughly 400 billion stars. Could these other stars also have planets orbiting around them? In fact, as of May 2010, at least 453 planets have been discovered, orbiting around 385 stars. There could be many more.

ONE REALLY BIG PLACE

The Milky Way is one of many galaxies bunched together to form a group called the Local Group. The Local Group is a small part of a bigger group called Virgo Cluster. Virgo Cluster and other galaxy clusters are all strung together like a huge web. Scientists estimate that there are more than 100 billion galaxies scattered throughout the visible universe. Well, you get the picture—space is one big place.

TAKE a LOOK

For as long as humans have been on Earth, we've wanted to explore the huge mystery known as space. Over the years we've developed telescopes and increasingly sophisticated tools to send images and information back. We've also sent people in space shuttles and rocket ships. As you explore this section and discover planets, stars, and moons and learn about the scientists and explorers who have brought that information to us, make a list of the kinds of questions that are still unanswered. Maybe you'll be the one to find the answers.

CHECK IT OUT!

Pluto was considered a major planet until scientists reclassified it as a dwarf on August 24, 2006. Why was Pluto demoted? One of the judging standards was the ability to "clear the neighborhood." That means a planet must have a strong enough gravitational force to pull nearby space "junk," such as particles of ice and dust, down to its surface. Pluto's gravitational field didn't have enough muscle. The other dwarf planets are Ceres, Haumes, Makemake, and Eris.

The Solar System
(with distances from the Sun*)

Mars
141.6 million miles
(227.9 million km)

Earth
92.9 million miles
(149.6 million km)

Venus
67.2 million miles
(108.2 million km)

Mercury
36.0 million miles
(57.9 million km)

SUN

Space

*Distances rounded to nearest tenth

250

Neptune
2.8 billion miles
(4.5 billion km)

Uranus
1.8 billion miles
(2.9 billion km)

Saturn
885.5 million miles
(1.4 billion km)

Jupiter
483.7 million miles
(778.4 million km)

CHECK
IT OUT
!

The Sun is the closest star to Earth. It is 270,000 times closer than the next-nearest star.

Basic Facts About the Planets in Our Solar System

Planet	Average distance from Sun	Rotation period (hours)	Period of revolution (in Earth days)	Diameter relative to Earth	Average surface or effective temperature	Planetary satellites (moons)
Mercury	36.0 million miles (57.9 million km)	1,407.5 hours	88 days	38.2%	332°F (166°C)	0
Venus	67.2 million miles (108.2 million km)	5,832.2 hours*	224.7 days	94.9%	864°F (462°C)	0
Earth	92.9 million miles (149.6 million km)	23.9 hours	365.24 days	100%	59°F (15°C)	1
Mars	141.6 million miles (227.9 million km)	24.6 hours	687 days	53.2%	-80°F (-62°C)	2
Jupiter	483.7 million miles (778.4 million km)	9.9 hours	4,330.6 days	1,121%	-234°F (-148°C)	at least 62
Saturn	885.9 million miles (1.4 billion km)	10.7 hours	10,755.7 days	944%	-288°F (-178°C)	at least 62
Uranus	1.8 billion miles (2.9 billion km)	17.2 hours*	30,687.2 days	401%	-357°F (-216°C)	at least 27
Neptune	2.8 billion miles (4.5 billion km)	16.1 hours	60,190 days	388%	-353°F (-214°C)	at least 13

*Retrograde rotation; rotates backward, or in the opposite direction from most other planetary bodies.

Space

Basic Facts About the Sun

Position in the solar system	center
Average distance from Earth	92,955,820 miles (149,597,891 km)
Distance from center of Milky Way galaxy	27,710 light-years
Rotation Period	25.38 days
Equatorial diameter	864,400 miles (1,391,117 km)
Diameter relative to Earth	109 times larger
Temperature at core	27,000,000°F (15,000,000°C)
Temperature at surface	10,000°F (5,538°C)
Main components	hydrogen and helium
Expected life of hydrogen fuel supply	6.4 billion years

Top 10 Largest Bodies in the Solar System

Ranked by size in equatorial diameter

1. Sun
864,400 miles
(1,391,117 km)

2. Jupiter
88,846 miles
(142,984 km)

3. Saturn
74,898 miles
(120,536 km)

5. Neptune
30,776 miles
(49,528 km)

6. Earth
7,926 miles
(12,755 km)

4. Uranus
31,764 miles
(51,118 km)

7. Venus
7,521 miles
(12,104 km)

9. Ganymede
(moon of Jupiter)
3,280 miles
(5,262 km)

10. Titan
(moon of Saturn)
3,200 miles
(5,149 km)

8. Mars
4,222 miles
(6,794 km)

Astronomy Terms and Definitions

Light-year (distance traveled by light in one year)	5.880 trillion miles (9.462 trillion km)
Velocity of light (speed of light)	186,000 miles/second (299,338 km/s)
Mean distance, Earth to Moon	238,855 miles (384,400 km)
Radius of Earth (distance from Earth's center to the equator)	3,963.19 miles (6,378 km)
Equatorial circumference of Earth (distance around the equator)	24,901 miles (40,075 km)
Polar circumference of Earth (distance around the poles)	24,860 miles (40,008 km)
Earth's mean velocity in orbit (how fast it travels)	18.5 miles/second (29.8 km/sec)

Fast Facts About the Moon

Age	4.6 billion years
Location	solar system
Mean distance from Earth	238,855 miles (384,400 km)
Diameter	2,160 miles (3,476 km)
Period of revolution	27 Earth days

Interesting features:
The Moon has no atmosphere or magnetic field. Most rocks on the surface of the Moon seem to be between 3 and 4.6 billion years old. Thus the Moon provides evidence about the early history of our solar system.

Space

Top 10 Known Closest Comet Approaches to Earth Prior to 2009

5. Biela
December 9, 1805
3,402,182.5 miles
(5,475,282 km)

6. Comet of 1743
February 8, 1743
3,625,276.5 miles
(5,834,317 km)

4. Halley
April 10, 837
3,104,724.0 miles
(4,996.569 km)

7. Pons-Winnecke
June 26, 1927
3,662,458.7 miles
(5,894,156 km)

3. IRAS-Araki-Alcock
May 11, 1983
2,900,221.5 miles
(4,667,454 km)

8. Comet of 1014
February 24, 1014
3,783,301.1 miles
(6,088,633 km)

2. Tempel-Tuttle
October 26, 1366
2,128,687.8 miles
(3,425,791 km)

9. Comet of 1702
April 20, 1702
4,062,168.8 miles
(6,537,427 km)

1. Lexell
July 1, 1770
1,403,632.1 miles
(2,258,927 km)

10. Comet of 1132
October 7, 1132
4,155,124.7 miles
(6,687,025 km)

The Phases of the Moon

The Moon's appearance changes as it moves in its orbit around Earth.

First quarter

Waxing gibbous

Waxing crescent

Full moon

New moon

Waning gibbous

Waning crescent

Last quarter

Major Constellations

Latin	English	Latin	English
Aries	Ram	Lynx	Lynx
Camelopardalis	Giraffe	Lyra	Harp
Cancer	Crab	Microscopium	Microscope
Canes Venatici	Hunting Dogs	Monoceros	Unicorn
Canis Major	Big Dog	Musca	Fly
Canis Minor	Little Dog	Orion	Orion
Capricornus	Goat	Pavo	Peacock
Cassiopeia	Queen	Pegasus	Pegasus
Centaurus	Centaur	Phoenix	Phoenix
Cetus	Whale	Pictor	Painter
Chamaeleon	Chameleon	Pisces	Fish
Circinus	Compass	Piscis Austrinus	Southern Fish
Columba	Dove	Sagitta	Arrow
Corona Australis	Southern Crown	Sagittarius	Archer
Corona Borealis	Northern Crown	Scorpius	Scorpion
Corvus	Crow	Sculptor	Sculptor
Crater	Cup	Scutum	Shield
Crux	Southern Cross	Serpens	Serpent
Cygnus	Swan	Sextans	Sextant
Delphinus	Dolphin	Taurus	Bull
Dorado	Goldfish	Telescopium	Telescope
Draco	Dragon	Triangulum	Triangle
Equuleus	Little Horse	Triangulum Australe	Southern Triangle
Gemini	Twins	Tucana	Toucan
Grus	Crane	Ursa Major	Big Bear
Hercules	Hercules	Ursa Minor	Little Bear
Horologium	Clock	Virgo	Virgin
Lacerta	Lizard	Volans	Flying Fish
Leo	Lion	Vulpecula	Little Fox
Leo Minor	Little Lion		

Galaxies Nearest to the Sun

1. Canis Major Dwarf Galaxy
25,000 light-years

2. Sagittarius Dwarf Elliptical Galaxy
70,000 light-years

3. Large Magellanic Cloud
179,000 light-years

4. Small Magellanic Cloud
210,000 light-years

CHECK IT OUT!

It would take the spacecraft *Voyager* about 749,000,000 years to get to Canis Major Dwarf Galaxy, the closest galaxy to ours.

Stars Closest to Earth

1. Proxima Centauri
4.22 light-years

2. Alpha Centauri A and B
4.35 light-years

3. Barnard's Star
5.9 light-years

4. Wolf 359
7.6 light-years

5. Lalande 21185
8.0 light-years

6. Sirius A and B
8.6 light-years

7. Luyten 726-8A and 726-8B
8.9 light-years

⊛ Sports ◯ ⊕

Outstanding in Their Fields

Do you wish you could bend it like Beckham? Ever since there have been sports to play, there have been players who stand out and inspire. Some remarkable athletes have worked especially hard to overcome great odds. Lance Armstrong won seven Tour de France bicycle races in a row (1999–2005) after battling cancer. Rachel Scdoris became the first legally blind athlete to race the grueling 1,100-mile (1,770 km) Iditarod Trail Sled Dog Race.

FAN-tastic!

Millions of fans follow the games, seasons, and statistics of their favorite teams and athletes. Most major cities have professional football, baseball, basketball, hockey, or soccer teams. These sports and others bring in big bucks through ticket sales and team merchandise.

X Marks the Spot

What if you love skateboarding, street luging, or speed climbing? Before 1995, there was no national competition for these extreme action sports. Then ESPN executive Ron Semiao founded the X Games, in which athletes compete in events such as bicycle stunts, in-line skating, snowboarding, and skateboarding.

Snowboarding superstar Shaun White holds the record for Winter X Game gold medals, with a total of ten. In 2010, Shaun clinched his second Olympic gold with his trademark trick, the tomahawk.

PHENOMS FOREVER

Every generation has its heroes—athletes whose talents and star power leave a permanent mark in history. Baseball legend Babe Ruth was the superstar of the 1920s. Boxing champ Muhammad Ali reigned in the '60s. The '90s had basketball phenom Michael Jordan and hockey idol Wayne Gretzky. Today, powerhouses Venus and Serena Williams and Rafael Nadal rock the tennis court. LeBron James tears up the basketball court. Who will the heroes be next year?

(TAKE a LOOK)

Whether you're playing a pickup game of hoops or running around the block, sports are a great way to play, stay healthy, and have fun. What gets you up and at 'em? Take a look through this section and see how your favorite sports measure up. Maybe you'll be inspired to try something new.

CHECK IT OUT !

Which athletes do kids admire most? At the 2010 Nickelodeon Kids' Choice Awards, skateboarder Ryan Sheckler was voted Favorite Male Athlete and pro volleyball player Misty May-Treanor scored for Favorite Female Athlete.

PRO FOOTBALL

League Leaders 2009

Passing Yards
Matt Schaub, Houston Texans — 4,770

Rushing Yards
Chris Johnson, Tennessee Titans — 2,006

Receiving Yards
Andre Johnson, Houston Texans — 1,569

Touchdowns
Adrian Peterson, Minnesota Vikings — 18

Kick Returns
Jerious Norwood, Atlanta Falcons — 117 returns, 2,987 yards

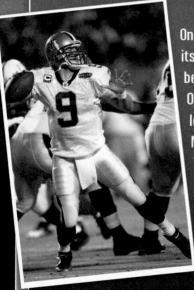

Super Bowl XLIV

On February 7, 2010, the National Football League staged its championship pro football game, Super Bowl XLIV, between National Football Conference (NFC) leaders New Orleans Saints and American Football Conference (AFC) leaders Indianapolis Colts at the Sun Life Stadium in Miami, Florida. The Saints brought the prized Lombardy Trophy home for the first time in Super Bowl history with a 31–17 win over the Colts. MVP Quarterback Drew Brees completed 32 of 39 passes for 288 yards and 2 touchdowns.

New Orleans Saints (NFC) 31
Indianapolis Colts (AFC) 17

The Pittsburgh Steelers made NFL history in February 2009 when Pittsburgh won the Super Bowl for the sixth time—the most Super Bowl victories by any single team. They claimed the Lombardy Trophy in Super Bowls IX, X, XIII, XIV, XL, and XLIII. The San Francisco 49ers (XVI, XIX, XXIII, XXIV, XXIX) and the Dallas Cowboys (VI, XII, XXVII, XXVIII, XXX) are the other league leaders, with five championships each.

Sports

CHEC
IT OU
!

COLLEGE FOLLOWING

COLLEGE FOOTBALL

Sports

Bowl Championship Series (BCS)

National Championship Game 2009
Alabama 37, Texas 21

Major Bowl Games 2009–2010

Game	Location	Teams/Score
Capital One Bowl	Orlando, FL	Penn State 19, LSU 17
Chick-fil-A Bowl	Atlanta, GA	Virginia Tech 37, Tennessee 14
Champs Sports Bowl	Orlando, FL	Wisconsin 20, Miami (FL) 14
Fiesta Bowl	Glendale, AZ	Boise State 17, TCU 10
Gator Bowl	Jacksonville, FL	Florida State 33, West Virginia 21
MAACO Bowl	Las Vegas, NV	BYU 44, Oregon State 20
Meineke Car Care Bowl	Charlotte, NC	Pittsburgh 19, North Carolina 17
Orange Bowl	Miami, FL	Iowa 24, Georgia Tech 14
Rose Bowl	Pasadena, CA	Ohio State 26, Oregon 17
Sugar Bowl	New Orleans, LA	Florida 51, Cincinnati 24

Heisman Trophy 2009

Heisman Trophy winner Mark Ingram of the Alabama Crimson Tide ran 116 yards and scored 2 touchdowns, defeating the Texas Longhorns 37–21 for Alabama's first victory in college football.

261

BASEBALL

Top Players 2009

Rookies of the Year
American League	Andrew Bailey, Oakland Athletics
National League	Chris Coghlan, Florida Marlins

Managers of the Year
American League	Mike Scioscia, Los Angeles Angels
National League	Jim Tracy, Colorado Rockies

Most Valuable Player Awards
American League	Joe Mauer, Minnesota Twins
National League	Albert Pujois, St. Louis Cardinals

Cy Young Awards
American League	Zack Greinke, Kansas City Royals
National League	Tim Lincecum, San Francisco Giants

Gold Glove Winners 2009
(selected by managers and players)

American League
Pitcher	Mark Buehrle, Chicago White Sox
Catcher	Joe Mauer, Minnesota Twins
First Baseman	Mark Teixeira, New York Yankees
Second Baseman	Plácido Polanco, Detroit Tigers
Third Baseman	Evan Longoria, Tampa Bay Rays
Shortstop	Derek Jeter, New York Yankees
	Torii Hunter, Los Angeles Angels
	Adam Jones, Baltimore Orioles
Outfielders	Ichiro Suzuki, Seattle Mariners

National League
Pitcher	Adam Wainwright, St. Louis Cardinals
Catcher	Yadier Molina, St. Louis Cardinals
First Baseman	Adrian Gonzalez, San Diego Padres
Second Baseman	Orlando Hudson, Los Angeles Dodgers
Third Baseman	Ryan Zimmerman, Washington Nationals
Shortstop	Jimmy Rollins, Philadelphia Phillies
	Shane Victorino, Philadelphia Phillies
	Michael Bourn, Houston Astros
Outfielders	Matt Kemp, Los Angeles Dodgers

Sports

League Leaders 2009

American League

Batting Average	Joe Mauer (.365), Minnesota Twins
Home Runs	Carlos Peña (39), Tampa Bay Rays
Runs Batted In	Mark Teixeira (122), New York Yankees
Wins	Justin Verlander (19), Detroit Tigers
Earned Run Average	Zack Greinke (2.16), Kansas City Royals
Saves	Brian Fuentes (48), Los Angeles Angels

National League

Batting Average	Hanley Ramirez (.342), Florida Marlins
Home Runs	Albert Pujols (47), St. Louis Cardinals
Runs Batted In	Prince Fielder (141), Milwaukee Brewers
Wins	Adam Wainwright (19), St. Louis Cardinals
Earned Run Average	Chris Carpenter (2.24), St. Louis Cardinals
Saves	Heath Bell (42), San Diego Padres

World Series 2009

The New York Yankees scored their 27th world championship with a 4–2 win over the Philadelphia Phillies in Game 6 of Major League Baseball's 2009 World Series. Left fielder Hideki Matsui earned the Most Valuable Player award with his 6 RBIs. Matsui tied the record with Bobby Richardson, another Yankee who set the record in 1960 for most RBIs in a World Series.

Little League World Series 2009

Chula Vista, California, earned the LLWS Title, defeating Chinese Taipei 6–3 in the Little League World Championships, played in South Williamsport, Pennsylvania, August 21–30. California's comeback victory was the second of its kind in a World Series final, making it the fifth straight win for the United States. The longest winning streak for the U.S.A. was 8 games, from 1959 to 1966.

NBA Championship Finals 2009

On Sunday, June 14, 2009, the Los Angeles Lakers clinched the National Basketball Association championship with a 4–1 win vs. the Orlando Magic in a best-of-seven series played at the Amway Arena in Orlando, Florida. The victory made the 10th win for Lakers coach Phil Jackson, who topped former record-holder Celtics Red Auerbach's 9 wins for most championships by a coach in NBA history. Most Valuable Player Kobe Bryant scored 30 points, holding a 27.1 per game average.

NBA Top Scorers 2009

NAME	TEAM	GAMES	AVG. POINTS
1. Dwyane Wade	Miami Heat	79	30.2
2. LeBron James	Cleveland Cavaliers	81	28.4
3. Kobe Bryant	Los Angeles Lakers	82	26.8
4. Dirk Nowitzki	Dallas Mavericks	81	25.9
5. Danny Granger	Indiana Pacers	67	25.8

WNBA Championship Finals 2009

The Phoenix Mercury defeated the Indiana Fever in five games, winning the Women's National Basketball Association (WNBA) title 94–86. Most Valuable Player, guard/forward Diana Taurasi averaged 19.0 points, 7.0 rebounds, and 2.5 assists. A record 82,018 spectators attended the event, making the 2009 WNBA Finals the most-attended finals in league history. The series' 931 combined points sets a WNBA Finals record for most points in a series.

WNBA Top Scorers 2009

NAME	TEAM	GAMES	AVG. POINTS (per game)
1. Diana Taurasi	Phoenix Mercury	31	20.4
2. Becky Hammon	San Antonio Silver Stars	31	19.5
3. Lauren Jackson	Seattle Storm	26	19.2
4. Cappie Pondexter	New York Liberty	34	19.1
5. Sophia Young	San Antonio Silver Stars	33	18.2

Sports

COLLEGE BASKETBALL

NCAA Men's Division I Championship 2010

The Duke Blue Devils beat the Butler Bulldogs 61–59 to earn the fourth national title of the National Collegiate Athletic Association (NCAA). The Final Four college basketball championships in Indianapolis, Indiana, on April 5, 2010, may be remembered as the near-greatest ending in sports history: a midcourt 3-point shot that Butler's Gordon Hayward threw—and missed—in the last 3.6 seconds of the game. Instead, he lost the game by a bounce. Brian Zoubek rebounded Hayward's miss in the remaining time and ended Butler's 25-game winning streak to clinch the title. The Duke–Butler series was the 11th championship game in NCAA history to be decided by a margin of 2 points or

NCAA Championship Game Leaders

	Duke		Butler	
Points	Kyle Singler	19	Shelvin Mack	12
Rebounds	Brian Zoubek	10	Gordon Hayward	8
Assists	Jon Scheyer	5	Willie Veasley	3
Steals	Lance Thomas	2	Shelvin Mack	2

NCAA Women's Division I Championship 2010

On April 6, 2010, the University of Connecticut Huskies scored their 78th straight win at the NCAA women's basketball championship against the Stanford Cardinals at the Alamodome in San Antonio, Texas. The victory marked the seventh NCAA women's basketball championship for coach Geno Auriemma. Outstanding player Maya Moore scored 23 points and 11 rebounds to help UConn rally from a losing first half to beat Stanford 53–47 for a second straight undefeated season.

OLYMPICS

Locations of the Modern-Day Summer Olympics

Year	Location	Year	Location	Year	Location
1896	Athens, Greece	1932	Los Angeles, California, USA	1972	Munich, Germany
1900	Paris, France	1936	Berlin, Germany	1976	Montreal, Canada
1904	St. Louis, Missouri, USA	1940	Canceled	1980	Moscow, USSR
1906	Athens, Greece	1944	Canceled	1984	Los Angeles, California, USA
1908	London, UK	1948	London, UK	1988	Seoul, South Korea
1912	Stockholm, Sweden	1952	Helsinki, Finland	1992	Barcelona, Spain
1916	Canceled	1956	Melbourne, Australia	1996	Atlanta, Georgia, USA
1920	Antwerp, Belgium	1960	Rome, Italy	2000	Sydney, Australia
1924	Paris, France	1964	Tokyo, Japan	2004	Athens, Greece
1928	Amsterdam, Holland	1968	Mexico City, Mexico	2008	Beijing, China
				2012	London, UK

Vancouver 2010 Winter Olympics

Vancouver, Canada, won the bid against seven other cities to host the XXI Olympic Winter Games. The event made history as the first social media Olympic games, enabling Olympic fans all over the world to follow on social media platforms Facebook, Twitter, and YouTube. There were 15 winter sports, 86 medal competitions, 615 medals awarded, and 2,632 registered athletes. The Olympic and Paralympic Winter Games included curling, figure skating, ice hockey, sledge hockey, short track speed skating, and wheelchair curling.

Medal Count Leaders

Country	Gold	Silver	Bronze	Total
United States	9	15	13	37
Germany	10	13	7	30
Canada	14	7	5	26
Norway	9	8	6	23
Austria	4	6	6	16
Russian Federation	3	5	7	15
Korea	6	6	2	14
China	5	2	4	11
Sweden	5	2	4	11
France	2	3	6	11

Tragedy Hits Athletes

• Nodar Kumaritashvili, a 21-year-old Georgian luge slider, suffered a fatal crash during a training run for the luge event. He died on impact after hitting a pole, traveling at speeds greater than 90 miles per hour (144.8 km) before the game's opening ceremonies.

• Canadian figure skater Joannie Rochette won a bronze medal in ladies' short program figure skating just days after her mother died unexpectedly.

Locations of the Modern-Day Winter Olympics

Year	Location	Year	Location
1924	Chamonix, France	1968	Grenoble, France
1928	St. Moritz, Switzerland	1972	Sapporo, Japan
1932	Lake Placid, New York, USA	1976	Innsbruck, Austria
1936	Garmisch-Partenkirchen, Germany	1980	Lake Placid, New York, USA
		1984	Sarajevo, Yugoslavia
1940	Canceled	1988	Calgary, Alberta, Canada
1944	Canceled	1992	Albertville, France
1948	St. Moritz, Switzerland	1994	Lillehammer, Norway
1952	Oslo, Norway	1998	Nagano, Japan
1956	Cortina d'Ampezzo, Italy	2002	Salt Lake City, Utah, USA
1960	Squaw Valley, California, USA	2006	Turin, Italy
1964	Innsbruck, Austria	2010	Vancouver, Canada
		2014	Sochi, Russian Federation

Shining Stars 2010

• In one of the greatest moments in hockey history, Canadian Sidney Crosby scored the winning point 7:40 into overtime, and claimed the gold for Canada, beating out the United States 3–2. It was the first men's hockey gold for a host nation in 30 years, and the record-breaking 14th Winter Olympics gold for Canada.

• South Korea's Yu-Na Kim dominated the ice with her gold-winning ladies' free skate performance, featuring six perfect triples, including a triple lutz—triple toe combination.

• U.S. Alpine skier Lindsey Vonn suffered a performance-threatening shin injury days before the games but recovered enough to take a gold.

Historic Feats

• The United States took the gold in bobsled for the first time since 1948.

• American Apolo Ohno became the most-decorated athlete of any Winter Games in history. His bronze win in the men's 5000 meter relay short track speed skating event won him his 8th medal.

• Canada set a new Olympic record with 14 gold medals, beating the previous high of 13 golds at any Winter Games (Soviet Union 1976, Norway 2002).

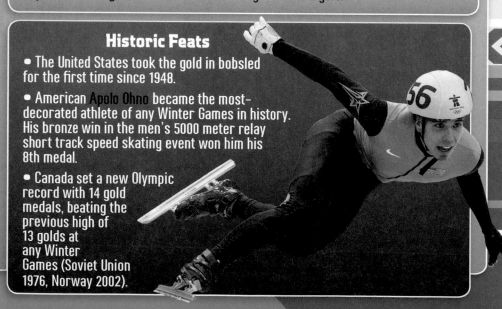

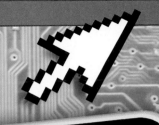

Technology & Computers

The World at Our Fingertips

Can you imagine a day in your life without watching TV, surfing the Web, listening to your MP3 player, or using your cell phone? Technology makes all of these things possible. Through the advancements in technology, we can download our music in a matter of seconds, watch our favorite TV show on Hulu anytime we want, or access information from any part of the globe with the mere touch of a finger.

Social Climbing

We can keep connected, too. The popularity of social media continues to grow the world over. From January to July 2009, Facebook usage increased 80 percent in the United States alone. Social media, like Facebook and Twitter, allow people to stay connected and know what's happening with their friends at any time of day. Through YouTube, they can view videos or upload their own. Skype allows people to speak with their friends around the world through their computer.

From Old Phone to Smartphone

Times have changed since Alexander Graham Bell invented the first modern telephone. Bell, who was awarded the first U.S. patent for the invention of the telephone, used a liquid transmitter and electromagnetic receiver to make the first successful phone call on March 10, 1876. Today, due to wireless technology and new operating systems—like the Apple iPhone and Google-powered Android—people can simultaneously access the Internet from their cell phone while they're using the phone to speak with someone.

No Ordinary Notepad

Released on April 3rd, 2010, Apple's iPad is the latest multimedia technology, revolutionizing the way that people communicate. The iPad comes with several built-in applications, including: Safari, YouTube, iPod, iTunes, iBooks, and more. The ultimate multipurpose portal, the iPad allows people to access their e-mail, read books, store photos and videos, listen to and download music, manage their contacts and calendar—all on a single device.

TAKE a LOOK

Since the introduction of the original color television in 1953, no other innovation has done as much to enhance the visual quality of television as High Definition (HD) TV. Today, cable and satellite program providers are in a race to see who can offer the most HD content on their network. Do you enjoy watching life in High Def?

CHECK IT OUT !

More and more, Americans are choosing to leave their landlines behind in favor of their cell phones. In 2009, 21 percent of U.S. households used only cell phones for their communication—no landlines. What else do teenagers use their cell phones for besides talking? Check out page 277.

Where Do Americans Get Their Data?

There are so many bits and pieces of data available today, in the form of the words and pictures that make up news stories, games, entertainment, gossip, reference, mail, pictures, movies, and more. What percentage of the available data do Americans access through different media?

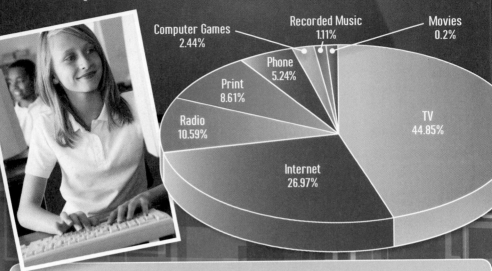

Computer Games 2.44%
Recorded Music 1.11%
Movies 0.2%
Phone 5.24%
Print 8.61%
Radio 10.59%
TV 44.85%
Internet 26.97%

U.S. Internet Usage vs. Population Growth

Year	Population	Users	% of Population
2000	281,421,906	124,000,000	44.1 %
2001	285,317,559	142,823,008	50.0%
2002	288,368,698	167,196,688	58.0%
2003	290,809,777	172,250,000	59.2%
2004	293,271,500	201,661,159	68.8%
2005	299,093,237	203,824,428	68.1%
2007	301,967,681	212,080,135	70.2%
2008	303,824,646	220,141,969	72.5%
2009	307,212,123	227,719,000	74.1%

U.S. Internet Users by Age

Age Group	Percentage Using
18–29	91%
30–49	81%
50–64	70%
65+	35%

U.S. Internet Users by Gender

Gender	Percentage Using
Male	74%
Female	74%

Average Monthly Time Spent Using Internet by Age

Age	Hours:Minutes:Seconds
2–11	5:21:00
12–17	11:32:00
18–24	14:19:00
25–34	31:37:00
35–44	42:35:00
45–54	39:27:00
55–64	35:49:00
65+	28:34:00

Adult Broadband Users by Age

Age	Percentage of Age Group Who Connect by Broadband
18–29	76%
30–49	67%
50–64	56%
65+	26%

Adult Wireless Internet Users by Age

Age	Percentage of Age Group Who Connect by Wireless
18–29	80%
30–49	66%
50–64	42%
65+	16%

HD TV Users

Number of households with HD TVs	33%
Number of households with HD TVs and HD TV programming	28.8%

Top 10 Most Visited Websites

Google sites (YouTube; Blogger)
Microsoft sites
Yahoo! sites (Flickr; del.icio.us)
Facebook
America Online sites
Fox Interactive Media sites (MySpace; Photobucket)
Ask Network sites (Bloglines; Excite; iWon)
eBay sites (PayPal; Shopping.com; Skype)
Amazon sites (IMDb)
Wikimedia Foundation sites (Wikipedia)

Top 10 Search Providers

Provider	Share of Searches
Google Search	65.2%
Yahoo! Search	14.1%
MSN/Windows Live/Bing Search	12.5%
AOL Search	2.3%
Ask.com Search	1.9%
My Web Search	1.0%
Comcast Search	0.6%
Yellow Pages Search	0.3%
NexTag Search	0.3%
WhitePages.com Network Search	0.3%

Top 10 Most-Searched Terms

2009	2008
facebook	myspace
myspace	craigslist
craigslist	ebay
youtube	google
yahoo mail	myspace.com
google	yahoo
yahoo	youtube
ebay	yahoo mail
facebook login	yahoo.com
myspace.com	facebook

Top 10 Social Networking Websites

Facebook
MySpace
YouTube
Tagged
Twitter
Yahoo! Answers
Yahoo! Profiles
myYearbook
Meebo
Windows Live Home

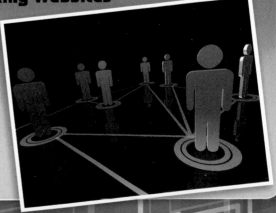

Monthly Social Network Usage by Country
(Combined Home & Work)

Country	Hours:Minutes:Seconds per Person
Italy	6:27:53
Australia	6:25:21
United States	6:02:34
United Kingdom	5:50:56
Spain	4:50:49
Brazil	4:27:54
France	4:12:01
Germany	3:47:24
Switzerland*	3:26:00
Japan	2:37:07

*Home only

Monthly Global Social Network Traffic

Website	Sessions per Person	Hours:Minutes:Seconds per Person
Facebook	19.16	5:52:00
Myspace	6.66	0:59:33
Twitter	5.81	0:36:43
Classmates Online	3.29	0:13:55
LinkedIn	3.15	0:12:47

U.S. Mobile Social Network Usage by Age

Age	Percentage Who Access Social Network on Mobile
13–17	5%
18–24	16%
25–34	34%
35–54	36%
55–64	7%
65+	2%

10 Top Online Video Sources

YouTube
Yahoo!
Facebook
MSN/WindowsLive/Bing
Hulu
CNN Digital Network
Fox Interactive Media
AOL Media Network
ESPN Digital Network
CBS Entertainment Network

10 Top Online Video Sources by Video Streams

YouTube
Hulu
MSN/WindowsLive/Bing
Yahoo!
CNN Digital Network
Turner Sports and Entertainment Digital Network
Nickelodeon Kids and Family Network
ABC Television
CBS Entertainment Network
Fox Interactive Media

Where Do Americans Watch Video Programming?
(by age)

Source	2–11	12–17	18–24	25–34	35–49	50–64	65+
On TV	10%	6%	7%	13%	22%	24%	18%
On the Internet	6%	8%	9%	15%	30%	23%	9%
On Mobile Phones	N/A	18%	13%	32%	27%	9%	1%

Monthly Time Spent Watching Online Videos by Age

Age	Hours:Minutes:Seconds
2–11	1:48:43
12–17	3:05:57
18–24	5:35:58
25–34	4:44:13
35–44	3:30:33
45–54	2:05:33
65+	1:13:34

U.S. Average Number of Apps by Device

Device	Number of Apps
Apple iPhone	37
Android	22
Other	16
Palm	14
Microsoft Windows Mobile	13
BlackBerry	10

U.S. Mobile Phone Device Averages

Regular cell phone	45%
Smartphone (BlackBerry, iPhone, etc.)	55%

U.S. App Store Usage by Provider

Provider	Percentage of market
Apple App Store	25%
Blackberry App World Store	16%
Verizon Application Store	15%
AT&T Application Store	12%
Sprint Application Store	10%
T-Mobile Application Store	8%
Other Service Provider App Store	5%
Windows Marketplace Store	4%
Android Market Store	2%
Palm App Store	1%
Fandango Website	1%

How Does a U.S. Teen Use Media Each Day?

Medium	Time Spent
TV	3 hours, 20 minutes
PC	52 minutes, including applications
Console gaming	25 minutes
Internet	23 minutes
DVD	17 minutes
Mobile video	13 minutes
DVR	8 minutes
Online video	6 minutes
Mobile voice	6 minutes
Text messages	96 sent or received

How Many Teens Use . . . ?

Device or Medium	Number who use daily
Audio-only MP3 player	1 in 3
Mobile web	1 in 3
Video in an MP3 player	1 in 4
Console games	1 in 10

Daily Teen TV Viewing by Country

Country	Hours:Minutes:Seconds
South Africa	5:02:01
Venezuela	4:53:55
Indonesia	4:25:24
Ireland	4:20:56
Lebanon	3:47:57
Poland	3:47:20
Italy	3:23:41
United States	3:20:04
Australia	3:07:42
Taiwan	2:47:29

U.S. Teen Mobile Media Usage
(exclusive of phone calls)

Usage	Percentage
Text messaging	83%
MMS picture or video file included	56%
Pre-installed games	45%
Ringtone downloads	43%
Instant message	40%
Mobile Internet	37%
Screensavers download	33%
Picture download	32%
Game download	29%
Software download	29%
Text alert	29%
E-mail	28%
Video messaging	26%
Content upload	26%
Music download	23%
Mobile video	18%
Online game	18%
Streaming audio	17%
Location-based service	16%

Top Genres of Mobile Video Consumption by Teens

Genre	Percentage
Music	54%
Comedy	48%
User-generated	39%
Sports	37%
Animated	36%

U.S. Teen Mobile Usage

Teens with own mobile	77%
Teen mobile borrowers	11%
Teens with no mobile	12%

How Do Teens Around the World Listen to Music?

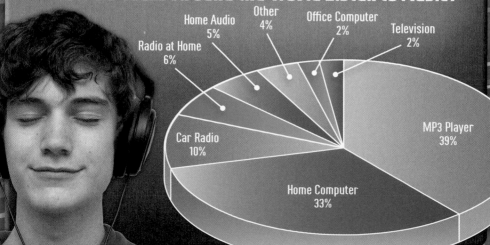

Home Audio 5%
Other 4%
Office Computer 2%
Television 2%
Radio at Home 6%
Car Radio 10%
MP3 Player 39%
Home Computer 33%

277

U.S. Government

We, the People

Government is a system under which a nation, state, organization, or other group of people is managed. Different countries have different kinds of government. A nation may be ruled by a king or a queen (monarchy). A single person can rule by himself or herself (dictatorship). In some rare instances, a country has no government at all (anarchy). The United States government is a representative democracy, ruled by the people themselves through their elected leaders. But this wasn't always the case.

Birth of a Nation

Before the United States were either united or states, they were colonies controlled largely by the English monarchy. The colonists wanted a different kind of government—one in which the people had a voice. After successfully fighting a revolutionary war of independence, they formed a new nation of their own. In 1787, they adopted the U.S. Constitution, a set of organizational rules and individual rights that serve as the foundation of our government to this day. It established three branches—the executive (president), the legislative (Congress), and the judicial (Supreme Court). The three branches work together while keeping a balance of political power among themselves.

The United States Capitol

FORM A LINE

The United States has had 44 presidents. Four of them died in office of natural causes:
- William Henry Harrison (1841)—of pneumonia
- Zachary Taylor (1849—1850)—of cholera
- Warren G. Harding (1921—1923)—of pneumonia
- Franklin D. Roosevelt (1933—1945)—of a cerebral hemorrhage

And four were assassinated:
- Abraham Lincoln (1861—1865)
- James Garfield (1881)
- William McKinley (1897—1901)
- John F. Kennedy (1961—1963)

If a president dies or can't complete his/her term, the vice president steps in. But what happens if the vice president can't take on the job either? You may be surprised at how many officials are in line for the job. (See page 284.)

TAKE a LOOK

If a picture is worth a thousand words, then whose picture is worth a thousand bucks? The faces of U.S. presidents and other leaders appear on our money, but do you know who's on what? If you had four Ulysses S. Grants, two Andrew Jacksons, a William McKinley, and five Abe Lincolns in your pocket, how much money would you have? Take a look at page 288 and count 'em up.

4 + **2** + **1** + **5** =?

CHECK IT OUT!

How can a presidential candidate win the election without getting the most votes from the people? Rutherford B. Hayes in 1876, Benjamin Harrison in 1888, and George W. Bush in 2000 are all proof that it can happen. (See page 286.)

The Branches of Government

Executive

The President

- Symbol of our nation and head of state
- Shapes and conducts foreign policy and acts as chief diplomat
- Chief administrator of federal government
- Commander-in-chief of armed forces
- Has authority to pass or veto congressional bills, plans, and programs
- Appoints and removes nonelected officials
- Leader of his or her political party

Legislative

The Congress:
The Senate
The House of Representatives

- Chief lawmaking body
- Conducts investigations into matters of national importance
- Has power to impeach or remove any civil officer from office, including the president
- Can amend Constitution
- The Senate is made up of 100 senators—2 from each state
- The House of Representatives is made up of 435 congressional representatives, apportioned to each state according to population

Judicial

The Supreme Court

- Protects Constitution
- Enforces commands of executive and legislative branches
- Protects rights of individuals and shields citizens from unfair laws
- Defines laws of our nation
- Can declare laws unconstitutional

Highest Federal Salaries

Official	Salary
President	$400,000
Vice President	$227,300
Speaker of the House	$223,500
Chief Justice of the Supreme Court	$223,500
Associate justices	$213,900
President Pro Tempore of the Senate	$193,400
Senate majority and minority leaders	$193,400
House majority and minority leaders	$193,400
Appeals court judges	$184,500
Senators	$174,000
Representatives	$174,000
District judges	$174,000

CHECK IT OUT!

For most of the years between 1789 and 1855, members of Congress received no yearly salary at all. Instead they were paid $6.00 to $8.00 a day when Congress was in session. Benjamin Franklin proposed that elected government officials not be paid anything for their service, but his proposal didn't win much support.

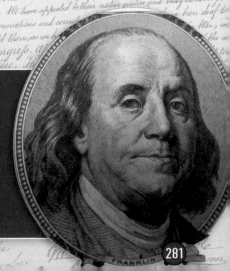

How a Bill Introduced in the House of Representatives Becomes a Law

How a Bill Originates

The executive branch inspires much legislation. The president usually outlines broad objectives in the yearly State of the Union address.

Members of the president's staff may draft bills and ask congresspersons who are friendly to the legislation to introduce them.

Other bills originate independently of the administration, perhaps to fulfill a campaign pledge made by a congressperson.

How a Bill Is Introduced

Each bill must be introduced by a member of the House. The Speaker then assigns the bill to the appropriate committee.

The committee conducts hearings during which members of the administration and others may testify for or against the bill.

If the committee votes to proceed, the bill goes to the Rules Committee, which decides whether to place it before the House.

The House Votes

A bill submitted to the House is voted on, with or without a debate. If a majority approves it, the bill is sent to the Senate.

Senate Procedure

The Senate assigns a bill to a Senate committee, which holds hearings and then approves, rejects, rewrites, or shelves the bill.

If the committee votes to proceed, the bill is submitted to the Senate for a vote, which may be taken with or without a debate.

Results

If the Senate does not change the House version of the bill and a majority approves it, the bill goes to the president for signing.

If the bill the Senate approves differs from the House version, the bill is sent to a House–Senate conference for a compromise solution.

If the conference produces a compromise bill and it is approved by both the House and Senate, the bill goes to the president for signing.

When a Bill Becomes Law

The bill becomes law if the president signs it. If the president vetoes the bill, two-thirds of both the House and Senate must approve it again before it can become law. If the bill comes to the president soon before Congress adjourns, the president may not do anything at all. If the bill is not signed before Congress adjourns, the bill dies. This is called the president's "pocket veto."

U.S. Government

(A similar procedure is followed for bills introduced in the Senate.)

State and Federal Court Systems

U.S. Supreme Court

State Courts

Federal Courts

State Supreme Court

U.S. Court of Appeals

State Court of Appeals

U.S. District Court

State General Trial Court
(Jury Court)

Municipal Court
(misdemeanors and minor civil cases)

District or Justice of the Peace Court

The Sequence of Presidential Succession

If the president dies, resigns, is removed from office, or can't carry out his or her duties, the vice president assumes the president's duties. If the vice president dies or becomes unable to serve, who is next in line? The order of presidential replacements is below.

1. **Vice President**
2. **Speaker of the House**
3. **President Pro Tempore of the Senate**
4. **Secretary of State**
5. **Secretary of the Treasury**
6. **Secretary of Defense**
7. **Attorney General**
8. **Secretary of the Interior**
9. **Secretary of Agriculture**
10. **Secretary of Commerce**
11. **Secretary of Labor**
12. **Secretary of Health and Human Services**
13. **Secretary of Housing and Urban Development**
14. **Secretary of Energy**
15. **Secretary of Education**

U.S. Government

Voting

Basic Laws and Requirements

- You must be 18 years of age or older before an election in order to vote in it.
- You must be an American citizen to vote.
- You must register before voting.
- You must show proof of residence in order to register.

How to Register

- Registering often only requires filling out a simple form.
- It does not cost anything to register.
- You need not be a member of any political party to register.
- To find out where to register, you can call your town hall or city board of elections.
- You can find out more about voting and registering at:

www.eac.gov/voter

Voter Turnout: 1960–2008

Year	Percent of citizens who voted
2008*	64.0%
2000*	54.2%
1990	36.5%
1980*	52.6%
1970	46.6%
1960*	63.1%

*Presidential election year

The Electoral College

Although people turn out on Election Day and cast their votes for president, the president and vice president are only indirectly elected by the American people. In fact, the president and vice president are the only elected federal officials not chosen by direct vote of the people. These two officials are elected by the Electoral College, which was created by the framers of the Constitution.

Here is a basic summary of how the Electoral College works:

- There are 538 electoral votes.
- The votes are divided among the 50 states and the District of Columbia. The number of votes that each state has is equal to the number of senators and representatives for that state. (California has 53 representatives and 2 senators; it has a total of 55 electoral votes.)
- During an election, the candidate who wins the majority of popular votes in a given state wins all the electoral votes from that state.
- A presidential candidate needs 270 electoral votes to win.

You may have heard that it is possible for a presidential candidate who has not won the most popular votes to win an election. This can happen if a candidate wins the popular vote in large states (ones with lots of electoral votes) by only a slim margin and loses the popular votes in smaller states by a wide margin.

Electoral Votes for President

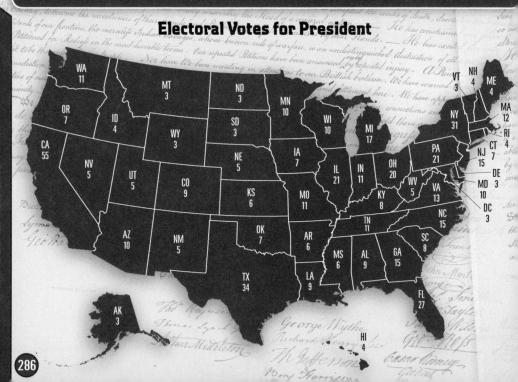

U.S. Government

U.S. Presidents with the Most Electoral Votes

President		Year	Number of electoral votes
Ronald Reagan	🐘	1984	525
Franklin D. Roosevelt	🐴	1936	523
Richard Nixon	🐘	1972	520
Ronald Reagan	🐘	1980	489
Lyndon B. Johnson	🐴	1964	486
Franklin D. Roosevelt	🐴	1932	472
Dwight D. Eisenhower	🐘	1956	457
Franklin D. Roosevelt	🐴	1940	449
Herbert Hoover	🐘	1928	444
Dwight D. Eisenhower	🐘	1952	442

🐘 = Republican

🐴 = Democrat

U.S. Presidents with the Most Popular Votes

President		Year	Number of popular votes
Barack H. Obama Jr.	🐴	2008	69,297,997
George W. Bush	🐘	2004	62,039,073
Ronald Reagan	🐘	1984	54,455,075
George W. Bush	🐘	2000	50,456,062
George H. W. Bush	🐘	1988	48,886,097

Who Is on Our Paper Money?

$1
George Washington

$2
Thomas Jefferson

$5
Abraham Lincoln

$10
Alexander Hamilton

$20
Andrew Jackson

$50
Ulysses S. Grant

$100
Benjamin Franklin

$500*
William McKinley

$1,000*
Grover Cleveland

$5,000*
James Madison

$10,000*
Salmon P. Chase

$100,000*
Woodrow Wilson

*Bills above $100 are no longer made.

Who Is on Our Coins?

Dime
Franklin D. Roosevelt

Half-dollar
John F. Kennedy

Penny
Abraham Lincoln

Nickel
Thomas Jefferson

Quarter
George Washington

Dollar
Sacagawea

Presidents of the United States

1. George Washington

Born: Feb. 22, 1732, Wakefield, Virginia
Died: Dec. 14, 1799, Mount Vernon, Virginia
Term of office: April 30, 1789—March 3, 1797
Age at inauguration: 57
Party: Federalist
Vice President: John Adams
First Lady: Martha Dandridge Custis Washington

2. John Adams

Born: Oct. 30, 1735, Braintree (now Quincy), Massachusetts
Died: July 4, 1826, Braintree, Massachusetts
Term of office: March 4, 1797—March 3, 1801
Age at inauguration: 61
Party: Federalist
Vice President: Thomas Jefferson
First Lady: Abigail Smith Adams

3. Thomas Jefferson

Born: April 13, 1743, Shadwell, Virginia
Died: July 4, 1826, Monticello, Virginia
Term of office: March 4, 1801—March 3, 1809
Age at inauguration: 57
Party: Democratic Republican
Vice President: Aaron Burr, George Clinton
First Lady: Martha Skelton Jefferson

4. James Madison

Born: March 16, 1751, Port Conway, Virginia
Died: June 28, 1836, Orange, Virginia
Term of office: March 4, 1809—March 3, 1817
Age at inauguration: 57
Party: Democratic Republican
Vice President: George Clinton, Elbridge Gerry
First Lady: Dolley Todd Madison

CHECK IT OUT!

George Washington is the only president who was unanimously elected. He received every single vote!

5. James Monroe
Born: April 28, 1758, Westmoreland County, Virginia
Died: July 4, 1831, New York City, New York
Term of office: March 4, 1817—March 3, 1825
Age at inauguration: 58
Party: Democratic Republican
Vice President: Daniel D. Tompkins
First Lady: Elizabeth Kortright Monroe

6. John Quincy Adams
Born: July 11, 1767, Braintree, Massachusetts
Died: Feb. 23, 1848, Washington, DC
Term of office: March 4, 1825—March 3, 1829
Age at inauguration: 57
Party: Democratic Republican
Vice President: John C. Calhoun
First Lady: Louisa Johnson Adams

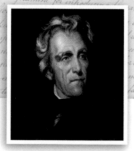

7. Andrew Jackson
Born: March 15, 1767, Waxhaw, South Carolina
Died: June 8, 1845, Nashville, Tennessee
Term of office: March 4, 1829—March 3, 1837
Age at inauguration: 61
Party: Democrat
Vice President: John C. Calhoun, Martin Van Buren
First Lady: Rachel Robards Jackson

8. Martin Van Buren
Born: Dec. 5, 1782, Kinderhook, New York
Died: July 24, 1862, Kinderhook, New York
Term of office: March 4, 1837—March 3, 1841
Age at inauguration: 54
Party: Democrat
Vice President: Richard M. Johnson
First Lady: Hannah Hoes Van Buren

9. William Henry Harrison
Born: Feb. 9, 1773, Berkeley, Virginia
Died: April 4, 1841, Washington, DC*
Term of office: March 4, 1841—April 4, 1841
Age at inauguration: 68
Party: Whig
Vice President: John Tyler
First Lady: Anna Symmes Harrison

10. John Tyler
Born: March 29, 1790, Greenway, Virginia
Died: Jan. 18, 1862, Richmond, Virginia
Term of office: April 6, 1841—March 3, 1845
Age at inauguration: 51
Party: Whig
Vice President: (none)**
First Lady: Letitia Christian Tyler,
Julia Gardiner Tyler†

11. James Knox Polk
Born: Nov. 2, 1795, Mecklenburg, North Carolina
Died: June 15, 1849, Nashville, Tennessee
Term of office: March 4, 1845—March 3, 1849
Age at inauguration: 49
Party: Democrat
Vice President: George M. Dallas
First Lady: Sarah Childress Polk

12. Zachary Taylor
Born: Nov. 24, 1784, Orange County, Virginia
Died: July 9, 1850, Washington, DC*
Term of office: March 5, 1849—July 9, 1850
Age at inauguration: 64
Party: Whig
Vice President: Millard Fillmore
First Lady: Margaret (Peggy) Smith Taylor

CHECK IT OUT !

William Henry Harrison had the longest inauguration speech and the shortest term of any president. After giving a speech lasting 105 minutes in the cold rain, he developed pneumonia and died 32 days later.

* Died in office, natural causes
** Vice President Tyler took over the duties of the president when William Henry Harrison died in office, leaving the vice presidency vacant.
† President Tyler's first wife died in 1842. He remarried in 1844.

13. Millard Fillmore
Born: Jan. 7, 1800, Cayuga County, New York
Died: March 8, 1874, Buffalo, New York
Term of office: July 10, 1850—March 3, 1853
Age at inauguration: 50
Party: Whig
Vice President: (none)*
First Lady: Abigail Powers Fillmore

14. Franklin Pierce
Born: Nov. 23, 1804, Hillsboro, New Hampshire
Died: Oct. 8, 1869, Concord, New Hampshire
Term of office: March 4, 1853—March 3, 1857
Age at inauguration: 48
Party: Democrat
Vice President: William R. King
First Lady: Jane Appleton Pierce

15. James Buchanan
Born: April 23, 1791, Mercersburg, Pennsylvania
Died: June 1, 1868, Lancaster, Pennsylvania
Term of office: March 4, 1857—March 3, 1861
Age at inauguration: 65
Party: Democrat
Vice President: John C. Breckenridge
First Lady: (none)**

16. Abraham Lincoln
Born: Feb. 12, 1809, Hardin, Kentucky
Died: April 15, 1865, Washington, DC†
Term of office: March 4, 1861—April 15, 1865
Age at inauguration: 52
Party: Republican
Vice President: Hannibal Hamlin,
Andrew Johnson
First Lady: Mary Todd Lincoln

U.S. Government

* When Zachary Taylor died, Millard Fillmore became the second vice president to inherit the presidency, leaving the vice presidency vacant.
** Buchanan was the only president who never married. A favorite niece, Harriet Lane, acted as White House hostess during his administration.
† Assassinated

17. Andrew Johnson

Born: Dec. 29, 1808, Raleigh, North Carolina
Died: July 31, 1875, Carter Station, Tennessee
Term of office: April 15, 1865—March 3, 1869
Age at inauguration: 56
Party: Democrat (nominated by Republican Party)
Vice President: (none)*
First Lady: Eliza McCardle Johnson

18. Ulysses Simpson Grant

Born: April 27, 1822, Point Pleasant, Ohio
Died: July 23, 1885, Mt. McGregor, New York
Term of office: March 4, 1869—March 3, 1877
Age at inauguration: 46
Party: Republican
Vice President: Schuyler Colfax, Henry Wilson
First Lady: Julia Dent Grant

19. Rutherford Birchard Hayes

Born: Oct. 4, 1822, Delaware, Ohio
Died: Jan. 17, 1893, Fremont, Ohio
Term of office: March 4, 1877—March 3, 1881
Age at inauguration: 54
Party: Republican
Vice President: William A. Wheeler
First Lady: Lucy Webb Hayes

20. James Abram Garfield

Born: Nov. 19, 1831, Orange, Ohio
Died: Sept. 19, 1881, Elberon, New Jersey**
Term of office: March 4, 1881—Sept. 19, 1881
Age at inauguration: 49
Party: Republican
Vice President: Chester A. Arthur
First Lady: Lucretia Rudolph Garfield

CHECK IT OUT!

On March 1, 1872, Ulysses S. Grant established Yellowstone as the country's first national park.

* Andrew Johnson became president when Abraham Lincoln was assassinated, leaving the vice presidency vacant.
** Assassinated

21. Chester Alan Arthur

Born: Oct. 5, 1829, Fairfield, Vermont
Died: Nov. 18, 1886, New York City, New York
Term of office: Sept. 20, 1881—March 3, 1885
Age at inauguration: 51
Party: Republican
Vice President: (none)*
First Lady: Ellen Herndon Arthur

22. Grover Cleveland

Born: March 18, 1837, Caldwell, New Jersey
Died: June 24, 1908, Princeton, New Jersey
Term of office: March 4, 1885—March 3, 1889
Age at inauguration: 47
Party: Democrat
Vice President: Thomas A. Hendricks
First Lady: Frances Folsom Cleveland

23. Benjamin Harrison

Born: Aug. 20, 1833, North Bend, Ohio
Died: March 13, 1901, Indianapolis, Indiana
Term of office: March 4, 1889—March 3, 1893
Age at inauguration: 55
Party: Republican
Vice President: Levi P. Morton
First Lady: Caroline Scott Harrison
(died in 1892)

24. Grover Cleveland

Born: March 18, 1837, Caldwell, New Jersey
Died: June 24, 1908, Princeton, New Jersey
Term of office: March 4, 1893—March 3, 1897
Age at inauguration: 55
Party: Democrat
Vice President: Adlai E. Stevenson
First Lady: Frances Folsom Cleveland

CHECK IT OUT!

Grover Cleveland is the only president elected
to two nonconsecutive terms.

*Chester Alan Arthur became president when James Garfield was assassinated, leaving the vice presidency vacant.

25. William McKinley
Born: Jan. 29, 1843, Niles, Ohio
Died: Sept. 14, 1901, Buffalo, New York*
Term of office: March 4, 1897—Sept. 14, 1901
Age at inauguration: 54
Party: Republican
Vice President: Garret A. Hobart,
Theodore Roosevelt
First Lady: Ida Saxton McKinley

26. Theodore Roosevelt
Born: Oct. 27, 1858, New York City, New York
Died: Jan. 6, 1919, Oyster Bay, New York
Term of office: Sept. 14, 1901—March 3, 1909
Age at inauguration: 42
Party: Republican
Vice President: Charles W. Fairbanks
First Lady: Edith Carow Roosevelt

27. William Howard Taft
Born: Sept. 15, 1857, Cincinnati, Ohio
Died: March 8, 1930, Washington, DC
Term of office: March 4, 1909—March 3, 1913
Age at inauguration: 51
Party: Republican
Vice President: James S. Sherman
First Lady: Helen Herron Taft

28. (Thomas) Woodrow Wilson
Born: Dec. 28, 1856, Staunton, Virginia
Died: Feb. 3, 1924, Washington, DC
Term of office: March 4, 1913—March 3, 1921
Age at inauguration: 56
Party: Democrat
Vice President: Thomas R. Marshall
First Lady: Ellen Axon Wilson,
Edith Galt Wilson**

*Assassinated
**Wilson's first wife died early in his administration and he remarried before leaving the White House.

29. Warren Gamaliel Harding

Born: Nov. 2, 1865, Corsica (now Blooming Grove), Ohio
Died: Aug. 2, 1923, San Francisco, California*
Term of office: March 4, 1921—Aug. 2, 1923
Age at inauguration: 55
Party: Republican
Vice President: Calvin Coolidge
First Lady: Florence Kling De Wolfe Harding

30. (John) Calvin Coolidge

Born: July 4,1872, Plymouth Notch, Vermont
Died: Jan. 5, 1933, Northampton, Massachusetts
Term of office: Aug. 3, 1923—March 3, 1929
Age at inauguration: 51
Party: Republican
Vice President: Charles G. Dawes
First Lady: Grace Goodhue Coolidge

31. Herbert Clark Hoover

Born: Aug. 10, 1874, West Branch, Iowa
Died: Oct. 20, 1964, New York City, New York
Term of office: March 4, 1929—March 3, 1933
Age at inauguration: 54
Party: Republican
Vice President: Charles Curtis
First Lady: Lou Henry Hoover

32. Franklin Delano Roosevelt

Born: Jan. 30, 1882, Hyde Park, New York
Died: April 12, 1945, Warm Springs, Georgia*
Term of office: March 4, 1933—April 12, 1945
Age at inauguration: 51
Party: Democrat
Vice President: John N. Garner, Henry A. Wallace, Harry S Truman
First Lady: Anna Eleanor Roosevelt

CHEC IT OU !

Two presidents, John Adams and Thomas Jefferson, died on the same day—July 4, 1826. Another president, James Monroe, died on July 4, 1831. A fourth, Calvin Coolidge, was born on July 4, 1872.

*Died in office, natural causes

33. Harry S Truman

Born: May 8, 1884, Lamar, Missouri
Died: Dec. 26, 1972, Kansas City, Missouri
Term of office: April 12, 1945–Jan. 20, 1953
Age at inauguration: 60
Party: Democrat
Vice President: Alben W. Barkley
First Lady: Elizabeth (Bess) Wallace Truman

34. Dwight David Eisenhower

Born: Oct. 14, 1890, Denison, Texas
Died: March 28, 1969, Washington, DC
Term of office: Jan. 20, 1953–Jan. 20, 1961
Age at inauguration: 62
Party: Republican
Vice President: Richard M. Nixon
First Lady: Mamie Doud Eisenhower

35. John Fitzgerald Kennedy

Born: May 29, 1917, Brookline, Massachusetts
Died: Nov. 22, 1963, Dallas, Texas*
Term of office: Jan. 20, 1961–Nov. 22, 1963
Age at inauguration: 43
Party: Democrat
Vice President: Lyndon B. Johnson
First Lady: Jacqueline Bouvier Kennedy

36. Lyndon Baines Johnson

Born: Aug. 27, 1908, Stonewall, Texas
Died: Jan. 22, 1973, San Antonio, Texas
Term of office: Nov. 22, 1963–Jan. 20, 1969
Age at inauguration: 55
Party: Democrat
Vice President: Hubert H. Humphrey
First Lady: Claudia (Lady Bird) Taylor Johnson

*Assassinated

37. Richard Milhous Nixon

Born: Jan. 9, 1913, Yorba Linda, California
Died: April 22, 1994, New York City, New York
Term of office: Jan. 20, 1969–Aug. 9, 1974*
Age at inauguration: 56
Party: Republican
Vice President: Spiro T. Agnew (resigned), Gerald R. Ford
First Lady: Thelma (Pat) Ryan Nixon

38. Gerald Rudolph Ford

Born: July 14, 1913, Omaha, Nebraska
Died: Dec. 26, 2006, Rancho Mirage, California
Term of office: Aug. 9, 1974–Jan. 20, 1977
Age at inauguration: 61
Party: Republican
Vice President: Nelson A. Rockefeller
First Lady: Elizabeth (Betty) Bloomer Warren Ford

39. James Earl (Jimmy) Carter

Born: Oct. 1, 1924, Plains, Georgia
Term of office: Jan. 20, 1977–Jan. 20, 1981
Age at inauguration: 52
Party: Democrat
Vice President: Walter F. Mondale
First Lady: Rosalynn Smith Carter

40. Ronald Wilson Reagan

Born: Feb. 6, 1911, Tampico, Illinois
Died: June 5, 2004, Los Angeles, California
Term of office: Jan. 20, 1981–Jan. 20, 1989
Age at inauguration: 69
Party: Republican
Vice President: George H. W. Bush
First Lady: Nancy Davis Reagan

41. George Herbert Walker Bush

Born: June 12, 1924, Milton, Massachusetts
Term of office: Jan. 20, 1989–Jan. 20, 1993
Age at inauguration: 64
Party: Republican
Vice President: James Danforth (Dan) Quayle
First Lady: Barbara Pierce Bush

CHECK IT OUT!

There have been two father-son presidential combinations: John Adams and John Quincy Adams, and George H. W. Bush and George W. Bush. In addition, President William Henry Harrison was the grandfather of President Benjamin Harrison.

*Resigned

42. William Jefferson (Bill) Clinton

Born: Aug. 19, 1946, Hope, Arkansas
Term of office: Jan. 20, 1993—Jan. 20, 2001
Age at inauguration: 46
Party: Democrat
Vice President: Albert (Al) Gore Jr.
First Lady: Hillary Rodham Clinton

43. George Walker Bush

Born: July 6, 1946, New Haven, Connecticut
Term of office: Jan. 20, 2001—Jan. 20, 2009
Age at inauguration: 54
Party: Republican
Vice President: Richard B. (Dick) Cheney
First Lady: Laura Welch Bush

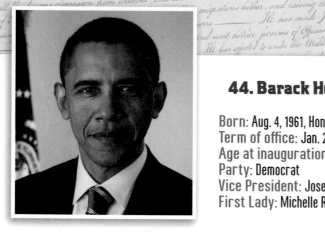

44. Barack Hussein Obama Jr.

Born: Aug. 4, 1961, Honolulu, Hawaii
Term of office: Jan. 20, 2009—
Age at inauguration: 47
Party: Democrat
Vice President: Joseph R. (Joe) Biden Jr.
First Lady: Michelle Robinson Obama

President Barack Obama was born in Honolulu, Hawaii, to a white mother who had grown up in Kansas and a black father from Kenya, Africa. As a young child, Obama was one of only a few black students at his school. He became an outstanding student at college and at Harvard Law School. After law school he worked to help poor families in Chicago, Illinois, get better health care and more educational programs. In 1996, he became an Illinois state senator, and in 2004, he was elected to the U.S. Senate. In 2008, Obama won the Democratic nomination for president and became the first African American to be elected to the highest office in the country.

Free to Be U.S.

For hundreds of years, the promise of freedom has attracted people to America from all over the world. Settlers came seeking the right to practice their chosen religions and to speak their minds without fear of punishment or government interference. They came for the right to make personal choices, large and small, and to live their lives as they pleased.

A Brave Declaration

In 1775, American colonists went to war for freedom. They wrote down their reasons for making war against their ruler, King George III of Britain, in the Declaration of Independence. The patriots who wrote this document were very brave. They knew that to revolt against Britain was treason, and that everyone who signed the Declaration could be hanged. Today the Declaration of Independence remains a symbol of freedom and courage, and a reminder that every person deserves the right to "life, liberty, and the pursuit of happiness."

Ten Top Rights

America won its independence in 1783. In 1787, members of Congress approved the U.S. Constitution, a document containing rules by which the new country would operate. Some members weren't completely happy with the Constitution. They thought it didn't say enough about people's rights. They wanted to add amendments that would guarantee citizens freedom of speech, of religion, and of the press, the right to a trial by jury, and other rights. In 1791, the Bill of Rights, consisting of the first ten amendments to the Constitution, was ratified by Congress.

★ STAR-SPANGLED COUNTRY ★

In September 1814, the United States was at war with Britain again. A lawyer named Francis Scott Key was aboard an American ship being held by the British as the ship began to bomb Fort McHenry in Maryland. The bombardment lasted all night. At dawn, Key saw the American flag still waving across the harbor and knew the attack had failed. The poem he wrote about it was published and set to the tune of an English song. But "The Star-Spangled Banner" didn't become our national anthem until March 3, 1931.

TAKE a LOOK

Read through the Bill of Rights on page 310. Key words and phrases are printed in red. Think about all the rights U.S. citizens enjoy. Are there other rights people should have? If you could add an amendment to the Constitution, what would it be?

In 1775, delegates from the colonies came together at the Second Continental Congress to prepare for war with Britain. John Hancock, the president of the Congress, was the first to sign the Declaration of Independence. Hancock signed his name in large, bold letters. Some people use the term *John Hancock* to mean a signature.

CHECK IT OUT!

c. 1000	Viking explorer Leif Ericson explores North American coast and founds temporary colony called Vinland.
1492	On first voyage to America, Christopher Columbus lands at San Salvador Island in Bahamas.

1513	Juan Ponce de Leon discovers Florida. Vasco Nuñez de Balboa crosses Panama and sights Pacific Ocean.
1520	Ferdinand Magellan, whose ships were first to circumnavigate world, discovers South American straits, later named after him.
1521	Hernán Cortéz captures Mexico City and conquers Aztec Empire.
1534–1539	Jacques Cartier of France explores coast of Newfoundland and Gulf of St. Lawrence. Hernando de Soto conquers Florida and begins three-year trek across Southeast.
1540	Francisco Vásquez de Coronado explores Southwest, discovering Grand Canyon and introducing horses to North America.

1541	Hernando de Soto discovers Mississippi River.

1572	Sir Francis Drake of England makes first voyage to Americas, landing in Panama.
1585	Sir Walter Raleigh establishes England's first American colony at Roanoke.
1603	Samuel de Champlain of France explores St. Lawrence River, later founds Quebec.
1607	First permanent English settlement in America established at Jamestown, Virginia. Capt. John Smith imprisoned by Native Americans and saved by Pocahontas, daughter of Chief Powhatan.
1609	Henry Hudson sets out in search of Northwest Passage. Samuel de Champlain sails into Great Lakes.
1620	Pilgrims and others board *Mayflower* and travel to Plymouth, Massachusetts. They draw up Mayflower Compact.
1626	Dutch colony of New Amsterdam founded on Manhattan Island, bought from Native Americans for about $24.
1675	Thousands die in King Philip's War between New Englanders and five Native American tribes.
1692	Witchcraft hysteria breaks out in Salem, Massachusetts, leading to 20 executions.

1754	French and Indian War begins.
1763	Treaty of Paris ends French and Indian War.
1765	Parliament passes Stamp Act (tax on newspapers, legal documents, etc.) and Quartering Act (requiring housing of British soldiers in colonists' homes).
1770	Five Americans, including Crispus Attucks, a black man said to be the leader, perish in Boston Massacre (March 5).

| 1773 | British Parliament passes Tea Act, leading to Boston Tea Party (Dec. 16). |

1775	American Revolution begins with battles of Lexington and Concord (April 19). Second Continental Congress appoints George Washington as commander of Continental Army.
1776	Second Continental Congress approves Declaration of Independence on July 4.
1777	Congress adopts Stars and Stripes flag and endorses Articles of Confederation. Washington's army spends winter at Valley Forge, Pennsylvania.

1783	Treaty of Paris signed, officially ending American Revolution (Sept. 3).
1787	Constitution accepted by delegates to Constitutional Convention in Philadelphia on Sept. 17.
1803	Louisiana Purchase from France doubles size of United States.

1804	Lewis and Clark expedition sets out from St. Louis, Missouri. New Jersey begins gradual emancipation of slaves. Alexander Hamilton killed in duel with Aaron Burr.
1812	War of 1812 with Britain begins by close vote in Congress.
1815	War of 1812 ends.
1825	Erie Canal opens.

1846	Mexican War begins when U.S. troops are attacked in disputed Texas territory.
1849	Gold Rush brings hundreds of thousands to California. Elizabeth Blackwell is first American woman to receive medical degree.
1860	Democratic Party splits into Northern and Southern wings. South Carolina is first Southern state to secede from Union after election of Abraham Lincoln.
1861	Civil War begins with attack on Ft. Sumter in South Carolina (April 12).
1862	Pres. Lincoln issues Emancipation Proclamation, freeing slaves in ten states.
1865	Gen. Lee surrenders to Gen. Grant at Appomattox Court House, Virginia (April 9). Pres. Lincoln assassinated by John Wilkes Booth in Washington, DC.
1870	Fifteenth Amendment, guaranteeing right to vote for all male U.S. citizens, is ratified (Feb. 3).
1898	After mysterious explosion of battleship Maine in Havana harbor (Feb. 15), Spanish-American War breaks out (April 25).

1903	Orville and Wilbur Wright conduct first powered flight near Kitty Hawk, NC (Dec. 17).
1909	Expedition team led by Robert E. Peary and Matthew Henson plants American flag at North Pole (April 6). W. E. B. DuBois founds National Association for the Advancement of Colored People (NAACP).
1917	Congress declares war on Germany (April 6) and Austria–Hungary (Dec. 7), bringing United States into World War I.
1918	Armistice Day ends World War I (Nov. 11).
1920	Nineteenth Amendment establishes women's right to vote (Aug. 26).
1927	Charles Lindbergh completes nonstop solo flight from New York to Paris (May 20–21).
1929	Stock market crash on "Black Tuesday" ushers in Great Depression (Oct. 29).
1932	Amelia Earhart is first woman to fly solo across Atlantic.
1941	Japanese planes attack Pearl Harbor, Hawaii, killing 2,400 U.S. servicemen and civilians (Dec. 7). United States declares war on Japan (Dec. 8). Germany and Italy declare war on United States (Dec. 11). United States declares war on Germany and Italy (Dec. 11).
1945	Germany surrenders, ending war in Europe (May 7). Atomic bombs dropped on Hiroshima (Aug. 6) and Nagasaki (Aug. 9); Japan surrenders, ending World War II (Aug. 14).
1950	North Korea invades South Korea, beginning Korean War (June 25).
1954	Supreme Court orders school desegregation in *Brown v. Board of Education* decision (May 17).
1958	In response to Soviet launch of *Sputnik*, United States launches *Explorer I*, first American satellite.
1962	Lt. Col. John H. Glenn Jr. is first American to orbit Earth.
1963	Dr. Martin Luther King Jr. delivers his "I Have a Dream" speech in Washington, DC (Aug. 28). Pres. Kennedy assassinated in Dallas, Texas (Nov. 22).

U.S. History

1965	Black nationalist Malcolm X assassinated in New York City (Feb. 21). Pres. Johnson orders U.S. Marines into South Vietnam (March 8).
1968	Dr. Martin Luther King Jr. is assassinated by James Earl Ray in Memphis, Tennessee (April 4). After winning California presidential primary, Sen. Robert F. Kennedy of New York is assassinated by Sirhan Sirhan in Los Angeles, California (June 5).
1969	Neil Armstrong and Edwin "Buzz" Aldrin of *Apollo 11* are first men to walk on Moon (July 20).
1972	Congress debates Equal Rights Amendment.
1973	Supreme Court disallows state restrictions on abortions (*Roe v. Wade*). United States signs Paris peace accords ending Vietnam War (Jan. 27). Vice Pres. Spiro Agnew resigns after threat of indictment for tax evasion (Oct. 10).
1974	Pres. Nixon resigns, elevating Vice Pres. Ford to presidency (Aug. 9).
1981	*Columbia* completes first successful space shuttle mission (April 12–13). Sandra Day O'Connor becomes first female Justice of Supreme Court.
1983	Sally Ride, aboard space shuttle *Challenger*, is first American female astronaut.
1986	Space shuttle *Challenger* explodes in midair over Florida.
1991	U.S. sends aircraft, warships, and 400,000 troops to Persian Gulf to drive Iraq's armed forces from Kuwait in Operation Desert Storm (Jan. 17). Ground war begins six weeks later and lasts only 100 hours (Feb. 24–28).
2001	On Sept. 11, hijackers overtake four U.S. planes, crashing two of them into World Trade Center in New York City. In all, 2,800 lives are lost.
2003	Suspecting weapons of mass destruction, United States declares war on Iraq (March 20). Official combat ends May 1.
2007	After hitting all-time high, stock market starts decline.
2008	United States is formally declared to be in recession.
2009	Sen. Barack Obama, first African American major presidential candidate, is inaugurated as president.

DECLARATION OF INDEPENDENCE

(Phrases in red are key ideas.)

IN CONGRESS, JULY 4, 1776

THE UNANIMOUS DECLARATION OF THE THIRTEEN UNITED STATES OF AMERICA

When in the Course of human events, it becomes necessary for one people to dissolve the political bands which have connected them with another, and to assume among the powers of the earth, the separate and equal station to which the Laws of Nature and of Nature's God entitle them, a decent respect to the opinions of mankind requires that they should declare the causes which impel them to the separation.

We hold these truths to be self-evident, that all men are created equal, that they are endowed by their Creator with certain unalienable Rights, that among these are Life, Liberty and the pursuit of Happiness. —That to secure these rights, Governments are instituted among Men, deriving their just powers from the consent of the governed, —That whenever any Form of Government becomes destructive of these ends, it is the Right of the People to alter or to abolish it, and to institute new Government, laying its foundation on such principles and organizing its powers in such form, as to them shall seem most likely to effect their Safety and Happiness. Prudence, indeed, will dictate that Governments long established should not be changed for light and transient causes; and accordingly all experience hath shown, that mankind are more disposed to suffer, while evils are sufferable, than to right themselves by abolishing the forms to which they are accustomed. But when a long train of abuses and usurpations, pursuing invariably the same Object evinces a design to reduce them under absolute Despotism, it is their right, it is their duty, to throw off such Government, and to provide new Guards for their future security. —Such has been the patient sufferance of these Colonies; and such is now the necessity which constrains them to alter their former Systems of Government. The history of the present King of Great Britain is a history of repeated injuries and usurpations, all having in direct object the establishment of an absolute Tyranny over these States. To prove this, let Facts be submitted to a candid world.

He has refused his Assent to Laws, the most wholesome and necessary for the public good.

He has forbidden his Governors to pass Laws of immediate and pressing importance, unless suspended in their operation till his Assent should be obtained; and when so suspended, he has utterly neglected to attend to them.

He has refused to pass other Laws for the accommodation of large districts of people, unless those people would relinquish the right of Representation in the Legislature, a right inestimable to them and formidable to tyrants only.

He has called together legislative bodies at places unusual, uncomfortable, and distant from the depository of their public Records, for the sole purpose of fatiguing them into compliance with his measures.

He has dissolved Representative Houses repeatedly, for opposing with manly firmness his invasions on the rights of the people.

He has refused for a long time, after such dissolutions, to cause others to be elected; whereby the Legislative powers, incapable of Annihilation, have returned to the People at large for their exercise; the State remaining in the mean time exposed to all the dangers of invasion from without, and convulsions within.

He has endeavoured to prevent the population of these States; for that purpose obstructing the Laws for Naturalization of Foreigners; refusing to pass others to encourage their migrations hither, and raising the conditions of new Appropriations of Lands.

He has obstructed the Administration of Justice, by refusing his Assent to Laws for establishing Judiciary powers.

He has made Judges dependent on his Will alone, for the tenure of their offices, and the amount and payment of their salaries.

He has erected a multitude of New Offices, and sent hither swarms of Officers to harrass our people, and eat out their substance.

He has kept among us, in times of peace, Standing Armies without the Consent of our legislatures.

He has affected to render the Military independent of and superior to the Civil power.

He has combined with others to subject us to a jurisdiction foreign to our constitution, and unacknowledged by our laws; giving his Assent to their Acts of pretended Legislation:

For Quartering large bodies of armed troops among us:

For protecting them, by a mock Trial, from punishment for any Murders which they should commit on the Inhabitants of these States:

For cutting off our Trade with all parts of the world:

For imposing Taxes on us without our Consent:

For depriving us in many cases, of the benefits of Trial by Jury:

For transporting us beyond Seas to be tried for pretended offences:

For abolishing the free System of English Laws in a neighbouring Province, establishing therein an Arbitrary government, and enlarging its Boundaries so as to render it at once an example and fit instrument for introducing the same absolute rule into these Colonies:

For taking away our Charters, abolishing our most valuable Laws, and altering fundamentally the Forms of our Governments:

For suspending our own Legislatures, and declaring themselves invested with power to legislate for us in all cases whatsoever.

He has abdicated Government here, by declaring us out of his Protection and waging War against us.

He has plundered our seas, ravaged our Coasts, burnt our towns, and destroyed the lives of our people.

He is at this time transporting large Armies of foreign Mercenaries to compleat the works of death, desolation and tyranny, already begun with circumstances of Cruelty & perfidy scarcely paralleled in the most barbarous ages, and totally unworthy the Head of a civilized nation.

He has constrained our fellow Citizens taken Captive on the high Seas to bear Arms against their Country, to become the executioners of their friends and Brethren, or to fall themselves by their Hands.

He has excited domestic insurrections amongst us, and has endeavoured to bring on the inhabitants of our frontiers, the merciless Indian Savages, whose known rule of warfare, in an undistinguished destruction of all ages, sexes and conditions.

In every stage of these Oppressions We have Petitioned for Redress in the most humble terms: Our repeated Petitions have been answered only by repeated injury. A Prince whose character is thus marked by every act which may define a Tyrant, is unfit to be the ruler of a free people.

Nor have We been wanting in attentions to our Brittish brethren. We have warned them from time to time of attempts by their legislature to extend an unwarrantable jurisdiction over us. We have reminded them of the circumstances of our emigration and settlement here. We have appealed to their native justice and magnanimity, and we have conjured them by the ties of our common kindred to disavow these usurpations, which, would inevitably interrupt our connections and correspondence. They too have been deaf to the voice of justice and of consanguinity. We must, therefore, acquiesce in the necessity, which denounces our Separation, and hold them, as we hold the rest of mankind, Enemies in War, in Peace Friends.

We, therefore, the Representatives of the united States of America, in General Congress, Assembled, appealing to the Supreme Judge of the world for the rectitude of our intentions, do, in the Name, and by Authority of the good People of these Colonies, solemnly publish and declare, That these United Colonies are, and of Right ought to be Free and Independent States; that they are Absolved from all Allegiance to the British Crown, and that all political connection between them and the State of Great Britain, is and ought to be totally dissolved; and that as Free and Independent States, they have full Power to levy War, conclude Peace, contract Alliances, establish Commerce, and to do all other Acts and Things which Independent States may of right do. And for the support of this Declaration, with a firm reliance on the protection of divine Providence, we mutually pledge to each other our Lives, our Fortunes and our sacred Honor.

The Bill of Rights

(Phrases in red are key ideas.)

The First 10 Amendments to the Constitution

(The first 10 amendments, known collectively as the Bill of Rights, were adopted in 1791.)

Amendment I

Congress shall make no law respecting an establishment of religion, or prohibiting the free exercise thereof; or abridging the freedom of speech, or of the press; or the right of the people peaceably to assemble, and to petition the Government for a redress of grievances.

Amendment II

A well regulated Militia, being necessary to the security of a free State, the right of the people to keep and bear Arms, shall not be infringed.

Amendment III

No Soldier shall, in time of peace be quartered in any house, without the consent of the Owner, nor in time of war, but in a manner to be prescribed by law.

Amendment IV

The right of the people to be secure in their persons, houses, papers, and effects, against unreasonable searches and seizures, shall not be violated, and no Warrants shall issue, but upon probable cause, supported by Oath or affirmation, and particularly describing the place to be searched, and the persons or things to be seized.

Amendment V

No person shall be held to answer for a capital, or otherwise infamous crime, unless on a presentment or indictment of a Grand Jury, except in cases arising in the land or naval forces, or in the Militia, when in actual service in time of War or public danger; nor shall any person be subject for the same offence to be twice put in jeopardy of life or limb; nor shall be compelled in any criminal case to be a witness against himself, nor be deprived of life, liberty, or property, without due process of law; nor shall private property be taken for public use, without just compensation.

Amendment VI

In all criminal prosecutions, the accused shall enjoy the right to a speedy and public trial, by an impartial jury of the State and district wherein the crime shall have been committed, which district shall have been previously ascertained by law, and to be informed of the nature and cause of the accusation; to be confronted with the witnesses against him; to have compulsory process for obtaining witnesses in his favor, and to have the Assistance of Counsel for his defence.

Amendment VII

In Suits at common law, where the value in controversy shall exceed twenty dollars, the right of trial by jury shall be preserved, and no fact tried by jury, shall be otherwise re-examined in any Court of the United States, than according to the rules of the common law.

Amendment VIII

Excessive bail shall not be required, nor excessive fines imposed, nor cruel and unusual punishments inflicted.

Amendment IX

The enumeration in the Constitution, of certain rights, shall not be construed to deny or disparage others retained by the people.

Amendment X

The powers not delegated to the United States by the Constitution, nor prohibited by it to the States, are reserved to the States respectively, or to the people.

Important Supreme Court Decisions

Marbury v. Madison (1803)
The Court struck down a law "repugnant to the Constitution" for the first time and set the precedent for judicial review of acts of Congress.

Dred Scott v. Sanford (1857)
Dred Scott, a Missouri slave, sued for his liberty after his owner took him into free territory. The Court ruled that Congress could not bar slavery in the territories. This decision sharpened sectional conflict about slavery.

Plessy v. Ferguson (1896)
This case was about the practice of segregating railroad cars in Louisiana. The Court ruled that as long as equal accommodations were provided, segregation was not discrimination and did not deprive black Americans of equal protection under the Fourteenth Amendment. This decision was overturned by *Brown v. Board of Education* (1954).

Brown v. Board of Education (1954)
Chief Justice Earl Warren led the Court to decide unanimously that segregated schools violated the equal protection clause of the Fourteenth Amendment. Efforts to desegregate Southern schools after the Brown decision met with massive resistance for many years.

Miranda v. Arizona (1966)
The Court ruled that Ernesto Miranda's confession to certain crimes was not admissible as evidence because he had been denied his right to silence and to legal counsel. Now police must advise suspects of their "Miranda rights" when they're taken into custody.

Roe v. Wade (1973)
In a controversial decision, the Court held that state laws restricting abortion were an unconstitutional invasion of a woman's right to privacy.

Chief Justices of the U.S. Supreme Court

Chief Justice	Tenure	Appointed by
John Jay	1789–1795	George Washington
John Rutledge	1795	George Washington
Oliver Ellsworth	1796–1800	George Washington
John Marshall	1801–1835	John Adams
Roger B. Taney	1836–1864	Andrew Jackson
Salmon P. Chase	1864–1873	Abraham Lincoln
Morrison R. Waite	1874–1888	Ulysses S. Grant
Melville W. Fuller	1888–1910	Grover Cleveland
Edward D. White	1910–1921	William H. Taft
William H. Taft	1921–1930	Warren G. Harding
Charles E. Hughes	1930–1941	Herbert Hoover
Harlan F. Stone	1941–1946	Franklin D. Roosevelt
Fred M. Vinson	1946–1953	Harry S Truman
Earl Warren	1953–1969	Dwight D. Eisenhower
Warren E. Burger	1969–1986	Richard M. Nixon
William H. Rehnquist	1986–2005	Ronald Reagan
John G. Roberts Jr.	2005–	George W. Bush

Weather

What Causes Weather?

Weather has a huge effect on our lives. It determines what kind of clothing we choose to wear, what we eat, and how we spend our day. Weather changes constantly, but all weather is a result of three key factors—pressure, temperature, and humidity (the amount of water in the air).

Warning: Contents Under Pressure

We walk around under an ocean—an ocean of air called the atmosphere, which is always pushing down on us. This atmospheric pressure keeps changing, and when it does, so does the weather. High air pressure produces clear, sunny weather. Low pressure brings cloudy, stormy weather. Meteorologists use an instrument called a barometer to measure the pressure.

Taking Some Heat

Every day the Sun heats up Earth and the air above it. The warm air rises and cooler air rushes in, which creates wind. If the air warms gradually and rises gently, we get a nice breeze. If it warms quickly, heavy-duty winds and storms can result.

It's Raining, It's Pouring

When the Sun strikes water—whether a puddle or an ocean—the heat turns water molecules into vapor. The vapor rises, cools, and condenses to form clouds. When the clouds become too heavy, water falls from them as rain or snow. This cycle of evaporation, condensation, and precipitation never stops. There is the same amount of water on Earth today as there was at the beginning. So the water you drink today could have been sipped by a dinosaur millions of years ago!

TAKE a LOOK

The water cycle never stops, but some places get more rain than others. Check pages 314–315 for the wettest and driest places in the United States and throughout the world.

CHECK IT OUT !

The line where cold and warm air masses collide is called a front. A cold front occurs when cold air pushes warm air out of its way. Cold fronts can bring stormy and even severe weather. A warm front occurs when warm air pushes away cold air, and it can bring gray, drizzly weather. (On a weather map, a cold front is indicated by a blue line with triangles below. Warm fronts are shown as red lines with half-circles above.)

U.S. Weather Extremes

The numbers below are based on 30-year averages of temperature, wind, snowfall, rainfall, and humidity at weather stations in the 48 continental states (not Alaska and Hawaii).

5 Driest Places

Location	Annual Precipitation
Yuma, AZ	3.01 in. (7.65 cm)
Las Vegas, NV	4.49 in. (11.40 cm)
Bishop, CA	5.02 in. (12.75 cm)
Bakersfield, CA	6.49 in. (16.48 cm)
Alamosa, CO	7.25 in. (18.41 cm)

5 Wettest Places

Location	Annual Precipitation
Mount Washington, NH	101.91 in. (258.85 cm)
Quillayute, WA	101.72 in. (258.37 cm)
Astoria, OR	67.13 in. (170.51 cm)
Mobile, AL	66.29 in. (168.38 cm)
Pensacola, FL	64.28 in. (163.27 cm)

5 Coldest Places

Location	Average Temperature
Mount Washington, NH	27.2°F (2.66°C)
International Falls, MN	37.4°F (3.00°C)
Marquette, MI	38.7°F (3.72°C)
Duluth, MN	39.1°F (3.94°C)
Caribou, ME	39.2°F (4.00°C)

5 Hottest Places

Location	Average Temperature
Key West, FL	78.1°F (25.61°C)
Miami, FL	76.7°F (24.83°C)
Yuma, AZ	75.3°F (24.05°C)
West Palm Beach, FL	75.3°F (24.05°C)
Fort Wayne, FL	74.9°F (23.83°C)

Weather

Worldwide Weather Extremes

Highest Recorded Temperatures by Continent

Temperature	Continent	Location	Date
136°F (57.8°C)	Africa	El Azizia, Libya	September 13, 1922
134°F (56.7°C)	North America	Death Valley, California, United States	July 10, 1913
129°F (53.9°C)	Asia	Tirat Tsvi, Israel	June 22, 1942
128°F (53.3°C)	Australia	Cloncurry, Queensland	January 16, 1899
122°F (50°C)	Europe	Seville, Spain	August 4, 1881
120°F (48.9°C)	South America	Rivadavia, Argentina	December 11, 1905
59°F (15°C)	Antarctica	Vanda Station	January 5, 1974

Lowest Recorded Temperatures by Continent

Temperature	Continent	Location	Date
-129°F (-89.4°C)	Antarctica	Vostok Station	July 21, 1983
-90°F (-67.8°C)	Asia	Oimekon, Russia	February 6, 1933
-90°F (-67.8°C)	Asia	Verkhoyansk, Russia	February 17, 1892
-87°F (-66.1°C)	North America	Northice, Greenland	January 9, 1954
-67°F (-55.0°C)	Europe	Ust'Shchugor, Russia	January*
-27°F (-32.8°C)	South America	Sarmiento, Argentina	June 1, 1907
-11°F (-23.9°C)	Africa	Ifrane, Morocco	February 11, 1938
-9.4°F (-23.0°C)	Australia	Charlotte Pass, New South Wales	June 29, 1994

*Day and year unknown

Highest Average Annual Precipitation by Continent

Amount	Continent	Location
467.4 in. (1,187.2 cm)	Asia	Mawsynram, India
405.0 in. (1,028.7 cm)	Africa	Debundscha, Cameroon
354.0 in. (899.2 cm)	South America	Quibdo, Colombia
340.0 in. (863.6 cm)	Australia	Bellenden Ker, Queensland
256.0 in. (650.2 cm)	North America	Henderson Lake, British Columbia
183.0 in. (464.8 cm)	Europe	Crkvica, Bosnia and Herzegovinia

Lowest Average Annual Precipitation by Continent

Amount	Continent	Location
0.03 in. (0.08 cm)	South America	Arica, Chile
0.10 in. (0.25 cm)	Africa	Wadi Halfa, Sudan
0.80 in. (2.03 cm)	Antarctica	Amundsen-Scott South Pole Station
1.20 in. (3.05 cm	North America	Batagues, Mexico
1.80 in. (4.57 cm)	Asia	Adan, Yemen
4.05 in. (10.28 cm)	Australia	Mulka (Troudaninna), South Australia
6.40 in. (16.26 cm)	Europe	Astrakhan, Russia

Weights & Measures

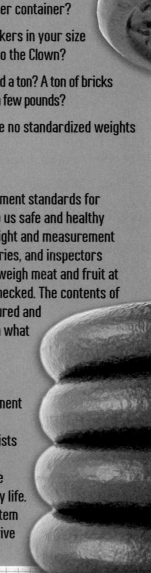

Weight and See

What if you never knew how many glasses of milk you could pour from a quart or liter container?

What if you bought a pair of sneakers in your size and they were big enough for Bozo the Clown?

What if a pound of peaches weighed a ton? A ton of bricks holding up a building weighed only a few pounds?

In other words, what if there were no standardized weights and measurements?

Standard Procedure

Every day we depend on measurement standards for precise information that will keep us safe and healthy and allow us to plan our lives. Weight and measurement standards are regulated by countries, and inspectors enforce the standards. Scales to weigh meat and fruit at the grocery store are regularly checked. The contents of boxed and canned food are measured and weighed to make sure they match what the label says.

Mainly Metric

The standard system of measurement for most developed nations is the metric system. In America, scientists and engineers use metric measurements, but people use the "inch-pound" system for everyday life. English colonists brought this system with them when they began to arrive in the 1600s.

A Perfect Ten

The metric system is based on the decimal system, whose foundation is the number 10. It lets us weigh and measure things more precisely than the American system. But every American measurement can be converted into metric, and vice versa. In 1959, the United States and other English-speaking nations agreed to make a foot equal exactly 0.3048 meters and a pound equal exactly 453.59237 grams.

1 FOOT = 0.3048 METERS
1 POUND = 453.59237 GRAMS

TAKE a LOOK

This chapter shows you how to convert most American measurements to metric, and vice versa. Use the information to go metric for a day, starting from when you wake up. Ask a family member to measure your height. Then measure everything else you use, eat, or drink all day. Measure your height again at night and convert all the measurements to metric. You may find something surprising in your results. (Learn more on page 350.)

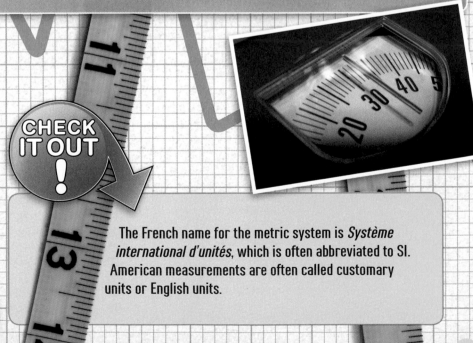

CHECK IT OUT!

The French name for the metric system is *Système international d'unités*, which is often abbreviated to SI. American measurements are often called customary units or English units.

Simple Metric Conversion Table

To convert	To	Multiply by
centimeters	feet	0.0328
centimeters	inches	0.3937
cubic centimeters	cubic inches	0.0610
degrees	radians	0.0175
feet	centimeters	30.48
feet	meters	0.3048
gallons	liters	3.785
grams	ounces	0.0353
inches	centimeters	2.54
kilograms	pounds	2.205
kilometers	miles	0.6214
knots	miles/hour	1.151
liters	gallons	0.2642
liters	pints	2.113
meters	feet	3.281
miles	kilometers	1.609
ounces	grams	28.3495
pounds	kilograms	0.4536

Converting Household Measures

To convert	To	Multiply by
dozens	units	12
baker's dozens	units	13
teaspoons	milliliters	4.93
teaspoons	tablespoons	0.33
tablespoons	milliliters	14.79
tablespoons	teaspoons	3
cups	liters	0.24
cups	pints	0.50
cups	quarts	0.25
pints	cups	2
pints	liters	0.47
pints	quarts	0.50
quarts	cups	4
quarts	gallons	0.25
quarts	liters	0.95
quarts	pints	2
gallons	liters	3.79
gallons	quarts	4

Temperature Conversions

Fahrenheit	Celsius
475	246.1
450	232.2
425	218.3
400	204.4
375	190.6
350	176.7
325	162.8
300	148.9
275	135.0
250	121.1
225	107.2
212	100.0
110	43.3
105	40.6
100	37.8
95	35.0
90	32.2
85	29.4
80	26.7
75	23.9
70	21.1
65	18.3
60	15.6
55	12.8
50	10.0
45	7.2
40	4.4
35	1.7
32	0.0
30	−1.1
25	−3.9
20	−6.7
15	−9.4
10	−12.2
5	−15.0
0	−17.8
−5	−20.6
−10	−23.3
−15	−26.1
−20	−28.9
−25	−31.7
−30	−34.4
−35	−37.2
−40	−40.0
−45	−42.8

Weights & Measures

Fractions and Their Decimal Equivalents

½	0.5000	²⁄₇	0.2857	⁵⁄₉	0.5556
⅓	0.3333	²⁄₉	0.2222	⁵⁄₁₁	0.4545
¼	0.2500	²⁄₁₁	0.1818	⁵⁄₁₂	0.4167
⅕	0.2000	¾	0.7500	⁶⁄₇	0.8571
⅙	0.1667	⅗	0.6000	⁶⁄₁₁	0.5455
⅐	0.1429	³⁄₇	0.4286	⅞	0.8750
⅛	0.1250	⅜	0.3750	⁷⁄₉	0.7778
⅑	0.1111	³⁄₁₀	0.3000	⁷⁄₁₀	0.7000
⅒	0.1000	³⁄₁₁	0.2727	⁷⁄₁₁	0.6364
¹⁄₁₁	0.0909	⅘	0.8000	⁷⁄₁₂	0.5833
¹⁄₁₂	0.0833	⁴⁄₇	0.5714	⁸⁄₉	0.8889
¹⁄₁₆	0.0625	⁴⁄₉	0.4444	⁸⁄₁₁	0.7273
¹⁄₃₂	0.0313	⁴⁄₁₁	0.3636	⁹⁄₁₀	0.9000
¹⁄₆₄	0.0156	⅚	0.8333	⁹⁄₁₁	0.8182
⅔	0.6667	⁵⁄₇	0.7143	¹⁰⁄₁₁	0.9091
⅖	0.4000	⅝	0.6250	¹¹⁄₁₂	0.9167

Length or Distance
U.S. Customary System

1 foot (ft.)	=	12 inches (in.)				
1 yard (yd.)	=	3 feet	=	36 inches		
1 rod (rd.)	=	5½ yards	=	16 ½ feet		
1 furlong (fur.)	=	40 rods	=	220 yards	=	660 feet
1 mile (mi.)	=	8 furlongs	=	1,760 yards	=	5,280 feet

An international nautical mile has been defined as 6,076.1155 feet.

Six Quick Ways to Measure If You Don't Have a Ruler

1. Most credit cards are 3⅜ inches by 2⅛ inches.
2. Standard business cards are 3½ inches long by 2 inches tall.
3. Floor tiles are usually manufactured in 12-inch squares.
4. U.S. paper money is 6⅛ inches wide by 2⅝ inches tall.
5. The diameter of a quarter is approximately 1 inch, and the diameter of a penny is approximately ¾ of an inch.
6. A standard sheet of paper is 8½ inches wide and 11 inches long.

World History

Ask Your Mummy

This chapter is about the history of the world since ancient times, before people wrote down accounts of events as a regular practice. Without recorded eyewitness accounts, how do we know what happened? Scientists and historians have learned a lot from their mummies!

A Cold Case

Take the case of Otzi, a 5,300-year-old mummy found in 1991, frozen in the Alps between Austria and Italy. Archaeologists could tell what Otzi had for his last meal, where he lived, and much more. They could also tell he knew something about natural medicine. They found a deep wound in his hand and several kinds of mosses in his stomach, including a kind known to have healing properties.

A Lot of Garbage?

Mummies of humans have been found on every continent except Antarctica. We can learn about the past not just from human remains but from what humans threw out when they were alive. Bone slivers and plant parts tell what families ate for supper and what they grew in their gardens. A broken fork or a splinter of pottery can reveal how civilized mealtimes were. What will our trash say about us in the future?

WORDS AND PICTURES

Today we have our pick of ways to study history. We can read journals, diaries, letters, ships' logs, and other primary-source documents to learn firsthand what people were experiencing. We can look at photographs or videos that capture a precise moment. We can even watch history as it's happening on the Internet or on TV. On January 20, 2009, millions of viewers around the world watched as Barack Obama was sworn in as the first African American president of the United States.

TAKE a LOOK

Behind every date and event in history are people—famous people and ordinary people. The more we know about the people, the more meaning history has. Pick a date or event in this chapter and do some research to learn more about the people involved. Or choose one of the famous people featured here and find some interesting details about him or her that aren't generally known.

CHECK IT OUT

There are various terms used for dating eras and periods in history. BC stands for "before Christ," or the years before Jesus Christ lived. The same period of time, which includes prehistoric times and ancient history, can also be called BCE ("before the common era"). CE means "common era." It refers to the same period of time as AD, which stands for "*anno Domini*." That means "in the year of our Lord," or after the birth of Christ.

Ancient History Highlights

Date	Event
4.5 billion BCE	Planet Earth forms.
3 billion BCE	First signs of life (bacteria and green algae) appear in oceans.
3.2 million BCE	*Australopithecus afarensis* roams Earth (remains, nicknamed Lucy, found in Ethiopia in 1974).
1.8 million BCE	*Homo erectus* ("upright man"). Brain size twice that of *australopithecine* species.
100,000 BCE	First modern *Homo sapiens* live in east Africa.
4500–3000 BCE	Sumerians in Tigris and Euphrates valleys develop city-state civilization. First phonetic writing.
3000–2000 BCE	Pharaonic rule begins in Egypt with King Menes. Great Sphinx of Giza constructed. Earliest Egyptian mummies created.
2000–1500 BCE	Israelites enslaved in Egypt.
1500–1000 BCE	Ikhnaton develops monotheistic religion in Egypt (circa 1375 BCE). His successor, Tutankhamun, returns to earlier gods. Moses leads Israelites out of Egypt into Canaan. Ten Commandments. End of Greek civilization in Mycenae with invasion of Dorians.
800–700 BCE	First recorded Olympic Games (776 BCE). Legendary founding of Rome by Romulus (753 BCE).
700–600 BCE	Founding of Byzantium by Greeks (circa 660 BCE). Building of Acropolis in Athens by Solon, Greek lawmaker (630–560 BCE).
600–500 BCE	Confucius (551–479 BCE) develops philosophy of Confucianism in China. Siddhartha Gautama or Buddha (563–483 BCE) founds Buddhism in India.
300–241 BCE	First Punic War (264–241 BCE). Rome defeats Carthaginians and begins domination of Mediterranean. Invention of Mayan calendar in Yucatán (more exact than older calendars). First Roman gladiatorial games (264 BCE). Archimedes, Greek mathematician (287–212 BCE).
250–201 BCE	Construction of Great Wall of China begins.
149–146 BCE	Third Punic War. Rome destroys Carthage.
100–51 BCE	Julius Caesar (100–44 BCE) invades Britain and conquers Gaul (France). Spartacus leads slave revolt against Rome (73 BCE). Birth of Jesus (variously given 7 BCE to 4 BCE).

People of Ancient History

Lucy

In 1974, in Hadar, Ethopia, scientists discovered a nearly complete skeleton of an *Australopithecus afarensis*, or early human being, which they named Lucy. The skeleton provided scientists with critical insight into the history of humans.

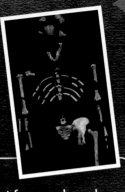

Tutankhamun

Tutankhamun, or King Tut, was one of the most famous pharaohs, or rulers, of ancient Egypt. He began ruling at age 10 and died at 19. There are no written records about his life. Until recently, most of the information known came from what Howard Carter discovered in King Tut's tomb in 1922. In 2010, results of a two-year study including DNA tests and CT scans of King Tut's mummy revealed the probable cause of his death as a leg injury complicated by bone disease and malaria.

Confucius

Confucius was a thinker and educator in ancient China. His beliefs and teachings about the way a person should live and treat others greatly influenced the Chinese culture and inspired the Ru school of Chinese thought. Later his beliefs spread to other parts of the world, and his type of belief system came to be known as Confucianism.

Buddha

Siddhartha Gautama was born the son of a wealthy ruler in what is modern-day Nepal. One day he was confronted with the suffering of people outside his kingdom, and he left his life of privilege. Siddhartha searched for enlightenment through meditation and eventually found his own path of balance in the world. He earned the title Buddha, or "Enlightened One," and spent the rest of his life helping others to reach enlightenment.

Julius Caesar

As a great politician, military leader, and dictator, Julius Caesar expanded the Roman Empire. He led Rome in conquering Gaul (France), ended the civil war, and instituted many social reforms. His rule ended with his assassination by many of his fellow statesmen on March 15, the Ides of March.

World History Highlights: 1–1499 CE

Date	Event
1–49 CE	Crucifixion of Jesus Christ (probably 30 CE).
312–337	Under Constantine the Great, eastern and western Roman empires reunite and new capital, Constantinople, is established.
350–399	Huns (Mongols) invade Europe (circa 360).
622–637	Muhammad flees from Mecca to Medina. Muslim empire grows (634). Arabs conquer Jerusalem (637).
c. 900	Vikings discover Greenland.
c. 1000	Viking raider Leif Erickson discovers North America, calls it Vinland. Chinese invent gunpowder.
1211–1227	Genghis Khan invades China, Persia, and Russia.
1215	King John of England forced by barons to sign Magna Carta, limiting royal power.
1231–1252	Inquisition begins as Pope Gregory IX creates special court to locate and punish heretics. Torture used (1252).
1251	Kublai Khan comes to prominence in China.
1271–1295	Marco Polo of Venice travels to China.
c. 1325	Renaissance begins in Italy.
1337–1453	English and French fight for control of France in Hundred Years' War.
1347–1351	About 25 million Europeans die from "Black Death" (bubonic plague).
1368	Ming dynasty begins in China.
1429	Joan of Arc leads French against English.
1452	Leonardo da Vinci, painter of *Mona Lisa* and other masterpieces, born near Florence, Italy.
1492–1498	Columbus discovers Caribbean Islands and Americas, returns to Spain (1493). Second voyage to Dominica, Jamaica, Puerto Rico (1493–1496). Third voyage to Orinoco (1498).
1497	Vasco da Gama sails around Africa and discovers sea route to India (1498). John Cabot, employed by England, explores Canadian coast.

World History

People of 1–1499 CE

Constantine

Known as Constantine the Great, he served as the emperor of Rome from 312 to 337. He created a "new" Rome by bringing religious tolerance to the empire and laying a foundation for Western culture. He moved the center of the empire from Rome to the Greek colony of Byzantium, which he renamed Constantinople.

Muhammad

As a prophet from Mecca, Muhammad worked to restore the faith of Abraham. He spread the religion of Islam and the belief in one true God, Allah. His teachings were recorded in the Koran. As his teachings spread, many aristocrats in Mecca began to oppose him. Muhammad fled to Medina, an event that marks the beginning of the Muslim calendar. In 629, he won over his opposition in Mecca. By the time he died in 632, most of the Arabian Peninsula followed his political and religious ideas.

Genghis Khan

Born around 1162 in Mongolia, Genghis Khan was a warrior and ruler who united the tribes of Mongolia and founded the Mongol Empire. He spent his life establishing and increasing his empire by conquering China, Russia, and parts of Persia.

Joan of Arc

At the age of thirteen, Joan of Arc heard the voices of saints telling her to help the French king defeat the English. She presented herself to the king and led the French army to victory at Orléans, forcing the English out of the region. She was later captured by the English, accused of heresy, and burned at the stake. Joan of Arc was hailed as a hero in France for her bravery and made a saint.

Leonardo da Vinci

Italian-born Leonardo da Vinci was one of the most farsighted, multitalented, and relentless thinkers of the time. He was a great artist, inventor, engineer, mathematician, architect, scientist, and musician whose works and insights influenced generations.

World History Highlights: 1500–1899

Date	Event
1509	Henry VIII becomes king of England.
1513	Juan Ponce de León explores Florida and Yucatán Peninsula for Spain.
1517	Martin Luther pins his 95 theses on door of Wittenberg Castle Church in Wittenberg, Germany, starting Protestant Reformation.
1520	Ferdinand Magellan discovers Straits of Magellan and Tierra del Fuego for Spain.
1547	Ivan IV, known as Ivan the Terrible, crowned czar of Russia.
1558	Elizabeth I, Henry VIII's daughter, becomes queen of England.
1585–1587	Sir Walter Raleigh's men reach Roanoke Island, Virginia.
1588	Spanish Armada attempts to invade England and is defeated.
1609	Henry Hudson explores Hudson River and Hudson Bay for England.
1632	Italian astronomer Galileo Galilei is first person to view space through a telescope and confirms belief that Earth revolves around Sun.
1687	Sir Isaac Newton publishes his theories on gravity and his laws of motion.
1721	Peter I, known as Peter the Great, crowned czar of Russia.
1756	Seven Years' War breaks out, involving most European countries.
1778	James Cook sails to Hawaii.
1789	Parisians storm Bastille prison, starting French Revolution.
1804	Scottish explorer John Ross begins expedition to find Northwest Passage in Arctic.
1821	Mexico gains its independence from Spain.
1845	Irish potato crops are ruined by blight, or fungus, creating famine that causes millions to starve to death or emigrate to America.
1859	Charles Darwin publishes On the Origin of Species.
1898	Spanish-American War begins.

World History

People of 1500–1899

Ferdinand Magellan

As a Portuguese explorer, Magellan sailed under both the Portuguese and Spanish flags. To find a route to India by sailing west, he sailed around South America to the Pacific Ocean, discovering the Strait of Magellan along the way. Although he was killed in the Philippines and did not complete the journey, his ships made it back to Spain and were the first to circumnavigate the globe.

Elizabeth I

Queen Elizabeth I ruled England, leading her country through war with wisdom and courage. She was a beloved queen who brought prosperity and a rebirth of learning to England, making the country a major European power. For this reason, the era in which she ruled became known as the Elizabethan Age.

Galileo

Galileo Galilei was a great Italian thinker whose contributions in philosophy, astronomy, and mathematics shaped the way we view the world. He helped develop the scientific method and establish the mathematical laws of falling motion. He advanced the development of the telescope to the point where he could use it to view objects in space and prove that Earth revolved around the Sun. His findings and beliefs were radical at the time and led to his excommunication from the Catholic Church.

Sir Isaac Newton

The contributions of this English physicist and mathematician laid the foundation of many modern sciences. Newton's discovery of white light and its composition of colors paved the way for studies in modern optics. His laws of motion gave a basis to modern physics and his law of universal gravity created a framework for classic mechanics.

Peter the Great

Crowned czar of Russia at the age of ten, Peter ruled jointly with his half brother until his brother's death. As sole ruler, Peter expanded the Russian empire to reclaim access to the Baltic Sea and establish trade with Europe. He reorganized government, founding the city of St. Petersburg as the new capital of Russia and creating the Russian army and navy.

World History Highlights: 1900–Present

Date	Event
1905	Albert Einstein formulates his theory of relativity.
1911	Marie Curie wins Nobel Prize for chemistry.
1914	Archduke Franz Ferdinand, heir to Austrian-Hungarian throne, assassinated in Sarajevo, setting off events that lead to World War I.
1918	Massive worldwide flu epidemic kills more than 20 million people.
1919	Treaty of Versailles signed, ending World War I.
1927	American Charles Lindbergh is first to fly solo across Atlantic Ocean.
1939	Germany invades Poland, sparking World War II. Britain and France declare war on Germany. United States remains neutral.
1941	Japan attacks United States by bombing American ships at Pearl Harbor, Hawaii. United States declares war on Japan and enters World War II.
1945	Germany surrenders. United States drops atomic bombs on two Japanese cities, Hiroshima and Nagasaki. World War II ends. United Nations, international peacekeeping organization, formed.
1948	Israel proclaims its independence. Gandhi, nonviolent leader of Indian Nationalist movement against British rule, assassinated.
1950	North Korea invades South Korea, starting Korean War.
1964	United States begins sending troops to Vietnam to assist South Vietnam during Vietnamese civil war.
1973	Paris Peace Accords signed, ending Vietnam War.
1989	Chinese army shoots and kills protestors in China's Tiananmen Square. Berlin Wall, separating East and West Germany, torn down.
1991	President Frederik Willem de Klerk negotiates to end apartheid in South Africa. Union of Soviet Socialist Republics (USSR) dissolved into independent states.
1994	Nelson Mandela elected president of South Africa in first free elections.
1997	Mother Teresa, champion of poor in Calcutta, India, dies.
2003	United States invades Iraq, aided by Britain and other allies.
2006	Iraqi dictator Saddam Hussein captured and killed for crimes against humanity.
2009	Swine flu epidemic sweeps world.
2010	Earthquakes in Haiti and Chile cause widespread death and destruction.

People of 1900–Present

Albert Einstein

Called the greatest scientist of the 20th century, physicist Albert Einstein developed revolutionary theories about how the world works, especially the connection between matter and energy. Einstein's knowledge was applied to the development of the atomic bomb, which he said saddened him. Today calling somebody an "Einstein" means that he or she is a genius, but young Albert Einstein was known more for playing tricks in school than for getting good grades.

Marie Curie

Polish-French chemist Marie Curie is best known for discovering the radioactive element radium, for which she won a Nobel Prize. She also discovered an element called polonium, named for her birthplace, Poland. Although radium is used to treat and diagnose diseases, repeated or excessive exposure can cause serious illness and even death. After years of working with radium, Marie Curie died in 1934 from radiation poisoning.

Mohandas Gandhi

To the people of India, Mohandas Gandhi was the Mahatma, or Great Soul. Gandhi believed in tolerance for all religious beliefs. He led peaceful protests to bring about social change and freedom from British rule. India was granted freedom in 1947, but fighting between Hindus and Muslims continued. Gandhi spoke out against the fighting, angering many and resulting in his assassination. In America, Dr. Martin Luther King Jr. modeled his nonviolent strategy of fighting racism on Gandhi's methods.

Nelson Mandela

In 1994, Nelson Mandela was elected the first black president of South Africa. That was the first year in which South Africans of all races could vote, thanks to of the end of the government's previous policy of racial segregation, called apartheid. Mandela had served many years in prison for leading protests against apartheid and became a world-famous symbol of racial injustice. After his release from prison, he led discussions with white leaders that led to the end of apartheid and to a nonracial form of government.

Mother Teresa

Born Agnes Gonxha Bojaxhiu, Mother Teresa was a Roman Catholic nun who became known as the "Saint of the Gutters" for her work with poor people. She founded a religious order in India to provide food, schools, health care, and shelters for the poor, sick, and dying. Mother Teresa received numerous awards for her work, including the Nobel Peace Prize. In 2003, Pope John Paul II approved the first step toward declaring Mother Teresa a saint in the Roman Catholic Church.

Homework Helpers

Use the tips, guides, definitions, examples, and ideas on the next four pages to help you ace spelling, writing, and every homework assignment.

Parts of Speech

Picking Up the Pieces

Pieces of a jigsaw puzzle need to be correctly connected to form a complete picture. Words need to be correctly connected to form a sentence. The part each word plays in a sentence is called its part of speech.

Part of Speech	Definition	Example
Noun	A person, place, or thing	kids, plates, spaghetti, meatballs
Pronoun	A word that replaces a noun	they
Adjective	A word that modifies a noun (*A*, *an*, and *the* are special types of adjectives called articles)	the, hungry
Verb	An action word	devoured, exclaimed
Adverb	A word that modifies a verb	quickly, loudly
Conjunction	A word like *but* or *and* that joins together groups of words or sentences	and
Preposition	A word like *in* or *of* that shows the relationship between one noun and another noun, verb, or, adverb	of
Interjection	An exclamation, usually a short part of speech that shows emotion or emphasis	Yum!

The hungry **kids** **quickly** devoured **plates** of **spaghetti** and **meatballs**. "Yum!" **they** exclaimed **loudly**.

Tip: A proper noun is a word for a particular person, place, or thing. Always use capital letters for proper nouns. Examples: Abraham Lincoln, Australia, Fourth of July

Vocabulary

Prefixes

A prefix is a group of letters that starts a word. If you know common prefixes, you can figure out meanings of new words and expand your spoken and written vocabulary. (Some prefixes have more than the one meaning given below.)

Prefix	Meaning	Example
anti–	against	antiterrorist
circum–	around	circumnavigate
co–	with	copilot
dis–	not	disappear
ex–	away from	expel
in–	not	incomplete
inter–	between	intersection
micro–	small	microchip
pre–	before	prefix
sub–	under	submarine
trans–	across	transform

Roots

Hidden within many words are parts of words called roots, which come from the Greek and Latin languages. Word roots can appear at the beginning, middle, or end of a word, but they always mean the same thing.

Root	Meaning	Example
audi	hear	audition
auto	self	automatic
bene	good	benefit
bio	life	biology
chrono	time	chronicle
dict	say	dictate
phil	love	philosophy
port	carry	portable
spec	see	spectacle
terr	earth	terrain

Spelling
Sounds Wrong to Me

Homophones are words that sound the same but have different spellings and meanings, like *know* and *no* and *bare* and *bear*. Avoid making these common homophone mistakes.

There Their They're

There is an adverb meaning a place.
Their is a pronoun that shows possession.
They're is a contraction that stands for they and are.

   They're riding *their* bikes over *there*.

To Too Two

To is a preposition that shows direction.
Too is an adverb meaning "also."
Two is a number.

   You *two* can come *to* the party, *too*.

Its It's

Its is a pronoun that shows possession.
It's is a contraction of it is or it has.

   It's a road known for *its* dangerous curves.

Punctuation
Use Your Comma Sense

Teachers say using commas incorrectly is the mistake students make most frequently. Here are three rules to remember:

1. Don't use a comma between the subject and verb.

Wrong:
Jennie, picked some flowers for her grandma.

Right:
Jennie picked some flowers for her grandma.

2. Use a comma before a conjunction to join two complete thoughts (independent clauses).

Jennie picked some flowers for her grandma, and then she put them in a vase.

3. Use commas around extra information (nonrestrictive clauses).

Jennie picked some flowers for her grandma, who was visiting, and then she put them in a vase.

Homework Helpers

Research and Study Skills
Book It

Got a report to write? The help you need to craft a perfect paper is as near as the library.

- Use an atlas to find maps of continents, countries, states, or cities.

- Use encyclopedias and almanacs for facts, figures, stats, and other information.

- Use a dictionary to find out a word's meaning and pronunciation, its origin, and its part of speech.

- Use a thesaurus to find synonyms (words that mean the same as other words) and antonyms (words that mean the opposite of other words).

- Ask a librarian (nicely, of course) for help if you get stuck. Librarians know a tremendous amount of information and are eager to point kids in the right direction.

Cool Tools Online

Dictionaries, thesauruses, and other reference materials are available online as well as in book form. In fact, you can find out almost anything you want to know online—the catch is, not all the information is correct. You can trust the information on these websites to be accurate, up to date, and especially good for kids.

Site:	www.ipl.org
What you'll find:	Information about almost everything, from animals to sports to school cancellations! Plus a chance to e-mail a librarian or connect with other kids
Site:	www.nal.usda.gov/awic/pubs/scifair.htm
What you'll find:	Science fair topics
Site:	www.kids.gov
What you'll find:	Information about U.S. history, government, the states, and more
Site:	www.nasa.gov/audience/forstudents/index.html
What you'll find:	Information on the planets, the stars, space research, and missions
Site:	www.scholastic.com/kids/homework
What you'll find:	Tips on writing, research, test-taking, and study skills
Site:	www.ala.org
What you'll find:	Keyword "great websites for kids" for a terrific assortment of sites, reviewed and selected by librarians

Tip: Don't copy and paste material directly from the Internet. Print it out and rewrite it in your own words to avoid plagiarism, which is using someone else's ideas and words as your own. Another tip: Use more than one source whenever you do research.

What's Next?

Welcome to Your Future

"Radio has no future.... Heavier-than-air flying machines are impossible....
X-rays will prove to be a hoax."
    —Lord Kelvin, inventor of the Kelvin scale of temperature measurement, 1899

When it comes to predicting the future, even brilliant scientists can get it wrong. The inventions on these four pages seemed impossible at one time, yet they exist today. There's no doubt they will lead to even more advanced inventions and discoveries—maybe one will be named after you!

Save Me a Space

Only about 500 people have flown into space, and almost all of them have been astronauts. However, by 2020 that number could grow to 15,000. These new travelers will not be space professionals, but ordinary people looking for the ride of their life.

Great Britain's Virgin Galactic company has been testing a six-passenger spacecraft called the *VSS Enterprise*, which company officials say will be ready for takeoff in 2011 or 2012. The *Enterprise* will fly to 50,000 feet (15,240 m) attached to a mother ship. Then it will be launched by rockets and soar another 65 miles (104.6 km) into the atmosphere. Although the craft won't carry passengers into orbit, the flight will let them experience weightlessness and get an unmatchable view of Earth.

More than 300 people have reserved seats on Virgin Galactic's first flights, currently priced at an out-of-this-world $200,000. However, in May 2010, a company named Space Adventures announced it would offer suborbital flights at $102,000. As more competitors get into the act, experts predict prices will drop even lower—perhaps all the way back down to Earth. What are you doing for summer vacation in 2025?

Let's Keep in Touch

Small touch screens on handheld devices put fun and information at our fingertips. Now touch screens are growing up, and growing large. Microsoft's Surface is a powerful networked computer that looks like a coffee table and has a touch screen built into the top. The Surface is big enough for a group to gather around it, and its technology lets everyone interact at the same time. Users can slide, stretch, and move pictures around—with both hands. They can surf the Net without a mouse or keyboard. They can download photos by simply placing a digital camera on top of the Surface and letting them jump out.

Microsoft says the Surface gives users a more natural way to interact with information than previous computers. Other companies have similar ideas in development, and experts say soon touch-sensitive computers will be built into desks, walls, and just about any available surface.

A Handful of 3-D

It's in the movies and on TV—now 3-D is in the palm of your hand! The new Samsung W960 has the first mobile 3-D display—and you can bet it won't be the last. According to one research company, there will be more than 70 million handheld 3-D devices in use by 2018.

Do You Mind?

Touch technology is exciting, but what if you could control a TV, a computer, or a robot just by thinking about it? By 2020, the Intel Corporation wants to develop brain implants that control devices directly by brain waves. Right now, Honda's new Brain-Machine Interface (BMI) helmet reads a person's thoughts by measuring changes in the brain. Then it transmits the data to its humanoid robot, ASIMO. The company says ASIMO—which can walk, talk, run, and climb stairs—follows instructions 90 percent of the time. The robot is specially designed to help people with limited mobility lead more independent lives.

Life-Saving Limbs

Losing a limb in a war or accident is a terrible tragedy. However, doctors and scientists now think a new kind of artificial limb may be possible—one that can feel sensations and be controlled by thoughts. In an experiment in Italy, electrodes were implanted into the remaining part of a car crash victim's arm. Then the electrodes were attached to a robotic arm. (The robotic arm was not attached to the man.) Over a month's time, the man learned to wiggle the robotic fingers, make a fist, and grab objects, just by concentrating.

In New York City's busy Times Square district, a robotic arm helped disable a bomb planted in a van on May 1. Police say thousands of people could have been killed or injured if the bomb had exploded.

A Turn for the Better

If computers can be built into our furniture, why not into our clothes? Shirts with bio-sensors are used in hospitals to monitor heart rates. Out on the road, you can safely communicate where you're turning without taking your hands off your bike's handlebars if you wear this hoodie that has a built-in turn signal.

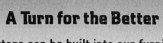

Bone Phone

How about a Bluetooth-enabled device for your phone that looks like a ring and can unfold into a headset when you get a call? It's called the ORB, and it conducts sound through the bones in your ear.

Robo-seals and Robo-saurs

Not all robots have to look metallic and hard-edged. Paro is a furry robotic baby harp seal that snuggles and mews when its head is scratched. In the United States, the robot is used to comfort elderly patients with Alzheimer's disease.

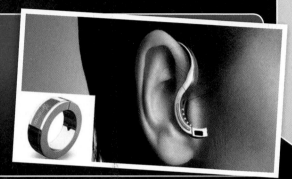

Pleo is the perfect pet—friendly, cute, and able to hear, see, show emotion, and detect objects. Pleo's abilities come from his built-in color camera, sensors, motors, and over 100 gears.

Index

Index

Answers

Animals, p. 7

In cats, camels, and giraffes, the front and back legs on each side of the body move together as a pair. In other animals, the two front legs move together, followed by the two back legs.

Flags & Facts, Countries of the World, p. 87

The four country flags that show the Southern Cross are Australia, New Zealand, Papua New Guinea, and Samoa.

Flags & Facts, States of the United States, p. 123

The 21 flags with a star or stars are Alaska, Arizona, Arkansas, California, Georgia, Illinois, Indiana, Kansas, Maine, Massachusetts, Mississippi, Nevada, New Hampshire, Missouri, North Carolina, North Dakota, Ohio, Rhode Island, Tennessee, Texas, and Utah.
The 26 flags on a solid blue background are Alaska, Connecticut, Delaware, Idaho, Indiana, Kansas, Kentucky, Louisiana, Maine, Michigan, Minnesota, Montana, Nebraska, Nevada, New Hampshire, New York, North Dakota, Oklahoma, Oregon, Pennsylvania, South Carolina, South Dakota, Utah, Vermont, Virginia, and Wisconsin.
The 8 flags with birds are Illinois, Iowa, Louisiana, Michigan, New York, North Dakota, Oregon, and Utah.
The flags of California and Missouri feature bears.
The flag of Maine is the only one with a moose.

Languages, p. 192

They that thrive well take counsel of their friends = It's good to get advice from your friends; Stand and unfold thyself = Tell me who you are; Mere prattle, without practice = It's all just talk; Headstrong liberty is lash'd with woe = Too much freedom can be trouble.

Weights & Measures, p. 317

You may find you're taller in the morning than at night. At night, when you're lying down, your spine relaxes and spreads out. During the day, gravity pulls your body down, pressing your vertebrae together and making you shorter.

Photo Credits

D'

UNIVERSITY PRESS OF FLORIDA

Gainesville · Tallahassee · Tampa · Boca Raton

Pensacola · Orlando · Miami · Jacksonville · Ft. Myers · Sarasota

Onramps and Overpasses

Florida A&M University, Tallahassee
Florida Atlantic University, Boca Raton
Florida Gulf Coast University, Ft. Myers
Florida International University, Miami
Florida State University, Tallahassee
New College of Florida, Sarasota
University of Central Florida, Orlando
University of Florida, Gainesville
University of North Florida, Jacksonville
University of South Florida, Tampa
University of West Florida, Pensacola

UNIVERSITY
PRESS
OF
FLORIDA